The Man who was Screaming Lord Sutch

The Man Who Was Screaming Lord Sutch

Graham Sharpe

To Pat and Ken Hellier:
no one cared more

Contents

Prologue

'I knew it would happen one day'
— ALAN HOPE, FIRST LOONY COUNCILLOR.

The man the world knew as Screaming Lord Sutch is holding court in the tiny town square of Llanwrtyd Wells, mid-Wales. It is a benign Saturday morning, 12 June 1999.

'Lord David Sutch, leader of the Official Monster Raving Loony Party,' is how he announces himself to a television interviewer. 'It's lovely here,' he exclaims. 'The mountains and the valleys, it's just great – it's nice, fresh air and I'd like to take it back in cans and sell it.' He goes on to boast that one party member has recently become a Loony councillor, and another is now the first Loony mayor. 'It's a good step forward, and backwards, and sideways – and we're going to keep the pound forever in Great Britain, but it's going to be the Loony Pound – and everyone should have a Loony Pound!' Behind him as he chats animatedly stands his partner, Yvonne Elwood, relaxed and smiling in a black jacket trimmed with leopardskin.

That summer Sutch had much to look forward to: a gig in Las Vegas, where he and Yvonne had perhaps planned to marry; money coming in from a lucrative breakfast cereal ad; the prospect of his best-ever electoral showing in the race to become mayor of London.

But, like so much in the life of this outwardly transparent and flamboyant character, the scene being played out in public was a façade. Unbeknown to onlookers, here was a man wrestling with private demons and coming to terms with a drastic resolution to an insoluble dilemma.

Two days earlier, complaining of flu symptoms, David Sutch had appeared at the Brixton Academy with his old pal Carlo Little, original drummer in his group, The Savages. He was singing with Little's band at a Rolling Stones convention, held to mark the superstar band's forthcoming shows at Wembley Stadium. A film of the gig shows an overweight Sutch wearing a long frock-coat over a baggy shirt, miming the playing of a piano as he shouts out the lyrics to 'Roll Over Beethoven'. It is not a vintage performance.

Carlo's daughter, Giselle, was close by when Sutch took the stage to perform: 'I heard him say in the dressing room earlier that he only wanted to do one number because he didn't feel so well. He went down a storm.' At which point, however, according to Carlo, he suddenly decided he wanted to play another song. Little, however, had been warned that there would be a severe financial penalty for over-running, so he had to prevent Sutch carrying on. He recalls: 'One of the last things he ever said to me was, "Oh, go on, just one more song."'

Early the next morning – 'I think it was before 9 a.m., which was unheard of for him' – Sutch rang former Savages guitarist Johnny Bedder. They had 'a one-hour conversation during which he told me about his dog dying. Otherwise he sounded optimistic and asked whether I could get him some work.'

David and Yvonne then travelled down to Llanwrtyd Wells for the annual Man Versus Horse Marathon, a unique event that pits horses and riders against humans over a gruelling twenty-two-mile course, with big prize money at stake for the first man ever to beat the horse. The bookmaking chain William Hill had, through my efforts as its media relations director, become involved as the event's sole sponsors, and for the previous eleven years I had arranged for Sutch to attend in the capacity of official starter. It had also become a tradition for him to play an impromptu gig in the local pub, the Neuadd Arms Hotel.

Over the years my secretary, Romaine Snijder, would watch him start the race, give out the prizes, do media interviews and perform in the evening, and had come to know David well. It enabled her to perceive a gradual change in him that would have eluded most of those present. 'As the years went by,' she said, 'it became obvious he was retreating inwards. He was always lively and smiling when he was 'on show', but whereas before he would enjoy the company of other people after his gig it got to the stage where he would come out of his room at the very last second and get back to his room as quickly as possible.

'This change in his behaviour went largely unnoticed, because in the first few years he had endeared himself to everyone by being sociable, affable and entertaining. I always came back with Loony Party banknotes that David gave me for my children, who were really pleased. David would seem disproportionately delighted to know this.

'In hindsight he seemed a little distracted [that night]. I remember that he even expressed some doubt as to whether he would make his traditional Saturday night appearance.'

Susannah Green, daughter of Gordon, owner of the Neuadd, agrees: 'He would always seek me out and give me a kiss when he arrived. But he wasn't at his best, and even snapped at me during the afternoon when he wanted an umbrella.'

Susannah's mother, Di, also noticed a difference: 'He barely spoke to me. In the past we had sat and talked for hours.'

The race started at about 10.30 a.m. that Saturday morning in front of a good turnout of spectators. Runners milled around, ready to get underway. Sutch, in three-quarter-length leopardskin jacket and white top hat, stood in front of them, waving his megaphone about, larking around, posing for pictures. He counted down the final seconds: 'Four – three – two – one – *go!* Good luck!' he called as the runners surged round and past him to charge down the road. 'Beat the horse!'

A few minutes later, the horses arrived for their own mass start. Sutch patted one, fondling the nose of another, chatting to the rider. The race announcer suggested that with the start imminent Sutch might want to shift himself –'unless you want to be trampled to death.'

'I'll move over to the side,' agreed Sutch. 'Bloody hell!'

A second countdown, and off trotted the horses down the road, Sutch jogging after them for a few yards in pursuit, megaphone aloft.

Some four hours later when, for the twentieth successive year, horse-power had proved superior to human endeavour, the race was over, and in weather now typically Welsh and wet, Sutch was making the presentations, sheltering under a large William Hill brolly. He handed over cheques, rosettes, silver plates, champagne – 'It's for later. Don't drink it, put your feet in it,' he advised one weary runner – and called kids over for pictures. Runners and riders alike were clearly delighted to meet him.

In the video footage of Sutch's interview in the town square, his face is a little puffy. His eyes look sunken, and there are dark rings round them. But it is early in the day for him and he is happy to chat, confirming that he has enjoyed this event 'for years and years and years'. He talks about the race with genuine interest. This is not a man just going through the motions.

'What do you get out of it?' asks the interviewer.

'I get a bit of excitement – and the opportunity to come down and get a bit of good quality air in my lungs, 'cos in London it's full up with diesel and petrol oil.'

As his last-ever TV interview concludes and the camera moves away a lime-green badge on his lapel becomes visible. It reads: 'Annie Emily Sutch Lives On.' His mother had died two years earlier.

I held an early evening buffet at the nearby Abernant Hotel for those involved in the race. I sat Sutch and Yvonne, who arrived late, with a garrulous, friendly Irishman called Tom Sheehan, a keen mountain biker who had a fellow cyclist with him.

'I had been anticipating a good giggle,' recalls Sheehan of his encounter with Sutch, 'but it is fair to say that I didn't have my ribs tickled. I held him in some regard as I knew he had helped to establish this race over the years, and when mountain bikers had taken part regularly, his presence lent such a new discipline additional prestige … He wasn't stand-offish at all, and Yvonne was quite chatty. David, though, seemed to be behind the conversation. He was just playing with a small plate of salad. In the light of future events I certainly feel that it was a case of a condemned man not eating a hearty meal.'

Despite David Sutch's earlier doubts about performing, the lure of the acclaim of a crowd won him over, and later on in the Neuadd, with a large, good-natured gathering of revellers and a band of local musicians, Screaming Lord Sutch took the microphone around midnight and hammered out three raucous rock 'n' roll numbers including, inevitably, 'Roll Over Beethoven', to massive applause and cheering. The photos Susannah Green and I took at that last gig show a man whose face is etched with anguish, who smiles with his mouth but not his eyes.

David and Yvonne drove back to Middlesex the next morning, and, that evening, 13 June, made their way to the Beck Theatre in Hayes, his local venue, where Clem Cattini, the original drummer in 1960s band The Tornados, renowned for their atmospheric hit 'Telstar', had organised a benefit concert for a singer called Lynn Alice, who had been struck down with cancer. The bill featured other names from the era such as Cliff Bennett, Brian Poole, Craig Douglas, Mike Berry, Billie Davis, and Jess Conrad. Clem hadn't asked Sutch to perform: 'If I'd invited everyone I knew it would have been a very long night.'

Cattini described him as 'dishevelled', and recalled that he 'appeared upset that I hadn't asked him. He looked very down, but I was extremely busy and only had time for a brief chat with him. Ever since, I've worried that maybe the fact I hadn't invited him to take part could have tipped him over the edge.'

'I had a bouquet of flowers to give to Lynn,' remembers the singer Billie Davis. 'I asked him to come on stage with me to present them, but he said no, and sat there with his head in his hands. When, a day or two later, I got the papers and read what he had done I just stood in my kitchen and shouted, "What did you want to do that for!"'

Cliff Bennett, who found fame in the 1960s with his band The Rebel Rousers, and who went back nearly forty years with Sutch ('We used to buy records from a shop Dave called "Froggy's" because he reckoned that's what the bloke who ran it looked like'), offered to cut his slot by a song or two when he saw how upset Sutch was at not being able to perform. 'When he was asked to walk on with flowers for Lynn he told Clem to "stick them up your fucking arse".'

Another long-term pal at the Beck was photographer Ron Long, who had once shared a house with Sutch. 'He seemed subdued and reckoned that he hadn't been the same since his beloved mum died,' he remembered. However, Sutch had talked 'eagerly' about a forthcoming 1960s show in Brighton, and Long had agreed to call him later to discuss his role. 'Don't ring too early – you know what I'm like,' was Sutch's parting comment.

Yvonne asked David whether he wanted to come back to their

home in Reading, but he told her he wanted to stay at his late mum's house, 10 Parkfield Road, South Harrow; they alternated between the two. 'I was going for a job interview the next day and he gave me a good luck card. It read: "To Eve, all my love to you. David xxxx." I kissed him goodnight and we had a long cuddle in the hallway. It was the last time I saw him alive.'

David must have gone indoors on his own, made a pot of tea, found a place in the cluttered house to sit down and wondered what the morning, and every subsequent morning, would hold in store for him.

Yes, he was doing OK at the moment. But however good or bad life was he couldn't tell his mum about it. Couldn't even tell the dog, Rosie, who had recently died, severing the final link with his mother. Couldn't tell his son, Tristan, who lived in the States. So, who was there to tell? Who really cared about what he did? Yvonne, for sure, but it seems he didn't know whether he could commit himself to a future with her. He might have felt the familiar embrace of depression enveloping him.

The next morning, a former girlfriend, Val Bird, was in South Harrow. 'I stood on the corner of Parkfield Road, toying with the idea of popping in for a cup of tea,' she recalls.

John Briggs, who ran a fan club for The Dave Clark Five, of which Sutch was an honorary member, had been surprised recently to be contacted by Sutch and asked if he would 'get all the info off the web about him'. It had taken him ages, but he'd done so, printed it out and sent it all off to him. Sutch rang Briggs that day, 'and asked me what my opinion was on all the stuff about him and we had a chat – there was no indication of anything untoward'.

The music photographer Steve Kramer was also surprised by a phone call from Sutch – they had never spoken before – to say how impressed he was by the photos Kramer had taken of Sutch's performance at a benefit gig for former Tornado Heinz, who was ill.

Sutch's next-door neighbour of fourteen years and professional Ali-G impersonator, Ray Wade, thinks he recalls seeing David that Monday – the only person who claims to have done so. 'The last few times I saw him he had said, "I can't sleep – my head, I've got such a headache, I'm exhausted from gigs." I was going away for a few days. He was obviously waiting for me to come out, and he said, "Which way

The Man who was Screaming Lord Sutch

are you going?" I said, "I'm going to Watford," and he said, "Oh, I wanted to go to Northolt." I said, "I can still give you a lift," but he said, "Oh, if you're not going that way, leave it," and went back in.' Yvonne called him that morning, and he told her he was 'a bit down', but by the evening he was 'feeling much better'.

The next day, Tuesday, 15 June, he was due to give a newspaper interview. He did not do it. This was completely out of character. But one thing David Sutch did do that day was to look out a leather jacket he had bought in 1987 while he was on tour in Germany with his friend Bill Roughley, alias the eponymous Faron of 1960s band Faron's Flamingos. Roughley had always admired that jacket, with its buttons decorated with skulls, and had joked every time he saw Sutch, 'When you die, you can leave me that jacket in your will.' Sutch parcelled it up, wrote Bill Roughley's address on it, and posted it, forgetting to put on any stamps.

Yvonne rang Sutch at 1 p.m. on Tuesday, got no reply, and tried again hourly until nearly midnight, when she finally got through to him. He told her he was OK, and about to go to bed. Annoyed that he hadn't phoned her, she decided to go over the following morning. Other friends like Carlo Little had also been trying unsuccessfully to contact Sutch.

By now I'd got back from Wales and returned to my office, and it crossed my mind to phone David to check he and Yvonne had got back OK and enjoyed the weekend. It seems he wasn't cutting himself off entirely from the world, however: he did speak to a friend, glamour model Samantha Kirli, 'Sammi', with whom he was supposed to be going to Royal Ascot that week, and he also spoke to his former long-term partner Giselle Menhennet, who now lived in France.

Sutch met 'Sammi' (aka Sam) in 1986, and they shared 'an on-off affair which lasted until 1993'. He helped progress her acting and singing career, she appeared on stage with him. He called her late and spoke at length: 'He was sounding really, really down.' This may well have been his final conversation. Samantha is adamant that this conversation ended early on the Wednesday morning at some time after 3 a.m., as she was so late getting to bed that she was exhausted all the next day at the races.

David had evidently made his mind up by now about the

complicated, shambolic succession of arrangements that passed for a life. There were too many people to please – but not enough that he genuinely wanted to. He was no longer even pleasing himself. There would never be a more appropriate time to act. His finances were in decent nick. Having not made a will, he must have known that everything would pass to Tristan, his son. He hadn't wanted to let anyone down, and had fulfilled his last remaining obligations – including the Man Versus Horse Marathon for me. There was the Hallowe'en gig in Las Vegas, but he hadn't yet signed the contract to perform.

In any case, he'd already taken the first steps towards taking his own life: first cutting out completely the long-term medication he'd been on to counter his persistent depression – and then taking twice as much as usual, perhaps hoping for Dutch courage. He probably did not give much thought to the fact that the day, Wednesday, 16 June, was the birthday of one of his best friends – Alan Hope, the first Loony Party mayor.

Sutch laid out a set of clothes on the bed: a grey Regency stage jacket with a yellow silk flower pinned to the lapel. He would have known, as he made those final preparations for his last public performance, that Yvonne Elwood would be the one to find him.

Yvonne opened the door at 10 Parkfield Road in the middle of that Wednesday afternoon. 'It looked like David was just standing on the stairs; he was dressed in ordinary, day clothes. It looked almost as though he had make-up on, because he was so pale. I called a greeting to him. I said, "David, what are you doing?" He didn't answer. I thought he was playing a joke on me and wanted me to take a photograph of him – so I did. Then I suddenly realised what he had done.'

There was a child's multi-coloured skipping rope around his neck.

chapter one

David's Dead

'The thing about Dave is that he'll probably be missed by everyone that ever met him, he was such a great person'

— CARLO LITTLE

Back in 1969, when I was a young reporter on the *Harrow Weekly Post*, I received a call: 'Graham! It's Dave here. Grab a photographer and get yourself down here. My house is on fire – it'll make a great story!'

'Well, OK, David, but by the time I can get round to you the fire will be out.'

'No, it won't.'

'Why not?'

'I haven't rung the Fire Brigade yet. I've got a bucket of water here – I'll wait till you arrive so you can take a shot of me pouring it over the flames.'

We arrived at his house in twenty minutes, and, to his delight, the blaze made the front page. Rapidly the activities of Screaming Lord Sutch became part of our staple diet. He was always turning up in the paper – and we co-operated obligingly – with some new idea, gimmick or statement. He would happily have been the lead story every week. There was never any trouble getting hold of him for a quote – though it wasn't worth calling him much before midday, as he kept rock musician's hours – and he would always want to chat about his recent media appearances.

I used to watch him play at the Clay Pigeon at Eastcote, hamming his way through his 'Jack the Ripper' act, flailing enthusiastically at anything that moved with an unconvincing-looking axe. Once, in the early 1970s, at the Railway Hotel in Wealdstone, he broke off from belting out his songs to lead all of us in the audience outside, carrying with him an effigy of the prime minister, Edward Heath, which he tossed onto a waiting bonfire: a typical stunt which predictably garnered the publicity he so loved.

David Sutch was never really able to sing. Nor did he ever fool himself that he could. 'I'm not the world's greatest singer,' he declared in 1991, 'but I am a good rock 'n' roll shouter.' He could bellow and rave it up, and, on a good night, just about cling to the vaguely recognisable outline of a song. In his earlier days, back in the early 1960s, when static, bland crooners or Elvis clones were the order of the day, he had always ensured that his own musical shortcomings were disguised by competent, often brilliant, backing musicians who played up a storm behind him. But as a performer: that was a different matter. He could transfix an audience. Sutch shattered the derivative image of early British rock 'n' roll. He was the first domestic wild, long-haired, uncontrollable, original, mould-breaking media magnet to burst on the scene.

After several years as a journalist I joined William Hill, working first in their betting shops, then in their press office, and my association with David Sutch was reinstated when I came up with the bright idea of letting him place a bet on the number of votes he would get as a Monster Raving Loony candidate at his next by-election. We set the number low, thus allowing David to win back the cost of his deposit and have a unique story for the papers into the bargain, which would benefit both of us. As the relationship was refined we increased our involvement to the point where David was standing for the Official Monster Raving Loony I Bet I Will Beat William Hill Party. We got involved with other Sutch exploits, too, including an Elvis Lookalike Competition and, memorably, a Monster Hunt Weekend held on the shores of Loch Ness, when we put up £250,000 as a prize for anyone who could come up with convincing proof of the existence of Nessie.

There were a number of serious hunters and one or two spoof bids, and then there was Screaming Lord Sutch, who turned up at the loch brandishing a Neptune trident and some British Rail sandwiches, which he dipped into the waters in an effort to entice the monster to the surface, to the delight of the accompanying media pack. In 1989, I introduced David to the Man Versus Horse Marathon, for which he would be the starter and prize-giver, and which we could now brand as the 'Looniest' race in the calendar.

And then, that Wednesday night, 16 June 1999, my phone rang at around midnight, hauling me out of a sound slumber. It was our mutual friend, Mary Murray: 'Graham, put the Ceefax on. David's dead.' David? David who? I thought. Downstairs I turned the television on to read: 'The veteran rock 'n' roller turned politician is believed to have committed suicide.'

David Sutch would have revelled in the wall-to-wall media coverage of his death: the banner headlines on the tabloid front pages; the prominent mentions in the broadsheets; the obituaries on television and radio. Publicity had driven his career, and stimulated his ego. It was a consistent trait during the thirty years that I knew him.

It was a tribute to David that the media treated him with such affectionate respect: 'The Campaigner Who Put a Smile into Politics' was the *Daily Mail*'s headline; 'Tragedy of Lord Sutch' – the *Telegraph*; 'A Loony Legend' – the *Mirror*; 'Politics Loses Colourful Clown' – *The Times*; 'Number 10 Tribute as Unique Loony Lord Sutch Dies' – the London *Evening Standard*.

Not everyone was shocked. A bizarre, scurrilous, but very funny website, www.stiffs.com, commented that Screaming Lord Sutch was 'what the British affectionately refer to as "an eccentric" and what we here in America call "a fucking nutcase"'. But *The Times*, in a lengthy obituary, disagreed:

His long and absurd career was an important reminder that in the true British electoral system anyone can stand, and the people are free to vote not for party nominees, but for individuals. For all his motley he was not altogether a fool. It is through the loophole he kept open that Martin Bell found his way into Parliament ... [Although] most of his political activities had more to do with self-publicity than ideology, Sutch was a very moral person who wanted to do what he saw as the right thing and to help young people. He was an early rock 'n' roller who was appalled by the drug squalor into which so many stars descended.

'When you watched *Election Night*,' said the presenter Johnny Vaughan on Channel 4's *The Big Breakfast*, 'the highlight was when you go to the prime minister's constituency and there's Screaming Lord Sutch, reminding us of how ludicrous politics, and all the sound and fury, signifying very little, really is. He's a genius.'

Around the corner from Parkfield Road, Keef Venness, the manager of the local charity shop, was sorting through a box labelled 'To Be Collected By Mr Sutch', which had been put to one side for him a few days previously. The box contained what most people would regard as useless tat: a 'Monster in my Pocket' bum-bag; bits of animal-print clothing; fluffy toys. 'He'd buy anything weird and wacky,' said Venness, who claimed that he and Sutch had been planning to open up a fancy dress shop to cash in on Millennium Night party fever.

Yvonne Elwood once described her job as 'looking after David', making her sound like a carer, but even the ghost-writer of Sutch's autobiography (*Life As Sutch*) former *Guardian* journalist Peter Chippindale, spoke of how he was 'notorious for the unreliability of his shambling progress through life'. Whenever Sutch carried out a function for me at William Hill we would wait, often in vain, for an official invoice, and eventually receive a grubby, hand-written bill, requesting some obscure amount. 'He's always late,' Sutch's infamous but loyal friend Cynthia Payne once said. 'Late for everything, and that does drive me mad. I once invited him round for 7.30 p.m. and he turned up at midnight. That's quite typical.'

I was knocked sideways by David's death. But what did I – or anyone else, for that matter – really know about his state of mind? On Thursday, 17 June 1999, Yvonne laid flowers outside 10 Parkfield Road. 'I feel very sad and angry at such a sad waste of a valuable life,' she told reporters. 'He had been fighting a constant battle against depression and I'm afraid in the end he just didn't feel he could carry on. We envisaged spending the rest of our lives together and it is something that is very hard to come to terms with. He had talked of suicide before,' she added, 'and always said that when you suffer from depression then you don't have to have a reason; the depression is the reason.'

At a brief preliminary inquest hearing on 23 June, Police Sergeant Stephen Burns said that the terraced house in Parkfield Road where Sutch lived, where his mum had lived, was in a disorganised state, full of old newspapers, suitcases and general clutter. The sergeant had had to negotiate some filing cabinets in the hallway at the foot of the stairs before he could even get to the body. Sutch 'was suspended from a rope tied around the banisters. His feet were on the third or fourth stairwell and he was slumped.'

'Yvonne tried to get David to clear out his mum's house,' 'Wild' Bob Burgos, an erstwhile Savage, later revealed, 'but he wouldn't touch a thing. He wanted it all left just as it was before she died – even the teacup with her lipstick marks remained untouched.'

David's former partner Thann Rendessy, the mother of his son, Tristan, would later tell me, startlingly, that he was unable to report his mother's death to the relevant authorities, that 'he even carried on paying her pension into her account'. She also said that twenty skips were needed to clear out the house.

The *Daily Telegraph* reported that two suicide notes were found, dated a week earlier and signed 'Lord David E. Sutch'. The hearing was told that he had been badly affected by the deaths of his mother two years previously and, more recently, of his dog, a Yorkshire terrier, Rosie, which had belonged to his mother and whose passing therefore marked the complete severance of direct links with her. Yvonne, however, complained to the *Harrow Observer* that 'he suffered eighteen years of depression, yet they've been suggesting he killed himself because of a dog. We're upset David's death has been trivialised.'

The inquest was adjourned for further inquiries to be made and to allow Tristan to travel to the hearing from his home in Texas.

In the *Independent* of 25 June the poet and rock musician Martin Newell paid tribute to David with a beautifully observed poem:

A world of lugging Selmer amps
And Hammond organs into vans

As pre-Profumo Britain rubbed its eyes.

The early discs, all plundered riffs
Whacked down in pegboard studios
To acetate, pressed-up, released and sunk.

But watch the pantomime begin
The coffin carried through the crowd
And see the startled front four rows jump back.

In top-hat, cloak, outrageous hair
Sutch blunders out, leaps off the stage
You had to be there really and fifteen.

To see his keyboard player got up
The wig skew-whiff and rouged-up cheeks
When Dave, as Jack the Ripper, raised the knife.

And brought it down, the awful scream
The swirl, the drums, the flashing lights
He did the same act every night for years.

If Mayall schooled the stars in blues
It's Sutch who trained them up for stage
A one-trick pony but a brilliant trick.

You'd heard the news and vainly hoped:
'Another stunt?' But not this time.
Go gentle with that coffin, boys. Just once.

David's funeral, on Monday, 28 June, at St Paul's in South Harrow, was a surreal experience. Not the quiet, or private occasion that Sutch's reclusive solicitor cousin Linda Oliver had tried unsuccessfully to arrange; she had been over-ruled by long-standing friends, led by Carlo Little.

The front cover of the Order of Service was adorned with a rosette, a guitar, a cross and a steaming cup of tea, the beverage he once described as 'a gift from God'. The considerable contingent of garishly dressed candidates and colleagues from the Loony Party included one who, for no apparent reason, was carrying a furry donkey's head on a stick. Dave Savage, a Sutch fan and member of The 'Northern' Savages (he had different bands for different areas), was dressed as Jack the Ripper. The younger generation was represented by thirteen-year-old Oliver Hewett, recently appointed as leader of the Young Loony Party. (He once chained himself to the railings of Downing Street to protest against compulsory homework.) But divisions and factions were already forming amongst the Loonies.

There were rock 'n' rollers from Sutch's past: P.J. Proby, who came with Billie Davis, and her daughter Celyn, who had 'loved him to bits'; Wee Willie Harris; Frank Allen; Tommy Bruce; Nick Simper; Cliff Bennett; Bruce Welch of The Shadows; Mick Green of Johnny Kidd's Pirates. One of Sutch's musicians says he saw Jimmy Page there, too. There was Rick Parfitt of Status Quo – although later reports suggested that he was a lookalike, as were, I imagine, the dead ringers for John Major and Elvis.

There was Doc Cox from the television programme *That's Life*, and the football agent and former music PR man Eric Hall, who claimed that Sutch 'stole my "Monster" catchphrase for his Loony Party, but I decided not to sue.' Dorothy Calvert, the widow of Sutch's early mentor and manager back in the early sixties, Reg Calvert, attended in a wheelchair, with her daughter Candy. Roger Daltrey of The Who sent a wreath and card that read 'Fondest Memories'. Captain Sensible wrote: 'Oi, Sutch, what about that fiver?' Political colleague Mark Boyle just asked: 'Why?' There were also flowers from Paul Nicholas, and Chas and Dave. One of Sutch's earliest Loony Party allies, Stuart Hughes – who had become a Conservative and from whom Sutch had later acrimoniously split – demonstrated a posthumous reconciliation by arriving in Loony regalia and with a huge wreath in the shape, colour and style of Sutch's famous, massive electoral rosettes.

The *Daily Telegraph* estimated the turnout at 500.

Thann Rendessy (by then Noey) was there with Sutch's son Tristan (who had inherited his father's estate of £399,405), as was Giselle Menhenett, with whom he had lived for over eighteen years, and Cynthia Payne, with whom he had lived platonically for around eighteen months.

Yvonne, accompanied by her daughter, Alex, had insisted on walking to the church behind a Lincoln Continental, escorted by some fifty of the bikers present. The note on her floral tribute, a furry leopardskin heart split down the middle, read: 'Thank you, Dave, for the best two years of my life. It took so long to make it and we'll never have the recipe again.' The last line was a quote from the Richard Harris hit 'MacArthur Park', written by Jimmy Webb, which, she said, was 'our song'.

The funeral convoy, reported the BBC, 'featured various floral tributes and a pair of the politician's leopardskin boots stuffed with a bouquet'. I managed to find a place inside the church, but many were left outside, where they had to listen to the service on loudspeakers. For the first time in many years there was standing room only at a Screaming Lord Sutch gig.

When the hearse arrived, carrying David's coffin, on which rested lilies and one of his top hats, it was impossible not to wonder whether this just might all be one wonderful, giant Sutch hoax. 'I was half expecting the coffin to open,' said former Searchers guitarist Frank Allen, a mate of Sutch's since 1960, 'and David to leap out screaming, "I fooled you all!"'

After the first hymn, the eulogy was delivered by John Tempest, Sutch's long-term PR manager and agent: 'I wish I hadn't been asked by Tristan, Linda and [her sister] Julie to give this eulogy,' he said.

> I wish David hadn't died. But he did; we are here, and it is, indeed, an honour to be invited to say a few words about David Sutch.
>
> David Edward Sutch was born at a very early age to a lady he never ever forgot. In fact, many of us remember attending his mum's funeral service in this very church just over two years ago. And at that service we were all impressed by his love for the lady who was always there when he needed her. But, let's not forget, he was there when she needed him.
>
> To many of David's friends from his early rock 'n' roll years – some of whom are here today – he showed the world a totally different way of performing. There are those who will rightly say that others, who have gone on to great things in the world of music, owe rather more than a nod of acknowledgement in David's direction.

I well remember the times he'd be at some by-election or another and he'd be shaking hands and asking people to vote for him. Up would come some lady and she'd probably say, 'I saw you at Scunthorpe Baths in 1965, I was in the front row and you smiled at me – do you remember?' Where others might have disregarded her, she'd be rewarded with a smile and one of his Loony Million-Pound notes, then he'd pose for a quick photograph for her family album …

David had an effect on all of us – and definitely for the better. He didn't like having to take sides. So it's perhaps fitting that we've all come together – a large family – here to celebrate the life of a father, a cousin, a friend and colleague, a leader and a man that the world will never see the like of again. Sutch was the way it was with him. And Sutch is why he will always be with us.

Reverend Alan Hulme of St Paul's gave the address, and began by saying: 'All funerals are unique, but some are more unique than others.' Sutch's 'great love of cups of tea', he went on, 'was not perhaps the standard image of a rock 'n' roll star – but one of his friends last week said a packet of tea would be a more fitting tribute than a bunch of flowers.' He told mourners that 'among all the fun and laughter there was a great sadness to Lord Sutch – he reached a moment when he thought there was no hope. It was a tragic moment.'

A recording of Chuck Berry's 'Roll Over Beethoven' was incongruously but movingly played, resulting in a spontaneous outbreak of jiving outside the church, with foot tapping and tears inside.

The burial at Pinner New Cemetery was designated for 'close friends and family' but an impressive motorbike guard of honour accompanied Sutch to his final resting place. Former Savage Ronnie Harwood sang 'Love Me Tender' at the graveside, and various items were thrown on top of the coffin as it was lowered into the grave he shares with his mother. Cynthia Payne dropped in a message, and a Loony rosette went down, with a pair of handcuffs from an infamous practical joke. There was an unfortunate spat between Sutch's closest female friends, smoothed over by the vicar. The wake featured a joyous jam by former Savages.

At the forty-five-minute inquest on 31 August 1999 the Hornsey coroner, Dr William Dolman, called David Sutch 'a comedian with tragedy at his heart' and said:

> He clearly was a man who had suffered from depression for a long period. The public saw his public face, a cheery, outgoing character, yet in the privacy of his room, his true character, his true sadness, appeared … The public saw one face of David Sutch, his close friends saw the other side of him. I suppose in a sense his life is a tragi-comedy. It has come to a sudden end – an end he had obviously planned.
>
> The entertainment and fun he brought to many people in what one might call the sometimes unsavoury world of politics, I hope, will be remembered longer than the events of June this year. I record that David Sutch killed himself, and, I'm going to add, while suffering from a depressive illness.

Yvonne Elwood told the inquest that Sutch had been taking tablets for depression for quite a long period when she first met him, and said 'he was a tortured soul'. His depression, she revealed, 'would affect him physically. His whole face would drop and he just couldn't cope. He had to cancel appointments, and nothing would make him happy. He would either go to bed, or sit being depressed, or walk about. He liked to go and sit in the park, feed the fish, things like that.' They had divided their time between Reading and Harrow, she explained, but she would return to Reading to take a bath as there were no facilities in his house. His bath, it emerged later, was full of gardening equipment.

On the calendar found in Sutch's house it was discovered that he had written a note on Tuesday, 15 June that read: 'Depression, depression, depression is too much.' He was 'found to have taken twice the therapeutic levels of Prozac and some Lithium' and, in a significant statement, Lynne Birmingham, a psychiatrist, said that Sutch, a manic depressive, had spoken as far back as July the previous year of 'feeling so low he was thinking of ending his life, though he had no plans at that time to do so.'

'He never slept properly,' Cynthia Payne told the inquest. Describing herself – when the coroner asked her to accompanying

A Service of Thanksgiving
for the life of

DAVID
EDWARD
SUTCH

(SCREAMING LORD SUTCH)

1940 – 1999

28th June 1999, 2pm
St Paul's Church, South Harrow

laughter what she did for a living — as an 'after-dinner guest speaker', she explained that 'he used to get up at three in the morning and go down to the kitchen and drink tea or cocoa. There was one occasion he woke up and was screaming coming down the stairs, with a nightmare. His mother told me that he did the same thing once at her house.'

I couldn't help but think of one of David's best-known songs, 'All Black And Hairy', which he wrote in 1966, and which concludes: 'And now at home I cannot sleep / As I'm always frightened of what I might meet.' He would repeat the last line four times and finish with a convincing scream.

Payne's evidence appeared to hint chillingly that Sutch had been planning his own death for some while. Several days before his death David had been contacted by a promoter concerned that he might not turn up for an upcoming gig. She said that Sutch had told the promoter: 'Don't worry about that. I shall be on the front pages of the newspapers next week.'

After the inquest, Yvonne Elwood was interviewed on the steps of the coroner's court and told TV cameras that Tony Blair should ban fox hunting.

chapter two

War Baby

'If you want to understand the adult, look in the childhood'
— JOHN REPSCH, *THE LIFE OF JOE MEEK*

The Second World War was under way, and the Battle of Britain recently won, when David Sutch was born at New End Hospital in Hampstead, north London (not Moscow, as one paper claimed in 1963) on 10 November 1940. His mother, Annie Emily (known to her family as Nancy) was a fan of Charles Dickens, and named her son after David Copperfield. Annie had come to London to go into service with a solicitor's family, from a Sheffield pit village, Woodhouse, five years earlier, at the age of eighteen. 'I was brought up in a very strict Victorian fashion,' she said later, and in 1995 told the *Daily Mail*: 'My in-laws are very religious people, and he's got an uncle who's a Baptist minister.'

David's birth certificate shows him to have been registered four days after his birth as David Edward, by William Joseph Sutch, Police Constable, of 241 Fordwych Road, Hampstead NW2. His mother's maiden name is revealed to have been Smith. According to David, his parents had been married in 1937, but their marriage certificate shows that the ceremony took place on 2 October 1939 at the register office in 'the Metropolitan Borough of Hampstead' just thirteen months before he was born.

Sutch's paternal grandfather was William Edward Sutch, a motor mechanic. His maternal grandfather, George Smith, was a munitions factory worker who had been gassed at the Somme; he was deceased by the time Annie married. (A photograph exists in which he is wearing a cape-like overcoat, with a Gladstone bag; it makes him look like Jack the Ripper.) David's dad William Sutch's profession was listed as 'drilling operator, motor works', and he was a War Reserve policeman. He was twenty-three at the time. Annie, then twenty-two, did not have a recorded occupation.

William's sister, Mary, recalls that they lived in two rooms at Fordwych Road: 'It was wartime and accommodation was difficult. They had a gas cooker installed on the landing and got water from our one and only bathroom. A short distance away was the Handley Page factory, producing bomber aircraft. Nearby was an important mainline railway, Cricklewood station. The German bombers were with us day and night, and seemed determined to destroy the factory and railway lines.

'Will, Nancy and David had the offer of caretaking a large house on the edge of Kenwood [the ostentatious Bishop's Avenue], which was much safer than Fordwych Road. The garden was a jungle, grass and trees out of control. It had been a beautiful house before it had been closed up – the owners had gone abroad. Will, with some of his brothers and friends, eventually managed to clear the jungle and they lived very happily out of the [way of the] continual bombing.

'Will, being a policeman, had often to be on night duty, so Nancy was alone with David in this huge house, so as often as we could, my mother and I would take a bus to Hampstead Heath and stay with her for company. I was about ten years old and spent a lot of time looking after David, and pushing him in a big pram on the Heath, and around Kenwood. My father was a chauffeur and drove a Rolls Royce during the daytime, and was not around a lot, as he had ARP duties at night. He always seemed to have his top hat on.'

Rolls Royce, top hat? It's tempting to think that's where David's sense of style originated.

In 1941, one of the most important events of David Sutch's life occurred. William crashed his motorbike on his way to Hampstead police station during the blackout, and he died on 15 September. Who knows how this affected David throughout his life? In an extraordinary admission over fifty years later, however, Sutch's mother hinted strongly that her short marriage was not exactly idyllic, revealing that David's dad never 'took much interest in him. I don't remember him ever nursing David, picking him up or playing with him.' In fact, she said, William's 'only real passion was canoeing'. You can understand how rumours that the young David was illegitimate may have started, and how history may have been repeating itself when similar whisperings arose when his own son was born.

At the time, though, David's mother was out of work, homeless and left to raise her son on her weekly widow's pension of 3/6d (17.5p). She found a room in a house in Glengall Road in Kilburn in return for carrying out domestic chores, and she also worked as a cleaner, a shop assistant, a cook and a waitress. 'I always managed to pay my bills,' she once said proudly, 'and was never in debt.' She told a national newspaper: 'After my husband's death I got myself a job doing official war work at the Smith's clock factory in Neasden, so I could get David into one of the government's day nurseries.'

'The enduring image I have of her,' David recalled, 'is working hard over the kitchen sink, washing up, cooking and cleaning.'

It appears that David spent up to three years of his early life back in Woodhouse – presumably at his maternal grandparents' home at 10, Coisley Road. This is not recorded in his autobiography, but perhaps his mum may never have told him that they had had to return, albeit temporarily, to south Yorkshire. Certainly by the end of the war, David had already become familiar with a style of clothing that would become his trademark: his gran had made him 'a lovely little siren suit, trimmed with leopardskin fabric, which I proudly wore when my mother took me down to the local park'.

David began his education back in London at Salusbury Road infant and primary school, near Queen's Park underground station, in 1946. Pat Greenberg, a fellow pupil, tells how she too had donned the compulsory green-and-yellow tie and navy jumper, and that she had shared membership of Grange 'house' with him. She recalls to this day the young lad with the straight, dark hair who was a 'happy rebel, not malicious or violent, but a bit of a showman even then, always acting the goat. I remember him being stood in the corner with his back to the teacher and turning round to pull faces. If you were caught misbehaving in those days even minor misdemeanours meant the ruler – David got the ruler plenty of times.'

He first showed an aptitude for entertaining when, in true Just

William style, he organised shows for friends in which he produced and starred in his own hand-puppet shows based on Punch and Judy. The *Kilburn Times* wrote about him and he 'had the thrill of giving my first show to an indoor audience' when he performed at a friend's birthday party.

Towards the end of the 1940s, David's mother began a relationship with a used car dealer, whom he called Uncle Benny. They remained 'engaged' for twelve years and he eventually rented them a flat in South Harrow. Annie didn't shout about this – indeed, her sister-in-law Mary knew nothing about it: 'I never heard the name of Benny. I assume this was kept quiet. Nancy [Annie] received a police pension if I remember rightly, and possibly would have lost it had she remarried, I'm not sure. I know David was encouraged to participate in police parties when young.'

Cynthia Payne knew about it, though: 'She loved the man – they went everywhere together – he took her cruising, which wasn't cheap in those days.'

Film footage of David, aged about eight, and his mum on holiday in Jersey with Benny shows them looking relaxed and happy. But later in the same reels there are bizarre scenes of the youngster playing around a large, carved figure resembling some sort of voodoo doll, and then happily wandering around a cemetery filled with the graves of German soldiers. Oddest of all is a brief shot of what appears to be a group of black-clad nuns or monks cavorting briefly and inexplicably in a country lane.

Benny was obviously not short of a bob or two: fascinating cine-film footage shows David's homely-looking mum in her late thirties or early forties – but, typically for that era, looking somewhat older – together with Benny, on glamorous trips on luxury liners, taking in places like Gibraltar, the South of France, Spain, Naples, Madeira, Portugal, even the States and what looks like the Caribbean. David seems to be missing from the cruises – perhaps he was shipped up to Yorkshire for the duration. Further footage reveals a teenage David showing off a new, light-blue motor scooter, taking mum and Benny up and down the road, his hair already unfashionably long.

But Annie's affair eventually ended when Benny met and married a much younger woman. 'My mother was torn apart by that,' Sutch later told an interviewer. 'She really loved him. I was a schoolboy boxer and

I threw a punch or two. He'd been a boxer in the army and could have flattened me, but he didn't.'

Significant details of this relationship are notable by their absence from his autobiography – at the express request of David's mum who 'swore Sutch to secrecy', according to Cynthia Payne. Thann Rendessy confirms that Mrs Sutch had hoped to marry Benny, but that 'he got rid of her for a younger woman, and that made her against marriage and men. That was why he – David – didn't ever want to get married to anybody. I think he was bitter that she was dumped, I think that bothered him.'

Having failed the Eleven Plus exam, David moved on in 1952 to Percy Road Boys' School in Kilburn, where he became notable for his sporting prowess. He was a member of the school boxing squad both in the Willesden and Middlesex competitions, and became a local and county champion. Sutch kept his boxing up even after leaving school, joining the Rotex Club in Willesden – 'You were never sure when the Willesden mob might attack you,' he explained. His teacher, Doug Rosewarne, now in his eighties, says he also joined school 'adventure tours' to south-east England, the Isle of Wight and Yorkshire, staying at Youth Hostels and enjoying the experience so much that he later joined the YHA himself. 'He was always popular and helpful,' says Rosewarne. 'He was a quiet lad, devoted to his mother and his home life.'

After Sutch had left school and begun to make a name for himself as a performer, Mr Rosewarne approached him to open officially the newly launched Percy Popalong Disco. Sutch agreed, and when Mr Rosewarne went to visit him, 'he explained how he'd visited many shows to see what worked, and decided as he wasn't a good singer, to "shock" by his dress and antics.'

Sutch himself reflected: 'I found myself irresistibly drawn to anything slightly spooky or with horror in it.' He had already come to understand that the first major event in his life had been the dreadful demise of his father; now his penchant for the macabre was being nurtured by visits to Madame Tussaud's Chamber of Horrors and the Tower of London.

Sutch's first public appearance took place in the summer of 1953, while he was still at school. Holidaymakers at Butlins in Clacton were treated to a rendering of 'How Much Is That Doggie in the Window?'

– which won him a clockwork mouse. He also contested an election to the school prefecture – and actually won: his first and last election victory. Arthur 'Nobby' Randall was at Percy Road at the same time as David: 'Attention was drawn to him because of his zany antics and jokes – he never took anything seriously.'

David – whose mother was now working at another local school as a dinner lady – then landed himself a part-time job, working for a local butcher in the evenings and at weekends. 'One of the perks was that he had the use of the delivery bicycle,' remembered another school pal, Don 'Sackie' Bromage. 'They used to have a large basket fixed over the front wheel. It was one of his favourite japes to trick one of the first-formers into taking a ride in the basket – news of these events spread through the school, so after 4 p.m. Percy Road would be lined on both sides with all the mugs that had previously fallen for the ruse. Dear old David would set off and gain a fair old lick of speed, and would suddenly leap off the bike, leaving the poor, unsuspecting wretch to his fate – which was usually ending up in a heap in the road, with the added attraction of grazed knees, elbows and pride.'

In 1956, shortly after leaving school, David and his mother moved from Kilburn to South Harrow in northwest London. He lasted less than a day in his first job, in a factory in Hanger Lane, Willesden, a pivotal moment he recalled a few years later, during a 1963 interview:

> The school sent me to a factory in north London where they had picked a job for me as a sheet metal worker. The foreman told me it was a good gaff to work in and took me around. 'This is where you'll be,' he said. My eyes got used to the dark and I saw all these geezers standing at machines. Then the foreman says I'll start at three quid a week, and explained about the pension – it was the pension that did it. I was going to have to spend forty years in this moody hole. They were going to buy my whole life for a few miserable quid. I told them to stuff the job and left.

Then he had a go at plumbing and basic car mechanics. 'My first job was working in a garage as an assistant mechanic,' he told Radio Cornwall. Jenny Wiggins lived opposite Sutch's workplace in those days: 'I'd come home from school and could hear him right at the end of the road – he was shouting and screaming as he was working away in the garage.'

Then Sutch took up window-cleaning, the round costing him £15 from an acquaintance called Big Ginger Bill. He took to the job straight away: 'I could work the hours I wanted and, if it was freezing cold or raining, I could stay in bed. The work gave me the freedom to be myself, let my hair grow long and wear whatever I liked as well as practise songs as I went on my rounds.' The round fulfilled other needs, too: 'There were always plenty of cups of tea and the odd leg-over. All the money I earned I kept. I was on my way.'

On 9 February 1958, David picked up his weekly pay of £6 1/4d from the Dayton Cycle Company, where he had worked for five months. I found his buff-coloured wage packet forty-five years later, discarded in the garden of his house in Watford Road, Sudbury. Even at this early stage of his life he had begun to hoard anything with his name on it.

There's something of the dog that didn't bark about the absence in Sutch's autobiography of any references to his National Service at the age of eighteen. Conscription survived until 1960, and he does note that his long hair caused people 'to get very angry and shout at you in the street to get it cut and that you should be put in the army', but he fails to address the question of why he wasn't. Flat feet or a bad chest may have been to blame.

By now, in any case, he had 'become a Radio Luxembourg junkie – it was such a relief after all those terrible years of listening to the BBC, where the nearest thing to rock 'n' roll was the Billy Cotton Band. Mother tolerated all this teenage music as long as I didn't play it too loud and disturb the neighbours.' He was starting to think about trying it himself.

David's favourite haunts were the local Cannibal Pot coffee bar and the Ace café on the North Circular Road, where he would risk the scorn of greasers, bikers and Hell's Angels by turning up on his second-hand BSA Bantam 125cc. A biker of Sutch's acquaintance now suggested he should head for a venue from which a number of rock 'n' roll stars had already emerged. Two Australian wrestlers, Ray Hunter and Paul Lincoln, had opened a coffee bar in Old Compton Street in London's West End, called the 2 I's (Two Eyes). Soon it was dubbing itself 'Home of the Stars'.

chapter three

I Must Be Seen and Heard

'He never claimed to be a singer in the conventional sense – not in any sense at all, as far as I could make out. But he was an entertainer. A great entertainer. No matter how brilliant the individuals in his band, you never looked at them when Screaming Lord Sutch was on stage. He dwarfed them'

— Ian Gillan, Deep Purple

From the time he first heard Bill Haley and The Comets playing 'Rock Around the Clock' Sutch was determined to become a rock 'n' roll star. Forty years later he would have entered *Pop Idol*, *Fame Academy* or *The X Factor*. In the late 1950s the way to do it was to make an impression at the 2 I's. 'It was just a cellar in a basement of a coffee bar, where they sold frothy coffee,' he was to recall, 'but it was a breeding ground for rock 'n' rollers. I got an audition. They said at the time that they didn't want any more guys just coming and copying Elvis. They said, "You've got to do something different."'

Passing a second-hand shop one day, Sutch spotted a pair of buffalo horns, and bought them 'for a couple of shillings'. He glued them onto a crash helmet, and borrowed a leopardskin coat from his aunt, which he cut up to make a loincloth. This, he decided, would be his 'Wild Man of Borneo look'. Coupled with his over-the-top vocal ravings, he decided he would stand out from the crowd at auditions.

It is a story – complete with the later consequences when his aunt asked for her coat back – that is pure 'Just William'. Yvonne confirmed that Sutch had come across Richmal Crompton's masterpieces at school, and David's mother once said of him: 'He was very naughty. I don't think he'll ever grow up. He's always playing jokes and messing about.' I wonder whether the eternal eleven-year-old, always getting into and out of scrapes and returning to the bosom of his loving family, was something of a secret role model, but he was aware that he gave his mum occasional cause for concern: 'I was certainly a handful for any mother to bring up on her own – a bit of a teenage tearaway. I'd spend too long at the fairground, or stay out with girls until all hours.'

Tom Littlewood, who then ran the 2 I's place with Paul Lincoln, remembered his first encounter with the would-be singer: 'One afternoon a strange individual came in, presenting himself as Mr Sutch [and] asked if he could do an audition. I was very much amazed when he arrived, looking like a rag-and-bone man. He had with him a large bundle of miscellaneous equipment – sheepskin, pair of buffalo horns, a man-trap, snow shoes and so forth.'

Flaunting his 'Wild Man' image, Sutch soon impressed at his audition, singing 'an obscure old number called "Bullshit Boogie" – I didn't give a fuck' – duly landed a spot singing at the venue, and began to pick up bookings for gigs. The exact date of his debut is impossible to pinpoint, but it would have been at the very end of the 1950s. Film taken in the 2 I's at the time shows a garishly-dressed Sutch looking as though he is in colour while all those around him are in shades of black and white. His lengthy hair is an extraordinary contrast with the short back and sides of the other men. He had hit on the recipe for success: being different. He'd stay different for the rest of his life.

Unquestionably, David Sutch's style was unique for the times. There were few, if any, similarly hirsute chaps about in those days, although why he had decided to grow it and risk the inevitable jibes is not clear. In his autobiography, he calls himself 'the first of the long-hairs … I had grown my locks to eighteen inches long and turned myself into a freak years before the hippies came along.' Fellow early rocker Jackie Lynton stresses Sutch's impact: 'Walking down the street, people would come towards us – and they would cross the road – they wouldn't walk past you. Because, seeing the first man having hair down to his shoulders – it was 1960, it was way before anybody. It was ridiculous.'

His startling appearance soon attracted the attention of the media. Iain McGregor, then a reporter for Bernsens International Press Service, BIPS, went along with photographer Frank Martin, to see this 'outrageously dressed singer', and thought he might make a story for the agency's international customers. 'I thought his performance was putrid, to be honest, and that he was a nonentity masquerading as a pop star, but we did the story and got him some of the publicity he came to love.'

'I went down there screaming and yelling,' boasted Sutch. 'Next thing it was all over the papers – "Newcomer Horns in on Rock 'n' Roll" – and I was launched.'

Carlo Little reckons it was on 6 February 1960 that he turned up at an old haunt of his, the Cannibal Pot coffee bar (named after a line in a Tommy Steele record) in Sudbury near Wembley, having just finished his National Service. He put a Buddy Holly record on the jukebox and was approached by a young lady called Gill, who correctly identified him, much to his surprise, and told him that her boyfriend Dave, who would be along in a minute, had similar tastes in music. 'He walked in, wearing a three-quarter-length Crombie coat and Biggles goggles with no glass in them over his long, lank hair.'

David and Carlo hit it off and talked about Carlo (who he apparently dubbed 'Little Slasher') starting a group, although in the early stages there was no indication that Sutch would participate musically. It was suggested that he might manage the band. However, during a rehearsal in a hall at the back of the Swan pub in Sudbury, Sutch, inspired by the high-pitched, wailing notes of guitarist Bernie Watson (who Sutch used to say looked like a schoolkid, and who subsequently brought his mate Nicky Hopkins into the band), suddenly launched into a wild flight of head-shaking, screaming and hollering, which left his band-mates almost speechless, but impressed. He was in as vocalist.

Sax player Pete Newman, who was there at the genesis of what became The Savages, recalled his sister Pat telling him, '"All you can do is scream, Dave: how about calling yourself Screaming Sutch?" Later he turned up at rehearsal with a top hat and I said, "Hey, Dave, you look like a Lord."'

Little has a variation on the derivation of their frontman's title: 'Dave had announced that his stage name would be Screaming Lord Sutch – the first word in tribute to Jay Hawkins [the American bluesman], and because he used to run up and down underground trains screaming when he was out with his mates on a Saturday night; the second inspired by the top hat he was wearing. I came up with Savages [they also played as The Raving Savages] as the ideal description of the way we wanted to sound.' (Hawkins, who wrote the classic 'I Put a Spell on You', dubbed himself 'Screamin'' and performed with accessories of skulls, coffins and voodoo paraphernalia. He later accused Sutch of 'taking a little something from me'.)

Yvonne told me that Lord Snooty, comic character in *The Beano*, and never seen without his top hat, was also an early Sutch favourite.

A period of intense one-to-one singing instruction now ensued in Little's front room, during which the drummer struggled (in vain?) to explain timing and key to Sutch. Together they succeeded in building up a repertoire of maybe a dozen songs. 'He knew all the lyrics to American hits anyway,' said Little – indeed, a diary from those days is full of hand-written song lyrics which Sutch had painstakingly copied down, either from the radio or from repeated listening to records.

As a lad Sutch had lived near the Gaumont State theatre in Kilburn and many years later he was to see the great Jerry Lee Lewis there. 'It was the most electrifying rock 'n' roll show I've ever seen,' he recalled. 'I've been a fan, and later a friend.' Indeed, before too long, Sutch would have the privilege of playing with Jerry Lee in Hamburg, on a bill where The Beatles would be the support band. 'My early influences were Jerry Lee, Chuck Berry, Little Richard and Bo Diddley,' he said. Rock 'n' roll would be Sutch's brief, and the wild abandon of Lewis and Little Richard his example.

According to his autobiography, David Sutch made his first public appearances with The Savages later in 1960 on the stage of the Park Royal Hotel on Hanger Lane and the Clay Pigeon pub at Eastcote. There, John Schollar, a guitarist who would later back him, 'was amazed to see Sutch run in, dressed as King Neptune, covered in "seaweed", jump on a table amongst screaming girls, leap off, land in a heap on the floor and commence singing.' But Carlo Little, who was there at the time, identifies the historic landmark as the British Legion in South Harrow, and also puts the cost of entry at two bob. They had spread the word by creating their own small posters to stick up over existing advertising billboards: 'A couple of dozen turned up. We made enough to buy a couple of drinks.'

Very quickly Sutch became a favourite of the tabloid papers. His always long, sometimes brightly coloured hair, leopardskin loincloth and many and varied stage props couldn't help but create a stir. All this, remember, in an era when, as John Osborne once remarked, 'you could attract outraged looks just by walking down a provincial High Street in a yellow cardigan.' Sutch didn't care. 'He used to be stared at all the time,' confirms early Savage Rick Brown. 'He called them gawpers. But he was carefree, everything was a huge laugh. That was his style.' On 28 September, 1960 the *Sunday Pictorial* ran a photograph of Sutch – arms outstretched, eyes shut, mouth wide open, hair hanging around his face, a hat adorned by bull horns – with the headline 'HE'S THE DAFTEST YET!' The story is very much of its time:

The weirdie wearing the horns is a rock 'n' roll performer – the latest to make a bid to become Britain's teenage rage. He's called Screaming Lord Sutch. And this is what he said: 'The horns are a great gimmick – the kids love 'em. It's strange. I've met people who could really sing, but they were getting nowhere. Now, I can't sing. Never could. I just scream. That's the way to put rock 'n' roll over. Scream, man. I haven't had a haircut for over a year. That helps a bit. My leopardskin clothes and bearskin jacket make the whole thing swing. Man, it's a riot! I'm making money. I've got a full diary of dates – and a record lined up.'

The nineteen-year-old screamer was plain David Sutch from South Harrow, Middlesex, when he asked rock star Vince Taylor for work with his group. Vince heard David scream and recommended him to his own backer, Tom Littlewood, who runs the famous 2 I's coffee bar in Soho – where Tommy Steele, Wee Willie Harris, Terry Dene, The Shadows and other rockers started out.

Tom advised the newcomer: 'Get a gimmick, and you're in'. So, plain David Sutch went away and bought a pair of buffalo horns in a second-hand shop for fifteen shillings. He fixed 'em in a hat, and returned to the 2 I's as Screaming Lord Sutch.

The eighteen-inch hair just grew, along with the gimmick, and now he is touring with Vince's group. Says Vince: 'When The Screamer starts work, the fans don't know whether to laugh, jive or run away.'

You think Lord Sutch is a bit much? Putting it mildly – HE'S A SCREAM!

Sutch, it turned out, had yet to admit to his mother what he'd been up to. 'I still thought he was cleaning windows,' said Annie. 'When the truth came out in conversation I was flabbergasted.'

Sutch described the group's style at that time as 'rock 'n' roll, wild and frantic', condemning the current sounds as 'timid', and later telling journalist Ritchie Unterberger: 'I always had good musicians plus a good visual show. I came from the music hall era, so I literally put musical vaudeville to rock 'n' roll.'

In June 1960, Carlo had temporarily joined semi-pro band Dougie Dee and The Strangers, as Sutch was now being backed, as the *Sunday Pictorial* reported, by Vince Taylor's Playboys, a ploy by Tom Littlewood, who 'just fired' The Savages from the 2 I's to save on costs. (Little would later, so the story goes, turn down a job with the Rolling Stones – writing the name of a friend, Charlie Watts, on a cigarette packet and handing it to Mick Jagger.)

Around this time promoter Lionel Digby booked Sutch to play on a tour of the West Country – his first gigs outside London. 'I remember going to an antiques shop with David,' he recalls, 'helping him look for a coffin for his act.'

Another of Sutch's first promoters was Bob Potter, now owner of the Lakeside Country Club in Surrey that has become famous in recent years for hosting the World Darts Championship. Potter included Sutch on one of his innovative 'package' shows. He played venues like the Agincourt Ballroom in Camberley, and Aldershot's Palais de Danse, before his West Country tour. Potter reminisces about obscure acts such as Baby Bubbly, Lance Fortune, Karl Danger and Mal Turner, a ventriloquist who once passed himself off as Gene Vincent, according to Potter, and whose use of blood in his act may well have given Sutch ideas. Potter laughed as he told me stories of being on the road: Sutch sleeping in the bath, his fur coat around him to keep warm; Sutch asking an elderly chemist for pills to thicken his hair then returning later to tell him it had worked very quickly – whipping off his hat and allowing his hair to tumble down over his shoulders; enraging a butcher by sticking a poster advertising a gig over his window, with the consequence that the butcher stormed out of his shop after Sutch, waving his meat cleaver.

When he had first met Sutch, Potter decided, 'You've got a gimmick – you'll do for me. Everyone thought he was crazy, but he was an intelligent man who was his own PR.' But he wasn't an instant hit with Potter, as the first Savages' bassist Rick Brown recalled: 'We played Camberley and Bob spent the show jumping up and down waving his fists at us – we were terrible, disastrous.'

But Sutch once even bailed Potter out of trouble. 'I was nicked for having the wrong licence for the coach I was driving,' he says. 'They took me in to the station, but Sutch came in, handed over "my card" to the copper and in his best posh voice demanded that I be charged or released and quoted the law at him. It worked – they let me out.'

Potter tried to encourage Sutch to expand his act, maybe move into promotion by running an agency. 'When he left me I knew he'd never have a hit record – a great live act doesn't always make for hit records.'

Carole Watt, a teenage girl Sutch met around this time in Weymouth, remembers 'helping to push the band's van through snow when it broke down'. They developed their relationship when he returned to the area, then blonde Carole and a friend, Little Carol, moved to London to be nearer to Sutch.

She recalls meeting up with him at the 2 I's where Tom Littlewood told her that 'Sutch was no good for me and that I'd be better off with him'. But she still became Sutch's girlfriend – or one of them. 'He did buy me a little ring, and people used to think we were engaged,' she says. They spent much of their time going to see films – 'not always horror movies' – 'snogging' in Soho doorways and 'making love'. Sutch also sent Carole explicit love letters when she lived in The Beach, the hotel that her parents owned in Weymouth. Terrified that her parents might find them she asked Little Carol to stash them away in 'a secret place we had in White Sands (Little Carol's parents' hotel)', later asking her to retrieve them.

Before she got round to it she moved away so, for all Carole knows, there is a bundle of her love letters from Lord Sutch lying around somewhere in Weymouth. 'It was just about having fun in those days,' she says. 'Dave was always happy. I never ever, ever saw him exhibit any symptoms of depression. I never saw him drunk and he never took drugs.'

The developing relationship was curtailed when Carole and Carol became involved in a minor altercation with police. They ended up arrested and sentenced to probation, with the proviso that they return to Weymouth. 'The day I left London I was sobbing my heart out,' she recalls. 'Dave was squeezing me as hard as he could and telling me that we would still meet up. I think if I'd been able to remain there we may well have stayed together – who knows?'

As she thought back to that day she began to cry again.

Sutch first met Bill Roughley around this time. Roughley was another aspiring rocker, front man for Faron's Flamingos, who had come down from his native Liverpool in an effort to make it. The two of them hit it off. Roughley stayed with Sutch, reciprocating when his pal visited Merseyside, and one night Sutch and his guitarist teamed up with Bill to visit the Casbah Club, run by Mona, mother of original Beatles' drummer Pete Best. 'George Harrison was in the club playing guitar, along with another rhythm guitarist,' recalled Roughley. 'After they played, the audience threw some money at them, which Dave thought was an insult – he said it was expected in boxing but not in music. Sutch wanted to get up and play, so I told George Harrison he was here. "Yeah, I've heard of him," said George, but he said he couldn't lend Sutch's guitarist his own instrument as he could not afford to replace any strings which might get broken. We managed to get a guitar for Sutch's man to play, though, and a little while later he got up to sing – he soon had the audience literally screaming at him. Then he jumped off the stage, came over to where I was and started writing in a little red notebook.

'Mrs Best then came in looking annoyed and demanding to know, "Who was it?" Sutch asked her to be quiet and said he was trying to write. But she insisted she wanted to know who it was who had thrown worms at the audience.

'Of course, it was Dave, who had been out in the garden digging up worms which he then threw at the girls while he was singing – they got stuck in their beehive hair-dos. He was thrilled and showed me what he had written down in his book: "Worms work better than maggots." Mrs Best promptly banned us from the Casbah.'

'By 1961 I was a personality and a star,' declared Sutch modestly in *Life As Sutch*. On 17 February he played the Granada in Grantham as part of an All Stars bill, also featuring Jess Conrad; Johnny Duncan and The Blue Grass Boys; Mark Wynter; The Four Jays; Vince Taylor and The Playboys; Mike and Bernie Winters; and, from the USA, Gene Vincent. Desmond Tyler paid 3/6d (17.5p) to get in and recalls Sutch billed as 'the new non-recording star'. Jess Conrad, the suave, good-looking crooner, remembers that, at the start of the tour in Bedford, 'We were all travelling together, but Sutch arrived late, in a horsebox he was living in – sleeping on straw in the back. We'd been betting amongst ourselves about how many numbers it would take us to get what we called a "run-down" – when the audience would rush the stage in response to one of our numbers.

'Sutch had turned up so late that he'd missed rehearsals, but he heard us talking and immediately said, "I bet you I can get the kids running to the front on my first number."

'When he went on stage, backed by The Flee Rekkers, he threw everything into his first song – and went rushing towards the front of the stage to wind up the audience. Unbeknown to Sutch the cinema people had covered up the orchestra pit with tarpaulin and we'd been told not to go on it. Sutch jumped straight on to it – and disappeared out of sight into the pit. He carried on singing but all you could see was his big buffalo horns sticking up.'

Off-stage Sutch seems also to have been attracting a certain notoriety. At the Golden Lion in Fulham the impact he made was rather too literal: connecting with and breaking a punter's nose with his axe and having to pay a gin and tonic as compensation. In March 1961 it was reported that a woman police sergeant had sent her seventeen-year-old daughter to Coventry – presumably not literally – for planning to marry Sutch. Newspapers reported mother telling daughter, 'Get that thing out of my house.' It seems probable that this girl, Gillian White, was the one responsible for introducing Sutch and Little, but she has, sadly, disappeared into obscurity. By July, though, Sutch appears to have quickly got over this romantic setback, as papers were carrying the news that he had tried to elope 'in his pink horsebox', to Gretna Green with a sixteen-year-old fan. The tryst was foiled, again, by Mum rushing to Scotland where, it was reported, she discovered her daughter and Sutch, the latter clad in Tyrolean hat, tartan shirt, Italian suit and cowboy boots.

A week later in this eventful year he was fined £12 for assault, following an on-stage brawl at a Dumfriesshire miners' club – not, one might have thought, the ideal environment for Sutch's act, particularly if he was still wearing the elopement gear. But he was learning how to deal with uncomplimentary audiences. He told a paper what happened when he was wolf-whistled by a bunch of workmen: 'I waved a dirty great bunch of fivers in their faces and said I might be a long-haired nit, but I didn't muck about in dirty holes for ten quid a week. That shut them up.'

In May 1961 The Savages were back in business and auditioning for guitarists. Several years before he found stardom and world fame with Deep Purple and Rainbow, guitarist Ritchie Blackmore became one of the first of a long and illustrious line of musicians to be offered their first break by Screaming Lord Sutch. 'Ritchie Blackmore, who could only have been fifteen or sixteen at the time, came along with his girlfriend and his dad,' remembered Carlo Little, who was now back in Sutch's band. 'We heard about seven or eight blokes, but it was a toss-up between Ritchie and Roger Mingay. Roger just had the edge, because he was older and more experienced.' He was teaming up with Little, pianist Andy Wren and bassist Ken Payne, although the line-up was pretty flexible. Blackmore would finally get in about a year later.

Rodney Johnson, who acted as a general factotum cum roadie for the band in these days, remembered that Sutch 'used to drink whisky & coke – almost always when someone else was paying. He was a mean man: you could tell by the way he ate eggs – never missed the least bit of the white. It took me a while to realise Carlo's real name, because when Sutch was around he always addressed him as 'F'fucksake Carlo' – it was "F'fucksake Carlo, what's happening? F'fucksake Carlo, where's this or that?"'

How good was Sutch in these days? In 1961 Chas Hodges of Chas and Dave was playing in Mike Berry's Outlaws. 'I'd heard of Sutch but never seen him,' he recalls. 'Roger Mingay [who subsequently left Sutch to play with The Outlaws] was always saying, "Sutch has the best act in the country." "Bollocks!' we'd say. 'Nobody can top us!" One day we were booked on the same bill. Doncaster Baths. Sutch and us. The same night. Now we'll see. And we saw. It was the most spectacular *show* I'd ever seen in my life. You could not take your eyes off of him.'

And he could also sell a song in those days, remembers Chas: 'The first time I ever heard "Roll Over Beethoven" Sutch was singing it live. I loved it and went out and bought Chuck Berry's. I was well disappointed. It didn't have the drive and guts of Sutch and The Savages. I still think of it as a Screaming Lord Sutch original.'

In his diary for those days, Sutch described under the heading 'Acts To Do' a sequence with 'Me dresed [sic] as Cave Man and Andy [Wren] as Cave Woman. I chase Andy over stage with club and we go back on stage sward [sic] fencing. Then boys come on in white coats and on the back of them is the word "Zoo" and then they drag me off.' Or for their rendition of 'Money': 'Me dressed as burglar with black mask and sack, Andy as copper. At end Andy grabs me and I say Wots Up, Wots Up, and Andy says can I see your driving licence, please.' For a song called 'Mercheen Man' (I imagine he meant 'Machine Man'): 'I control Andy with a black box – I say, you all think I'm mad – yes, you all think I'm mad. I'll show you, Mercheen Man (repeat) and then Andy walks on dressed as a robot man and I tell him to stop and pick up chair – which he does – and then I tell him to go and play the piano, which he does. And then I turn a knob too far and it comes off in my hand, so I bang the control box two times and Andy jumps two times. I shake it two times and Andy shakes two times, and goes mad.'

Just William would have approved.

Sutch was catching on to the value of publicity: 'The more I muck about and shock people and get bad publicity the more popular I become with the kids.' But he was also considering his own input: 'If you're in show business you must really believe in it and you must really feel it, otherwise the public themselves can tell.'

He was able to step up to playing bigger, more prestigious venues when he got on to another touring package that included Gene Vincent and Brenda Lee. 'Everywhere we went was a sell-out,' said Carlo Little. 'We were touring the whole country, even going up to Scotland. David was driving us – he owned what was called a "gown van" which had a tall rear end to store stage gear, and three of us were slung in the back with two or three on the bench seat at the front. But there were horrendous fumes coming into the van which we thought we were clearing by opening all the windows, but we were actually sucking them in by doing that. On occasions we had to sleep in the van, which was murder. Sutch gave us about four quid a gig and paid for the fuel etc, keeping the rest for himself – which pretty much represented about an average week's wages for him every time we played.'

Other reports have Sutch and the band travelling around 'in an ambulance with a large pink crocodile on top'. A West Country motorist spotted this apparition and promptly drove into a ditch. Indeed, an early advert plugging the first two Sutch singles depicts him and the group – including a very youthful Ritchie Blackmore – standing around, and even on, a deeply unrealistic-looking croc. Original bass player Rick Brown thought the croc was 'the first sign of the obsessive collecting' to which Sutch would later succumb: 'I once told him that I'd seen an elephant's foot in a junk shop – he was there, cash in hand, the next morning, waiting for them to open.'

Nicky Hopkins, a classically-trained pianist then in his mid-teens, joined Ricky Brown, Carlo Little and Bernie Watson in The Savages in September, and stayed with them for nine months before leaving to join Cyril Davies's All Stars and then Cliff Bennett's Rebel Rousers. Hopkins was another Sutch protégé who went on to much bigger things – in this case playing much-praised piano for The Rolling Stones on both their epic tours of the early 1970s and classic albums like *Exile on Main Street*. According to Sutch, in one of the presumably unintentional slips of the tongue that endeared him to so many, Hopkins 'was known as the sixth Beatle'.

That winter, Sutch launched his recording career, *Disc* magazine informing its readers that in the week of his twenty-first birthday, 'Screaming Lord Sutch has signed a five-year contract with Joe Meek's RGM sound recording organisation.' In those days an act would frequently first sign with a record producer, and together they would come up with the tapes of a single or an LP, and this would then be licensed to a record label for manufacture and distribution to the shops.

The independent producer Joe Meek, whose brief career would eventually become legendary, was an eccentric, innovative, driven and troubled genius, homosexual at a time – the early 1960s – when to be so was still illegal, and a producer of pop records by the dozen, including far more than his fair share of huge hits. His trademark sound – often achieved with primitive studio effects produced by the most ingeniously inventive means – was a reverberant, tremulous guitar or keyboard sound (best heard on The Tornados hit 'Telstar', which he produced) and eerie, echoing background ambience. Meek was fascinated by, and would become obsessed with, the occult and imagery of death and Satanism. Screaming Lord Sutch and his wild act and horror movie obsession was a natural match.

Earlier that month, Meek had produced and released a single by The Moontrekkers, 'Night of the Vampire', boasting that it was 'unsuitable for people with nervous dispositions'. The style he would evolve with Sutch was clearly already on his mind.

'When I went on a 2 I's package tour with Adam Faith and Joe Brown,' recalled Sutch later, 'we toured round the country. There was a talent scout who gave me a card for somebody by the name of Joe Meek, so I phoned up and the guy said, "Come over – I've heard all about you, your wild stage show. What material have you got that's not been recorded?" I had this number called "My Big Black Coffin" that I'd written. We put it together and recorded it.'

Brown remembered "good old Dave Sutch" affectionately – telling Radio 2 listeners after his death: "He was one of the great characters of rock 'n' roll – a royal loony. There will never be another. Acts on the bill always needed to get on the stage before him – because usually if they went on after him there was no stage left. The last gig I played with him, he set fire to the piano and I had to do my set with this thing smouldering away next to me.'

In his autobiography, Sutch described how, in his live performance of 'My Big Black Coffin', recorded as 'Till the Following Night', the band would begin by playing the Death March, and 'four monks [usually audience volunteers], led by Igor the bald-headed Mad Monk, bearing aloft a four-branch candelabra, carried a coffin in through the audience. I was in the coffin and Igor would slip in a mike so I could start screaming and yelling to a sound effects tape of weird noises. I would poke big rubber hands out of the coffin lid, before I leapt out to attack the girls in the first row.' Wearing thick, 'unearthly white' make-up, and clad in black dress jacket with top hat, he would round off the spectacle with 'a mouthful of green gunge which I spat over the audience'. There would follow flares, flashing lights, stage chases, broken blood capsules, clubbings, strangulations and bucketfuls of worms hurled over the audience as he sang:

> While the bats are a-flyin'
> And the cats are a-sighing
> And the zombies are a-dancin'
> And the skeletons p-rancin'
> I get back into my big black coffin
> Till the following night ...

'To my great satisfaction,' concluded Sutch in *Life As Sutch*, 'there seemed to be universal agreement that it was the ultimate in bad taste and quite disgusting.'

'It is easy to forget how dramatic his act was in those days,' says Cliff Bennett. 'When he came out of the coffin, make-up on, long hair flying, he frightened the life out of the audience.'

Asked later about Meek's contributions to his records, Sutch said, 'He could round them off and control us, because we would tend to go on for about ten minutes, so he would get them down to three minutes.' Carlo Little, who was drumming, recalls the following line-up cutting their first disc: Ken Payne on bass, Roger Mingay on guitar, Andy Wren on piano and Pete Newman on sax. 'Dave was given the lyrics, and we had to create the tune around them. We decided to do it as a twelve-bar, and before we got into the recording studio we knew it inside out.'

With lyrics like 'I got two horns on my head and a twinkle in my eye; I got two feet of hair and it make the chicks all sigh' this energetic song, whoever wrote it, is about Sutch himself.

Meek borrowed the atmospheric sound effects – amongst them

howling wind and coffin-like creaking – from his earlier near-hit, 'Night of the Vampire', and John McCready, an authority on Meek's work, describes how 'Joe surrounded Sutch with intensely detailed audio montages of creaking coffins and doors, with howls and screams echoing into infinity. With wires held together with chewing gum and a trusty spring echo, which was in fact a garden gate spring stretched out and nailed to a plank, on these records, 306 Holloway Road [Meek's studio above a leather goods shop] was as dangerous a place to be as it sounded.'

Sutch later reminisced:

Joe and I were both intrigued with horror. Playing in his studio was so relaxed that you never felt you were making a record – it was like being at home. It was incredible for anyone to have a studio in their flat – unheard of. He had hit after hit and the other studios couldn't understand it. His was the most independent and original sound of anyone at the time. To get the particular echo sound he wanted for one of my records he even made me go into the lavatory and sing with the door shut. He had wires and everything everywhere, it was so small – you were recording in his bedroom, he converted it to a studio. There was not enough room for the whole band and the drum kit, so the singer would have to go down and sing in the hall or, if it was too loud, sing right in the toilet – you had to have one foot in the bath, one foot on the toilet and sing. Maybe that summed up some of my early records. He was ten years ahead, and horror never dates.

Outside of his passion for music, the pill-popping Meek's sexual preferences at first mystified Sutch: 'He was always asking members of my band to stay over to do a bit of over-dubbing. They'd say, "I'm not going up there on my own." I was very naive – it was never the ugly sax player or the drummer without any teeth.'

Continuous gigging, building up a substantial following of fans, paid off when the band were handed a record deal by HMV, and on 14 December – surely rather too close to Christmas? – their first single 'Till the Following Night' hit the shops. ('Good Golly Miss Molly' was the B-side.) First pressings credited Sutch as the writer of 'Till the

Following Night', but the Performing Rights Society remain confused, confirming that 'most references state that Sutch wrote this tune [although] we have a registration in favour of James Wallace, published by Ivy Music'. (Ivy was Meek's publishing company.) The original title, 'My Big Black Coffin', was perhaps changed because it was feared the BBC might ban it. Perhaps just suggesting that as a reason sparked publicity. The label credited Screaming Lord Sutch and The Savages.

Disc's respected music critic Don Nicholl awarded it just one of the maximum five stars permitted. 'Lord Sutch has had plenty of publicity,' wrote Nicholl. 'Now's his chance to see if he can live up to it. He rocks through a gruesome graveyard piece and makes the most of the eerie effects. I couldn't like it even if it was for charity! A load of unpolished hokum.' Some rather more important people didn't like it either, according to the American music writer Matt Marchese at least: 'The song's violent imagery and unbridled horniness placed it in immediate conflict with the guardians of public morals at the BBC, and Auntie Beeb promptly banned it.'

On 12 January 1962, Screaming Lord Sutch was the advertised attraction at the New Brighton Tower Ballroom. When he failed to turn up, the organisers managed to persuade a local band to stand in for him at short notice: The Beatles. It was one of the first public examples of a problem that would dog Sutch throughout his life and exasperate many of those working with and for him. 'Tell him he needed to check in for a one o'clock flight at twelve and he'd often turn up at two,' said Carlo Little. Carlo's wife, Iris, recalled the time Sutch brought a writer to her house for an interview, 'made an excuse to leave for a few minutes, and turned up again some ten hours later'. This inability to stick to a schedule would cost him friends, family, gigs and money.

Nevertheless, Sutch was on a roll, with media reports suggesting he was now earning a thousand pounds a week on tour – when he turned up – as he did for a gig on Saturday, 13 January at Oxford Town Hall, billed as a 'Special Extraordinary Attraction. Tickets in advance 5/6d'. This was the first time that Nigel Molden, who subsequently became a good friend of Sutch, saw him live: 'I was thirteen. My father worked for the firm which provided the supplies for the bar. I received a free ticket. Sutch was already seen as something of a cross between an attraction and an oddity. It is important to remember that long hair was virtually unheard of but it did not carry many of the negative connotations it became associated with during the second half of the decade.

'Sutch became a regular visitor to Oxford and I made sure that I saw him on each occasion. I have a clear memory of the head-through-the-toilet-seat routine, the imagery of which escaped me at the time – and quite possibly does to this day!

'As time went on the horror rock element developed, and I can recall being perplexed as the roadies moved people away from the front of the stage to make space for Sutch to jump into the audience with his fake axe. The element of surprise was considerable – such things had never happened before in ballroom performances. Sutch was an innovator in that sense, with the roots of many of his ideas clearly stemming from pantomime routines.'

Roy Hankin, another fan, saw Sutch at the Blue Moon club in Hayes, Hounslow Baths, the Capital R club in Feltham and Eel Pie Island, Twickenham, and recalls the set including popular rock 'n' roll numbers like 'Train Kept A-Rollin'; 'Honey Hush', 'King Kong', 'Don't You Just Know It' and 'Oo Poo Pa Do'. But he was particularly struck, watching Sutch unload his gear at Southall Community Centre around this time, by his crepe-soled Eton Clubman Chukka Boots.

Trevor Fontane, who would become a friend, recollects that the first time he saw Sutch in action in Camborne in Cornwall, 'he'd been arrested after running through the streets drumming up interest in the gig, wearing his leopardskin and buffalo horns, banging on cars and screaming. He was marched up to the police station but they let him out eventually to play.'

Meanwhile, an up-and-coming promoter in the Sheffield area had just opened a new club, the Black Cat, and was so keen to put on this London-based band with the massive following that he was prepared to pay top dollar. 'I chased around to get the booking,' recalls Peter Stringfellow. 'And I was happy to go to fifty quid to get Sutch and The Savages – I'd had people ringing me up about them. They were a terrific band at that time – he always had great musicians in the group – and we were in awe of Sutch himself. He was a mad bastard – he'd start fires on stage and really get the audience going. He had such an impact that what we'd probably call tribute bands today, but 'copycat groups' in those days, started up – Frankenstein and The Monsters, and Count Lindsay the Third and The Skeletons. I managed them, and they just completely nicked Sutch's style of act. He certainly started off horror rock and was unique in his heyday – so many of the subsequently successful yet similar people like Alice Cooper, Ozzy Osbourne and Marilyn Manson must have been influenced by Sutch.'

Sutch became the first act to play live at Stringfellow's Talk of the Town – later the Hippodrome – and the club owner watched him over the years as 'he lost his early momentum. I saw him losing that rocking credibility that he'd had. He pushed the Loony Party thing so far that it went from being funny to a bit of a joke.'

On 13 April 1962, Hamburg's now-legendary Star Club – where the Beatles and many other bands would later play – opened its doors for the first time. The German-based magazine *Gorilla Beat* reported that 'Sutch arrived at Hamburg airport dressed in a leopardskin, two horns on his head and an oversized axe in his hands – and that's how he played the Star Club, and that's how he appeared in front of the disbelieving judges when he was sued for haunting Hamburg.'

'We were the headliners,' Sutch subsequently remembered, possibly unreliably, 'and The Beatles were the support band – them and Gerry and The Pacemakers. They were playing about four hours a night, and we would just do forty-five minutes – and we made more money.' According to Sutch, when he met John Lennon at the Star Club the Beatle 'was tickled by the theatrical side of my act'. Lennon would later be quoted as saying, 'Screaming Lord Sutch will go on forever.'

Ian Hunter, subsequently the frontman of Mott the Hoople, paid his dues in Hamburg and joined The Savages briefly on bass, after being head-hunted by keyboards man Freddie 'Fingers' Lee: 'I never made any money, the little I got I spent on food and drink. Our first show was at five in the afternoon, our last ended at five in the morning. Once we played nine hours non-stop.'

Cliff Bennett recalled seeing Sutch play at the Star Club. 'When he arrived I was backstage with one of the owners, Horst Fascher. Sutch stormed on and opened with "Great Balls of Fire", started a fire and burnt the nylon curtains on stage. The fire brigade was called while Horst was swearing and threatening to put Sutch on the first plane back.'

By now Ritchie Blackmore was in The Savages with Ricky Brown, pianist Andy Wren, Dave Wendels on guitar, and Carlo Little. 'We used to go down a storm,' Little remembers. 'All the bands who made it later used to come and see us. Ritchie was really great even then – used to do all these amazing runs which left the audience gaping.' Another future 'name' who would also join Sutch's band opened for them in June at Wembley Town Hall: Paul Dean, of Paul Dean and The Dreamers, who would later become known as Paul Nicholas. Their performance in Wembley attracted controversy and media coverage as scores of stiletto-heeled girls stood on their seats to see better, and punctured the leatherette-covered cushions. The Savages' repertoire now included Bobby Darin's 'Bull Moose', featuring Sutch plus fiercely-horned helmet; 'Blue Suede Shoes', which saw him don over-sized, blue-painted footwear; 'Splash Splash', for which he would strip down to a swimming costume; their recently released single, 'Till the Following Night', for which Sutch emerged from his coffin; and 'Great Balls of Fire', which saw him set fire to a biscuit tin.

They were touring hard now. Bernard Warner tells of a gig at the Yarborough Social Club near Doncaster – 'he set fire to the curtains' – where his dad, the concert secretary, had booked them for £45 and a capacity crowd of 200 resulted. He also recalls that 'the group liked to gamble amongst themselves – I saw Sutch paid on Saturday and skint by Sunday.'

Colin Standring was in a band called Kit and The Saracens and remembers supporting Sutch and The Savages at a 1962 gig at the Railway in Wealdstone. 'We were all still at school and were very impressed – the band kicked off with some heavy riff instrumental. The guitarist – Ritchie Blackmore, I think – and the bassist had bleached white hair and held their guitars almost vertical, staring menacingly into the audience. Sutch's show included him leaping around with a red toilet seat round his neck. [He introduced this baffling gimmick for the song 'I'm A Hog For You Baby' and kept it throughout his career.] At one point he was standing on a chair, then one of the band came up with a broomstick from behind and poked him up the bum and Sutch squealed, "Ooh, is that you, Cliff?"' This was cutting-edge stuff for its time, a hard rocking band fronted by a larger-than-life stage presence – not until Arthur Brown and Alice Cooper would Sutch have a visual rival.

Ritchie Blackmore played what was supposed to be his final gig with the band at Putney in October – only to return around Christmas 1966. He took his experiences with him to Deep Purple, where he told vocalist Ian Gillan 'how Screaming made the band change into their stage gear in the toilet on a small ferry in Scandinavia – apparently he had arranged for some press people to meet the boat. Imagine the scene: Ritchie and the other Savages in furry, off-the-shoulder, leopard-skin, caveman-type outfits, guitars in one hand, suitcases in the other, running madly down the ramp, to be greeted by a few bewildered children and a small dog.'

Blackmore looked back at those days again during a 1990 interview with *Guitarist* magazine:

> The most frustrating part was that Dave always sung totally out of key. It was just horrendous. For instance, 'Johnny B. Goode' we'd start playing in A and he'd have no relevance to that, he'd come on in E flat and just stay in E flat, very confidently.
>
> Dave Sutch taught me a lot – all the professional stuff. He made me get out front and push myself. It was a theatrical act – he scared me to death the first time he came out of a coffin. I just thought, this guy's nuts. And he's got to drive after the gig otherwise I can't get home. He's coming at me with a big dagger and I'm in a loincloth like Tarzan. I was so skinny all my bones were sticking out. I was embarrassed and frightened. I was only sixteen or seventeen. We used to make thirty pounds a week, which was unheard of then.

'When the bills started mounting up we went back to Sutch,' he told *Record Collector* in 1998:

> You'd get to the point where everybody in the band would say, 'I can't take this any longer, I can't back the Screaming Lord any

more.' And they would leave. You knew they were gonna come back. It's like breaking out of a prisoner-of-war camp. A month later they come back in. It was like a penance. But he was the only guy that paid any money. You could go with all the fancy bands, but they didn't pay any money, so it was back to Sutch.

Carlo Little quit the Savages in the autumn of 1962 to join bluesman Cyril Davies. 'I was going from five gigs a week for £20, to one for £2, but I knew that was the type of music I wanted to play.' Nicky Hopkins and Bernie Watson moved with him. But Davies would die of leukaemia within a year and Carlo returned to the Sutch fold. The Savages' new line-up branched out to spend three months in Rome, also visiting Sweden and Germany.

Around this time Sutch also met the man who would be his future partner-in-crime in the Loony Party. Alan Hope was performing as Kerry Rapid under the management of Bob Potter, who sent Sutch and Rapid out together on a rock 'n' roll tour of the Midlands from 1962 into1963, and the two got to know each other very well.

In September 1962 Sutch would also have noticed that 'Monster Mash' by Bobby 'Boris' Pickett and The Crypt Kickers had stormed into the upper reaches of the US charts. Horror rock was set to be the next big thing – and he had just the song to give him that big breakthrough.

chapter four

Vote for the Ripper

'Instead of being the rebel he was now the relic'
— ALWYN W. TURNER, FRIEND AND WRITER

The year of 1963 was a significant one both for pop music and for David Sutch. In February, The Beatles' 'Please, Please Me' hurtled towards the top of the hit parade. The Rolling Stones would not be far behind. The Searchers charted; so did Gerry and The Pacemakers, Freddie and The Dreamers and The Hollies. The world of pop changed irrevocably. For Sutch the year's two innovations were to sustain a whole career. The first was his second single, 'Jack the Ripper', the second his debut at the hustings.

Sutch's first single, 'Till the Following Night', had failed to make much of an impression, but its somewhat delayed follow-up, released in March, which would be the defining image of his whole performing life, created a stir from the off, by attracting perhaps the most coruscating review ever run by the prestigious and influential *Melody Maker*. Written by Ray Coleman and Laurie Henshaw, and headlined 'TRASH!' it read:

> Nauseating trash — that's the only description we can apply to Screaming Lord Sutch's 'Jack the Ripper'. It's a sordid saga, complete with all the horror squeals. Is this really music? No, it's undiluted tripe.

We smashed the record after one play. And we hope you never have the misfortune to hear such dire rubbish.

Another national paper review declared: 'It's sick, let's face it. But it's also different. A lot of people are going to hate it.'

Over-the-top rants like this – especially if you consider that the current chart contained such gems as 'Wayward Wind' by Frank Ifield at number two, 'Sukiyaki' by Kenny Ball at number ten and Susan Maughan's 'Hand a Handkerchief to Helen' at number fifty – certainly got Sutch noticed and perhaps confirmed his belief that there was no such thing as bad publicity. It also boosted his earning power: the very next week the *Melody Maker* ran a full-page advertisement proclaiming that J. and T. Marshall Ltd, London's leading musical instrument stockists, 'proudly announce the opening of their new showroom at 93 Uxbridge Road, Hanwell, W7 on Monday, 11 March at 2 p.m. by Decca Recording Star Screaming Lord Sutch.'

'Jack the Ripper' had been recorded on 25 October 1962. The B-side, 'Don't You Just Know It', was a Huey 'Piano' Smith song given a meaty arrangement and featuring a fine guitar solo, and one of Sutch's best and most strident vocal performances. Its call-and-response framework worked well, and in later years Savage Tony Dangerfield brought it back into Sutch's stage show. Chas Hodges believes to this day that given the right promotion it could have put him into the charts. 'Ripper' itself was written by Americans Clarence and Charles G. Stacy (some say Stacey), Walter Haggin and Joe Simmons, though Sutch, perhaps suffering from selective amnesia, would claim it in his autobiography as 'my composition'. (Charles G. also wrote the rather different 'Please Santa Take My Toys'.) 'Jack the Ripper' seems now to be the property of Northern Songs, but how this American song found its way to England, Meek and Sutch remains a mystery, despite extensive efforts to track down its provenance. Carlo Little claims that The Savages created the music even though they received no credit on the label. Nicky Hopkins, Bernie Watson and Rick Brown were the others playing.

Sutch had already proved no slouch at publicising himself, but he would tell Joe Meek's biographer John Repsch that it was 'Joe's idea for me to visit the streets of Whitechapel late at night dressed as Jack the Ripper; all the places frequented by Jack. I did it and got local publicity. He [Meek] was intrigued by graveyards and churches. He used to go walking around there, writing songs.'

One wonders how much thought was given to the song's subject matter. Tony Barrell would later describe it in the *Sunday Times* as 'a moment of supremely bad taste'. Sutch, I am sure, regarded his hammy, panto-villain stage performance as a burlesque piece of music-hall melodrama as he acted out such lyrics as:

> *There's a man who walks the streets of London late at night,*
> *With a little black bag that's oh, so tight ...*
> *When she walks down the streets he's never far behind*
> *With his little black bag and his one track mind*
> *Well, he really catches up when the lights go down*
> *Cause that's the time he starts his dirty chop-around.*

Presumably in a quest for veracity, Sutch described how he 'carried a Gladstone bag containing the tools of my wicked trade – a massive syringe, knives, scalpels and cut throat razors.' The number began, he said,

> with a girl in tarty gear running across the stage panting with fright ... Then I burst on and chased after her, lunging with a knife ... I caught the girl in the middle of the stage and plunged the knife into her breasts whilst she let out bloodcurdling screams ... I dragged her over to a table where I ripped her open in a mock operation, dragging out a plastic heart and lungs which I'd dipped in water to make them look authentic. To boost the bad taste factor I always gave these a quick lick before placing them in a silver kidney bowl ... If I was doing a big show I'd go to the slaughterhouse in Harrow and buy pigs' hearts, lungs and heads which I whirled round and round before sending them sailing into the auditorium.

Some years later Sutch said: 'At that time it was a terrifyingly frightening record and was banned by the BBC for being obscene. Now you can see it was just tongue-in-cheek.' But in an interview at the time he claimed: 'They [the audience] love it. They come to see horror. They pay five or six shillings to see me, the same as they'd go and see a horror film. They're looking forward all week to being frightened to death. We watch all the latest horror films and anything connected with horror and we put our ideas to these, then we put music to them and we have a kind of Victorian stage show.'

Despite the rubbishing in *Melody Maker*, *Disc* awarded 'Ripper' a three-star – 'Good' – rating for 'a steady rock number which Sutch husks competently'. But the debate about the track and, indeed, Sutch's whole act, reached national TV in 1964 when Sutch appeared on the BBC programme *Late Night Line-Up*. 'You don't think your act offends in any way?' he was asked. By now Britain had been horrified by the dreadful 'Moors Murders' (although Ian Brady and Myra Hindley were not arrested until the following year).

'No,' replied Sutch, the camera zooming in to a close-up of his face. 'I'm only out to give visual entertainment, something that a lot of singers nowadays don't. They just walk up to the microphone with a guitar, open and shut their mouth like a goldfish, and nothing happens. I like to put on a show as I'm doing the records, not just to sing it but to act it.'

Brought up on corny, black and white, badly acted and scripted 'horror' movies of the late 1950s and early 1960s, Sutch would have given scant consideration to the implications of acting out the lurid lyrics of the track. But his gleeful over-the-top performances suggest that, like the knife he wielded on stage, he was not, in intellectual or analytical terms, the sharpest implement to be found in the kitchen drawer.

Around this time Carlo Little left the band, and Pete Phillips was drafted in from the guitarist Stuart Taylor's old band, The Dreamers. 'This line-up wore bright orange or pink satin shirts, black trousers, white custom-made cowboy boots adorned with bells at the ankle – it was showbiz,' Taylor recalls, 'and we all bleached our hair white or blonde.'

Paul Nicholas was a Savage when 'Jack the Ripper' was still a novelty to the audiences. Sutch would come on 'and do the real show-stopping stuff,' remembers Nicholas, 'which was of course "Jack the Ripper". And "Jack the Ripper" really consisted of Dave dressing himself as the Ripper and painting his face completely white, with perhaps a little touch of deep rouge lipstick.'

'Paul [sometimes] doubled up as the woman in drag who was put on the slab on stage and disembowelled,' explains the guitarist, Stuart Taylor. 'He came ambling out from the wings during "Jack the Ripper" and was slain by Sutch and laid out on a table.' Then, as Sutch appeared to be making 'giant incisions with a massive fake knife, I would scrape my plectrum along the bottom two strings of the guitar, creating a terrifying tearing sound. He then pulled out huge red papier-mâché [or otherwise] internal organs and lurched towards the front row. The front thirty or forty people would recoil in horror.'

Sutch's 'creative' PR talent', as an admiring Taylor puts it, had not flagged. 'We were travelling to a show on the south coast,' he recalls, 'when a stone shattered our windscreen. As the roadie panicked Sutch rushed to a phone box and called the *News of the World* to tell them he had been "shot at".'

'Jack the Ripper' gained popularity and notoriety on the Cinebox film jukeboxes of the day, in which Sutch could be observed wearing a top hat and black cloak, carrying a butcher's knife and chasing comely young wenches. It didn't crack the charts here, yet, ironically, it eventually charted in Germany, in a cover version by Casey Jones and The Governors.

Casey's version is quite different from that of Sutch, whom it wrongly credits as the writer, even boasting different lyrics, more keyboards and a good guitar break. It is more of an up-tempo pop song rather than Sutch's darker, more atmospheric take. For an ephemeral novelty released to scorn and derision – rather like its performer – 'Jack the Ripper' stood the test of time and remained the one constant in Sutch's act from the day it was issued.

Although The Who's *Tommy* and *S.F. Sorrow* by The Pretty Things would collect the plaudits for being rock music's first concept albums, Sutch could well have stolen their thunder by several years had he listened to Joe Meek. His mentor, he recalled, 'did suggest that I did a whole revue with this "Jack the Ripper", and make it into like a mini-opera – and he'd have written some more music. He was saying I could make it into a big production for my stage show, stabbing women, running about with a big butcher's knife.'

Frustratingly, or maybe fortunately, rather like Mark Wirtz's

'Teenage Opera', the promise of expansion never materialised and other related tracks like 'Hands of Jack the Ripper', 'Son of Jack the Ripper' and 'Midnight Man' would only emerge spasmodically, never to be brought together. Yet.

'I think he was mystified by the continuing appeal of "Jack the Ripper",' Sutch's son Tristan says. 'He just did it as part of his act without reading anything deeper into it.' But just because he may have been oblivious to the undercurrent of sadist violence and misogyny implicit in such material, should we ignore it? Clearly it must have meant a great deal to him, otherwise why go back and re-write and re-record it? Perhaps here is an early indication of Sutch's tendency to lock himself into a 'Groundhog Day' of his own making by not bothering to change a winning formula.

The song brought problems. As early as 1974 at the Biba Rainbow Rooms in Kensington, with girlfriend Thann Rendessy set to play the Ripper's victim, they were forced to scrap the song when someone threw a glass at the stage, eventually prompting a fight, during which Sutch jumped into the audience and punched the heckler. Paul Nicholas recalls one occasion when 'they [the audience] really took exception to this whole act and they rushed the stage. I did a runner out of the stage door. I was halfway down the road with Dave and he was in a telephone box. I said, "Dave what are you doing?" and he said, "I'm phoning the press." I said, "They're coming down the road!" He said, "Coward."'

Flash forward to the late 1970s, by which time sexual politics and the boundaries of taste had changed a very great deal, and the tawdry and frivolous Ripper joke finally went sour on the Lord.

Sutch couldn't say he wasn't warned. Drummer and bassist Mike Crawford, who played with him in the late 1970s, remembers a gig at Bradford University in 1977. A woman had just been killed in Bradford by the Yorkshire Ripper. 'We didn't know, so we turned up to play to this audience of around eight hundred. Everything went well until Dave decided to do "Jack the Ripper". Eight or nine girls stormed the stage and grabbed him, while he had his artificial head, symbolising his victim, in his hands. Security battled to push them off, but they stormed the stage again, shouting that we were making money out of people being raped and murdered. David was quite taken aback.'

On 22 May 1981, Peter Sutcliffe, the Yorkshire Ripper, was finally convicted of the murders of thirteen women. Just one month later, on 22 June, Sutch opened for The Cramps at the Hammersmith Palais. Alwyn W. Turner, who subsequently ghost-wrote a joke election manifesto for Sutch, was present, and told me: 'I think it [the Sutcliffe case] was unique, partly because the murders were so awful, and went on for so long – and were public – and partly because it coincided with the moment when feminism really exploded.

'So, I was intrigued when I went to the Palais gig. I knew Sutch's act, which climaxed in a (very) extended version of "Jack the Ripper", and I was curious whether he would make any allowances for the circumstances. I mentioned this to the guy I was going to the gig with, and he laughed it off, certain that The Cramps' audience wouldn't care about such sensibilities.

'They bloody did.

'The first half of the set was received without much enthusiasm. Sutch's band was too pub-rock to satisfy the post-punk taste of the time. I could see why The Cramps had requested Sutch as support – the 'Hammerness' of His Lordship appealed to their love of kitsch horror – but I could equally see that an audience not as well versed in rock 'n' roll history might not understand why this middle-aged man was singing "I'm a Hog for You Baby" while wearing a loo seat around his neck.

'Then Sutch played "Jack the Ripper". No change, no compromise, no recognition that it might have a new and unwelcome resonance. And bored indifference on the part of the audience soon turned to outright fury. Within a couple of minutes – he spun the song out – the first beer glasses were starting to be thrown at the stage. And it didn't take long for the occasional missile to turn to a hailstorm. It was a sell-out, and there were maybe two or three thousand psychobillies united in their fury that this man was celebrating the mass murder of women.

'I don't think that Sutch had encountered this before. [Band members, however, suggest he had.] The audience was considerably younger than his normal crowd. They made no allowance for him and – more crucially – he made no allowance for them. I've seen some angry audiences, but nothing compared to that night. Sutch didn't manage to finish the song – the barrage was too great – but abandoned it halfway through and left the stage, leaving behind a hall full of hatred.

'The structure of the evening – presumably as requested by The Cramps – called for Sutch to introduce the headline band. To his immense credit, he returned to the stage to do so. His reappearance was greeted with a new hail of bottles and glasses, but he got his introduction out before departing at top speed.

'I was only nineteen, but I knew my rock 'n' roll, and I was intrigued. To me, it marked the point at which psychobilly – and alternative rock more generally – said: thus far and no further. The Cramps were happy to indulge in faux-sexism, while Nick Cave in their contemporaries, The Birthday Party, was happily singing about his 'Six-Inch Gold Blade', but the old school, epitomised by Sutch, was met with outright hostility. There was a definite shift. If there was a new orthodoxy, Sutch still wasn't a part of it, but instead of being the rebel, he was now the relic.

'It made, of course, bugger-all difference to his act. I'm not convinced that he even noticed why he aroused such righteous anger that evening. Perhaps, perversely, he saw it as reinforcing his status as an outsider.'

However, I think it was, perhaps, the point at which Sutch realised he had lost the youth market for good, and began to look around for an alternative audience. Soon his mind would turn to the idea of resurrecting his political career, which had been moribund for many years: an ideal way to project himself to a different, potentially far more welcoming constituency.

Dave Savage, then yet to become a Savage, tells of another gig a year later, in 1982, at Leeds University, where the Yorkshire Ripper had also killed. Sutch was supporting The Stray Cats, and seems to have learned from his chastening experience in Hammersmith the previous year: 'That was the first time I ever saw him live. He was very thoughtful to change the words of 'Jack the Ripper' to Doctor Jekyll, as the West Yorkshire area still had strong memories of Peter Sutcliffe.' (Sutch's drummer at the time, Jack Irving, though, recalls complaints from some audience members at the lyric change).

But in March that same year, 1982, Sutch composed his least tasteful, least tactful song, 'Midnight Man', which would not see the light of day for some twenty years (when it was posthumously released). Is it credible that, despite the slating he had received from The Cramps audience, Sutch would not only once more revamp the Ripper theme but also appear to give it a Peter Sutcliffe slant? It seems extraordinary, but he did just that. The track is made all the more unpleasant by a lyric which has none of the redeeming features of 'Jack the Ripper'; that could at least claim an over-the-top, 'spoof' feel and a distance of a century from its subject matter. 'Midnight Man' is alarmingly contemporary, played straight, but just not funny. Judge for yourself:

> *He jumps from the bushes with a knife in his hand*
> *Gonna send a woman to the promised land.*
> *Bodies all around from the maniac's hand ...*

These lines are followed by a couplet with which a psychiatrist might well have a field day:

> *Come over here, dearie,*
> *I'm gonna put something in your ear ...*

Just who did Sutch see in the role of the 'Midnight Man'? Himself? Who was the 'dearie'? Was it shorthand for all women, or for one particular woman to whom he had been unhealthily close all his life? Was this David Sutch permitting Screaming Lord Sutch to act out deep and troubling images which, for reasons beyond him, had haunted his innermost thoughts for years?

In 1988, exactly one hundred years since the notorious murders, and with the aim of giving 'Jack the Ripper' a new lease of life, Sutch filmed a video to accompany a re-recording of the track. His media agent of the time, Arthur Martin, recalls the shoot taking place in the Brick Lane area of London – close to Whitechapel where the original crimes had been committed – with Sutch and The Savages dressing up in appropriate gear: 'David had his cape, bag and top hat'. They had wanted to use the Truman Brewery for filming, but the company was not interested in being associated with the subject matter of the song. 'There was something of a backlash against the video' said Martin. 'No one wanted to play it. Eventually I think we got it onto one obscure channel late at night.'

Martin was right – in fact, there was a massive outcry after Sutch sent out invitations to 'A Party to Re-launch "Jack the Ripper" to be held at Stringfellows on Thursday, 12 May 1988'. The track was to be released on RCA/Ariola Records. Just a week later, *The Stage* and *Television Today* was reporting:

> Women's groups across London are outraged that a record entitled 'Jack the Ripper' is being re-released, together with a comic horror video, and are urging all major outlets to ban the 'sick and horrendous' products.
>
> Ann McMurdie, of Action Against the Ripper Centenary, a group formed two months ago to put a stop to the 'tasteless' celebrations, told *The Stage*, 'I am disgusted that Lord Sutch should even consider recording something of such bad taste. It is simply endorsing male violence against women, further glorifying the Ripper who has become some sort of a folk hero.
>
> 'As to filming it all on the original site, well, that just shows no sensitivity at all to women. I am completely horrified and think it is sick. This is just men jumping on the bandwagon and trying to make money out of something that was an obscene event and should not be remembered fondly.'

Sutch, in typically defensive mode, replied: 'It is supposed to be tongue-in-cheek. I have even changed it so that the girls I chase are over six feet tall, huge and a lot taller than me. It's not hard horror as I'm not doing it nastily. I'm sending it up really and I don't see anything wrong with that.'

Sutch would almost certainly have been naively baffled by the outcry and incredulous that anyone should take him or the song seriously. But it would appear that the furore frightened the record company, as there is no record of the single's re-release going ahead.

In 1990 Tom Hibbert crystalised the damage that the song had inflicted on Sutch's image in certain eyes, when he interviewed Sutch for *Q* magazine. Once again the subject of 'Ripper' and its accompanying stage act was raised. 'This all sounds in excessively poor taste,' the writer says. Sutch, 'with shaking hand, raises a lager shandy to his lips and takes on a puzzled look: "What do you mean? It was just a laugh. It was like a mini-opera before its time."' Hibbert watches him perform 'Jack the Ripper' and describes how he 'dawdles across the stage clutching in his hand, by the "hair", a papier-mâché model of a woman's severed head. "I'm Jack the Ripper!" he tells us. He strikes a somewhat pathetic figure. The social club's hall is not alight with smiles, nor with chilled screams. Nor with anything much at all.'

Poor taste, yes. Politically incorrect, too. But for Sutch and his early audiences, emerging from the depressingly grey, post-war fifties, it was FUN. He may have done the song and the act to death eventually. And he took a critical kicking as a result – but protests when The White Stripes included the Sutch track in their chart-topping Xmas 2004 DVD *Under Blackpool Lights* were thin on the ground.

But back to 1963. With some venues restricting entrance to Sutch's shows to over-twenties, girls screaming and fainting during his act and a blanket ban slapped on him by Granada when he managed to plummet through a cinema organ one night after jumping from the footlights to the orchestra pit, his name was seldom out of the news. One paper graphically evoked the whole spectacle for its readers:

> He is earning £65 per night. To the mournful strains of what he calls the 'Death March', he is wheeled on in a coffin to the accompaniment of ghostly winds, rattling chains, screams and moans. On the front of the coffin is a skull presented to him by a sailor from Japan, with lights which flash red and white. He was banned from a hall in Scotland for appearing in a Red Devil hat with a lavatory seat around his neck.
>
> He comes on Irving-like, with cloak, full Victorian gear, a doctor's bag acquired from an antique shop in Stepney and a butcher's knife. At first he used one of his girlfriends as the victim Mary and planted her in the audience. Having found her, he chased her around the hall and up on to the stage.
>
> This practice has had to cease since they were invariably followed by a pack of would-be heroes in hot pursuit, anxious to achieve fame by rescuing a damsel in distress.

In March 1963 a teenager in Grimsby, Pauline Cousins, formed the Screaming Lord Sutch Fan Club. Trevor Fontane became member 211, and received a membership card revealing an assortment of Sutch likes and dislikes:

Colour of eyes:	(1) Blue (2) Red (3) Yellow
Actor:	Popeye/ Jonathan Rouse
Drink:	Tizer/ Lobster Tea
Sport:	Marbles
Likes :	People with elongated heads
Dislikes:	People

There were more early signs of the obsessive collecting that would ultimately prompt concerns for his sanity. 'Outside of entertaining the youth of the nation,' noted the music writer Bunny Lewis, 'his main interest lies in going to horror films and collecting chains, coshes, mantraps, a genuine sailor's wooden leg and a life-sized crocodile with luminous eyes. Anything, in fact, which he describes as "manly".'

Though the emergence of more copycat groups like The Ghouls and The Grave Robbers testified to Sutch's influence, on promoters' bills he was already having to consort with the 'enemy': the new Merseybeat bands who would effectively kill off any chances of Sutch ever becoming a chart act. On 7 June, moreover, The Rolling Stones released their first single, 'Come On', and a mere minute-and-a-half's appearance on television on *Thank Your Lucky Stars* saw ABC-TV's switchboard jammed by viewers outraged by the band's scruffy appearance. Soon The Pretty Things would arrive, with an even more outrageous, anti-establishment attitude and a wild stage show. But for the moment Screaming Lord Sutch still had the longest hair around.

In April 1963 the film *Just For Fun* had hit the nation's big screens, featuring a plethora of pop stars and a plot about a bunch of teenagers forming a political party. I'm not sure whether Sutch saw it, but he was about to enact it in real life. He flew to Australia for a two-week tour 'carrying a pistol, a knife and a red plastic set of lungs', reported the media, and on his return, just as it was beginning to look as though he was never going to succeed as a hit-making pop star, was presented with the idea of standing for Parliament.

Sutch was still popular live, but on record much of his appeal was dissipated, as his mediocre voice struggled to match his top-class musical accompaniment. For someone with his taste for the limelight, therefore, turning to 'politics' was an inspired move: here was a high-profile business which invariably dominated the news agenda whenever by-elections and general elections were imminent.

'When I started up,' explained Sutch later, 'I thought only people with bowler hats, rolled umbrellas and striped suits could stand. I thought only snobs could stand, but I proved the point that anyone could stand ... Not only was I entitled to vote – I was also entitled to be voted for. So I decided to form the Sod 'Em All party, which was what I and the people I knew thought of politicians.'

He would never actually campaign under that banner, but it was his manager Reg Calvert's suggestion to stand in Stratford-upon-Avon, a very newsworthy constituency, following the resignation of defence minister John Profumo, who had been brought down by the Christine Keeler sex scandal. This catapulted Sutch into the headline-making news agenda of the day. It was a tactic destined to keep his name before the public for the next thirty-five years, during which time he would see other political and showbiz celebrities come and go, their profiles waxing and waning whilst his remained constantly elevated.

Sutch expanded on the rationale in a 1965 *Arena* TV documentary: 'I realised that the hair alone wasn't enough, and the bright-coloured clothes weren't quite enough. So something had to be found – something completely different.' A measure of just how seriously he took politics was his comment that he would 'rather have one thousand laughs than one thousand votes.' Another good line was his assertion that he stood 'for the four Rs: reading, writing and rock 'n' roll'.

Dressed in top hat and tails, Sutch turned up to hand in his nomination papers, only to discover that he was £25 short of the requisite deposit of £150 ('That was a lot of money, then. But I was on a good screw with my gigs and for me it was only the equivalent of a week's work'). After being refused permission to pay by cheque he had to dash off to collect the additional money.

Reg Calvert organised meetings and free local concerts. Pathé News filmed Sutch canvassing voters. Although in his later years he was rarely seen with an alcoholic drink, back then he would have a beer. 'I placed a jug of water on the table and a couple of glasses on top,' he said of one election meeting, 'and made sure the beer bottles were well out of sight.' But addressing a political meeting daunted the fearless self-publicist. 'I was petrified,' he said. 'I had never given a speech in my life.' His first public meeting, the local paper reported, was abandoned after 'an hour's noisy barracking'. At Stratford, the deputy mayoress stormed off in a huff when Sutch dared to sit in the mayoral chair.

He campaigned in a large van, festooned with slogans and loud-speakers, which he drove around the constituency, often accompanied by a police presence. Contemporary film footage shows huge crowds of fans and inquisitive members of the public gathering around him. In true canvassing mode he alleged that he was looking to buy a property in Stratford where he and his mother would live.

It is difficult now, when election oddities have become so familiar, to appreciate the impact Sutch's intervention caused back then. Peter Sterling went round with Sutch in his campaign car and his purple furniture van, filming him on the stump: 'People didn't like him heckling their meetings – although they came out to ask for his auto-graph – or using the footsteps and screams from his "Jack the Ripper" record to attract attention. There were complaints to the police, who stopped us on one of the housing estates.'

Cassandra, the nom de plume of the *Daily Mirror's* hugely influential political columnist, William Connor, was aghast at the whole spectacle of Sutch and fulminated on 14 August:

> Mechanics of British democracy get strained from time to time, but the intrusion of this ear-splitting fellow who has not the remotest chance of ever getting to Westminster, but who is exploiting the occasion for his revolting act, is a new debasement of politics in a constituency that surely has had enough after the Profumo Affair.

Sutch himself – whose campaign slogan, coined by Calvert, was the catchy 'Vote For the Ghoul; He's No Fool' – Connor described as 'a political freak who appears to be contesting the seat for the cynical and anti-democratic motive of self-advertisement'. Yet even that august and sober institution, *The Times*, was moved to admit that 'the candidacy of Lord Sutch has captured public interest'. Sutch's impact on the hidebound, moribund political world mirrored his reinvention of rock 'n' roll razzamataz: the strait-laced establishment hated him for rocking – and mocking – their boat.

Interviewed in *Record Mirror*, Sutch lapsed briefly into serious mode, admitting, 'Yes, I believe the death penalty is a deterrent', feeling that the H-bomb 'should be banned' and declaring that the 'most important issue of our time is the elimination of poverty throughout the world, starting here in Britain'. One of his main platforms was 'Votes At 18', which he later justified by describing a meeting with a young couple who had three kids, but told him that as they were only twenty years old they were unable to vote for him: 'I thought that was ridiculous. You have a whole family and you bring kids into the world and you can't even vote.' With equal prescience, Sutch wanted the legislation of commercial radio and the abolition of dog licences. Nor did he neglect local issues: in this case the number of public conveniences in Stratford.

The Stratford-upon-Avon by-election took place on 15 August 1963. Sutch polled 209 votes for his National Teenage (he was twenty-two at the time) Party. The Tory candidate Angus Maude – the first to describe Sutch in public as a lunatic – won with 15,846. Sutch viewed his own, modest total as 'a shattering disappointment after my ludicrously high expectations', and one wonders whether he might have considered – even for a short while – putting the campaign down to experience and returning permanently and exclusively to what he dubbed 'the comparatively sane world of rock 'n' roll'.

The PR dividends for his rock 'n' roll career were not long in materialising, however, and on 31 August, his picture graced the front cover of *Melody Maker*. An article also appeared in a magazine called *Today*, headlined 'I MAY BE MAD BUT I'M NOT INSANE AND I'VE GOT A CERTIFICATE TO PROVE IT'. Sutch claimed in the piece to have a certificate from a Harley Street doctor, confirming that 'Mr David Edward Sutch has consulted me about his mental health. My examination of him has revealed no psychiatric abnormality for which he would require treatment.'

'So, there you are,' Sutch triumphantly declared. 'I'm sane, I'm earning big money, I am loved by my mum and that's good enough for me.' Given that no one had seriously questioned Sutch's mental health, however, this was an extraordinary story, which may just have pinpointed the first stirrings within David of the malevolent mood-swings that would ultimately bring him down.

There was a further hint that Sutch would call a halt to his fledgling political career when he told *Fabulous* magazine that he was seeking someone else to carry his baton as, if he continued to be the front man, 'it would seem too much like a gimmick … We're going to get a college graduate to stand,' he added, revealing what seems to be a concern about his working-class roots, or his limited education. 'Somebody who's a marvellous speaker, because that would be half the battle.'

Three days after his discouraging election showing, Sutch boarded the 'Beat Boat', along with Gerry and The Pacemakers, Freddie and The Dreamers, Billy J. Kramer and The Hollies, to entertain pop fans who had paid the not insubstantial sum of £2 10/– to sail from London to Margate and back. The cruise would not even make it as far as Margate, bad weather and sea-sickness apparently curtailing the voyage at Southend, but as the *Royal Sovereign* floated down the Thames, perhaps the seeds of Sutch's next attention-grabbing-stunt – a pirate radio station – were sown.

chapter five

Pirate Wedding

'Other people think I'm eccentric, but I'm not eccentric. I'm quite normal; it's all the other people who are eccentric – and there's plenty of them, in those straight suits, collars and ties – they're the eccentric ones'

– SCREAMING LORD SUTCH

n spring 1964, having failed to interest stations such as Radio Luxembourg in his talents as a DJ – 'They really didn't want to know' – and noting the growing success of pirate stations Caroline and London, David launched Radio Sutch.

Years later, in an interview for *Offshore Echoes,* he explained to Chris Edwards how it had come about:

> We rented a trawler, *Cornucopia,* for about two weeks. So it was fishing and trawling in the mornings and then from twelve onwards it was a radio station. The only trouble was, it was covered with fish scales and stunk to heaven. The music being played on the BBC was very, very straight. They wouldn't play much rock 'n' roll, so we decided to set up our own station.

Predictably Sutch soon tired of the boat, but became aware that out in the Thames Estuary there were disused forts that had been built during the Second World War for anti-aircraft defence. 'We just took one over and claimed squatters' rights. It was like a hotel in the middle of the sea – they had proper toilets and bathrooms, it was like a holiday camp.' Sutch, the ubiquitous Reg Calvert and assorted friends were amongst Radio Sutch's presenters, with Calvert's teenage daughter Candy and her cousin Tamara Harrison also appearing, along with Chris Cross, Dick Dickson and Brian Paul.

Radio Sutch launched from the Shivering Sands fort on 27 May, broadcasting over 194–200 metres, with the jingle: 'For a little bit of Heaven, tune to 197.' Proceedings got underway with – inevitably – Sutch's own 'Jack the Ripper'. The media who gathered to report the arrival of Radio Sutch were very impressed with the strength of the station's signal. 'But what they didn't know,' revealed Sutch later, 'was that just literally three hundred yards away was Reg Calvert, just over the brow of a hill, under a tree with all the stuff – he was just doing it all on land!' Three days later Sutch received an official notice that he was trespassing on War Office property.

Those who listened to the station recall that Sutch would play his own records and read horror stories on air late at night – a further stage in his quest to outrage and push the bounds of taste, and gain the inevitable publicity into the bargain. 'We broadcast *Lady Chatterley's Lover* and *Fanny Hill* to break up the nights,' said Sutch. 'We used to play a lot of Max Miller albums, which at the time were banned from the BBC, just because he was a bit saucy.' The station appeared to operate in much the same haphazard way as Sutch's life. 'Broadcasting hours tended to vary, sometimes due to DJs oversleeping and at other times due to equipment breakdowns,' reported a documentary CD, *The Radio Forts*. 'For most of its short life Radio Sutch operated off equipment powered by banks of car batteries.' The occupants of the fort washed in seawater.

Bizarrely, in addition to the local advertising the station attracted, American evangelists bought substantial air-time – 'five or six hundred pounds a week', Sutch claimed – in order to transmit taped Bible classes in the early hours, which covered Radio Sutch's expenses.

The link between the fort and the mainland was Sutch's agent's offices in Denmark Street, London, and everything 'was ticking over OK until the government started getting more and more stroppy and threatening to close us down. We had threats from the Navy at one stage – the government told them to get us off. We refused and we had all the press supporting us.' In Sutch's subsequent recollection, exaggerated only a little, matters climaxed in a dramatic naval battle: 'In the middle of threatening us, they just pulled up anchor, this huge battleship, and cleared off. The headlines the next day were "SUTCH TURNS BACK THE NAVY".'

Not all the dramas were of such magnitude. Sutch also remembered the time when DJ Colin Mills contracted food poisoning: 'He started to turn green and purple, so we did an SOS over the radio and they sent a helicopter.'

Having given up the unequal struggle, together with an alternative plan to turn the fort into a nudist colony called Sutch Island, and been invited to tour Australia and New Zealand, Sutch sold the station in September 1964 to Reg Calvert for a reported £5,000. When Calvert took over and re-named the station Radio City it broke new ground by broadcasting live stage acts – one of which, but of course, was Sutch's performance of 'Jack the Ripper' at the Kings Hall in Herne Bay.

Reg Calvert was one of the great 'hustlers' of the 1950s and 1960s music scene, who managed a stable of groups and solo singers – Sutch amongst them. His widow Dorothy credits him with smoothing the way for rock 'n' roll to take off in Britain, importing records from America and playing them to youngsters during intervals in the dance band shows the couple organised around the country, which became known as Teenage Party Nights. Their dances and shows needed plenty of artists and Sutch was one of them.

'I put him on for the first time in Exmouth in a disused cinema,' Dorothy recalled – 'oh, it must have been in the late fifties. He and his musicians probably earned twenty quid for the show – OK, he wasn't much of a singer, but then, how many of those boys could really sing? Cliff was the best of the bunch. As a person I didn't particularly like [Sutch]. I found him scruffy, and a little dirty – his hair looked dark, but it was very greasy. I didn't much like his personal habits, but perhaps that was just me being prim and proper.'

Sutch was staying with her and Reg on the night that the idea came to her husband to put someone up for the Stratford by-election: 'Had Sutch not been there he'd have used someone else – and but for that idea, Sutch might well have ended up a five-minute wonder. I wrote the manifesto for David – well, I don't think he could have written one himself.' Sutch hired a dress suit and top hat for campaigning, but when Dorothy pointed out that he would need a clean white shirt he told her he didn't have such a thing, 'so I had to rush off to Marks & Spencer to get one. I really wasn't keen on him living in my house – not being very hygienic. But as an entertainer he was spot on. Whenever he played somewhere he kept a note of what he'd played, and made sure that if he went back there he varied the show.' Sutch's well-documented care with cash had revealed itself to Dorothy early on in their relationship. 'He never paid Reg any commission without a struggle. He was certainly very sensible when it came to money.'

But in June 1966 Reg Calvert was shot dead following a row over plans to merge Radio City with another station. In October 1966 the man accused of killing him was acquitted on grounds of self-defence. Radio Sutch itself was revived briefly during the summer of 1992 when Euronet, a London-based twenty-four-hour satellite radio station, broadcast sixty-minute-long Sutch programmes for a number of weeks, plugging his book, records and party.

Sutch was still touring relentlessly – a 1964 music magazine article named his band, along with Johnny Kidd and The Pirates, as 'the hardest working' in Britain. 'I joined on about thirty bob and a Mars bar a week,' recalls Tony Dangerfield, 'and went straight into a run of eight or nine weeks of gigs.' *Gorilla Beat* magazine described a typical night:

> The stage was dark, wind blew, and a monks' choir moaned from a tape. A black coffin was carried on stage; the lid opened with a deafening noise, first one hand, then the other hand, the hat, the distorted face of Sutch. All of a sudden he jumped out of his coffin and ran about the stage like a cretin, screaming and shouting, accompanied by fire, smoke, thunder and lightning.

But as guitarist Stuart Taylor remembered, the set also featured some innovative instrumentals: 'Hall of the Mountain King'; Duke Ellington's 'Caravan'; and a Duane Eddy B-side, '3.30 Blues'.

In the meantime Sutch was continuing to release singles, though to less than warm acclaim. A pig's-head mask and the symbolic toilet seat round the neck were the live manifestation of Screaming Lord Sutch's next release for Decca – his third, and once again produced by Joe Meek, 'I'm a Hog For You' in September, 1963. Written by the highly respected American songwriting duo Lieber and Stoller, and featuring Paul Nicholas on piano, it got two stars – 'ordinary' – from *Disc,* and three out of five from *Record Mirror.* The B-side, 'Monster in Black Tights', a spoof on the currently topical 'Venus in Blue Jeans', penned by Geoff Goddard (who also wrote 'Have I The Right?') and Meek, has an almost pantomime feel:

> *My monster in black tights*
> *You've got the kind of blood that I likes*
> *I remember the day*
> *You dragged me away*
> *And left me on a barbed-wire fence.*

Another line admits: 'I like you best when you're in your vest.'

'More camp than an Antarctic expedition' is how Meek expert John McCready puts it.

Sutch's next single, 'She's Fallen in Love with the Monster Man', released in July 1964, featured a youthful Jimmy Page on guitar – yet another rock hero given an early break by the Lord. Almost two decades later, The Revillos would almost have a hit with a re-make of this poppy track. TV's *Juke Box Jury* panelists voted the track a hit, and were each rewarded by Sutch, emerging from behind a screen, with a strand of his hair. But chart success eluded him, as it did when the catchy 'Dracula's Daughter' came out in October. Jeff Beck is believed to be playing on this one.

Sutch was no more successful in his PR-driven bid to become the new manager of Wolverhampton Wanderers in September (despite his complete lack of interest in football), when they sacked their legendary manager Stan Cullis. A month later he did succeed in causing the adjournment of a court case without even being present, when his road manager Colin Mills, in court to face driving charges, gave the name of his counsel, to giggles from children in the public gallery, as 'Lord Sutch'. 'You must be labouring under a misapprehension,' responded a stern clerk of the court, 'because this Lord Sutch has no legal qualifications.' But most grievous was the failure of his bid to stand against the Labour prime minister, Harold Wilson, in the October 1964 general election – on a platform of fighting discrimination against long hair, and calling for knighthoods for The Beatles – when his nomination papers were rejected on a technicality.

A fascinating glimpse of how Joe Meek and Sutch made their music together is given in the 1965 *Arena* TV documentary, an almost unheard-of tribute to a hitless pop star. As they work on recording the B-side to 'Dracula's Daughter', 'Come Back Baby' – the first definitely Sutch-penned number to appear on a single – Joe Meek is seen twiddling away with dials and knobs, and calling out 'Hold it!' to Sutch, who has just contributed a wild scream. 'Sorry, no – is that the level you want to give?'

'Yes,' says Sutch, firmly.

'Right. It's a bit over the top, OK? A bit weird that time.'

'Shall I cool it a bit?' asks Sutch.

'No, just like that – stand by,' says Meek as he vanishes back to his tapes and reels.

Sutch sings on – flatly – before screaming again, much the same as last time.

The gig footage with which the programme opens shows him using the same dance-steps and hand movements that would feature over thirty years later in his last gig, less than a week before he died. Hamming it up in a fur coat and buffalo horns, and carrying a huge axe, he jumps off the stage into the front rows of the audience rather like a footballer playing the crowd after scoring a goal. The audience looks partly amused, partly bemused.

Now the programme takes us into the swish new Watford Road, Harrow home he has bought for his mum and himself (Sutch told Savage Ronnie Harwood he paid £12,000 for White Lodge – which would probably sell for best part of £750,000 in the 2005 market). Sutch, shaving with his electric razor, addresses the question of his horror fixation: 'It's something born inside of me – I'm just interested in this type of film, or record, as long as it's got something to do with horror, or horror is behind it. A lot of it started way back when I was fourteen and used to watch TV – *Quatermass*, *1984*, this type of thing, and it's just built up and built up over the years, and now, I just live every day, more or less, horror.'

Around the walls of his room, pin-up pictures of Brigitte Bardot vie for space with posters for horror films. 'I've dug all the Frankenstein, Jack the Ripper-type films. I like the ones with a good story behind them,' Sutch continues as we see him trying on skull masks in a fancy dress shop. 'I like the good challenge-type horror that plays on the nerves, rather than monsters. Things that are built up in the imagination, and the way they can bend your imagination, done with terrific camera work and the right reaction at the right time.'

Back at the house Sutch turns on the radio, which pumps out 'Climb Every Mountain', and, while admiring the ornaments on display around him – knights in armour, muskets, sword, eagle – expounds his philosophy: 'I like the old way of life – stuff that's really strong and sturdy – it used to last. It was hand-built, well made. Nowadays, it's all tinny and thin layers of paint – anything to bodge it up and make it look nice and pretty. But when it comes down to a bit of wear and tear, it collapses.'

He could have been analysing his own ultimate demise.

Also in evidence is Sutch's self-deprecatory sense of humour as the programme shows him in 'normal' clothes, interviewing older members of the public about Screaming Lord Sutch: they are not very complimentary. The programme ends with Sutch musing, deadpan but perhaps a trifle fancifully, on his appeal: 'They like to see something different. I think there's too many, maybe feminine-type pop singers on the scene – they're too goody-goody. The young people of today like to rebel against society, so if they can go for somebody who has a James Dean-type act, this is the type of fan we get.'

The self-delusional comparison to the smouldering actor was typical, a trait that was to recur throughout his life.

The next two years saw Sutch maintaining his place in the public eye at every opportunity. He got his chance to take on the prime minister, as another general election took place in May 1965. Still just twenty-four years old, Sutch registered as a candidate for the 'National Independent Teenage Party' in Harold Wilson's constituency of Huyton. He had added the legalisation of commercial radio to his manifesto, along with cat licences and the removal of tax from motorbikes. To add a local angle he suggested 'preserving the Cavern Club as a national shrine'.

He was in optimistic mood: 'I'll save my deposit this time. There's a lot of feeling against Harold.'

'I was with him in Huyton,' recalled Paul Nicholas. 'Sutch had a great photograph done of him trying to shake hands with Harold Wilson; he released that as a Christmas card – he thought that was very funny.' Sutch had managed to wheedle his way into a photo opportunity with a bemused Wilson, who initially refused to shake his hand, but then relented and handed him a cigar. 'I tapped Harold on the shoulder,' Sutch explained. 'I said, "What about a light, then, 'arold?" And the picture of that went around the world.' He was rewarded with 585 votes.

He found himself appearing on bills with the biggest acts, both established and up-and-coming, from The Who to Graham Bond, but this next wave of rock acts were gaining ground on his brand of novelty rock 'n' roll. He was now represented by the Roy Tempest Organisation Ltd, 'Europe's Largest Band Agency', whose big names included Manfred Mann, The Kinks, The Animals and The Yardbirds. The latter would record a fiery version of 'The Train Kept A Rollin'', which Sutch covered and which was released by CBS in June 1965. It was his first 'straight' single, but had a muddy production, again by Meek, and a rock 'n' roll rather than beat feel that made this Tiny Bradshaw track seem oddly out of its time. 'Rock's coming back,' exclaimed an enthusiastic but sadly misguided Sutch. 'It's like when Bill Haley was great.'

His fan club was now being run by Jann Clayton-Fuller. She told me recently, 'I still have material from it in my loft. I also have some of David's hair.' I didn't ask from which part of his body.

In July 1965, he was dressed for all the world like Fred Flintstone, in a leopardskin off-the-shoulder dress, and carrying a hefty caveman's club. This was for an appearance at Willesden County Court in a case involving a hire-purchase agreement on a van. 'Is that the way you usually dress yourself?' he was asked by the judge, who invited him to sit down when told it was. The usher made him leave his club outside.

He was also able to cause a stir internationally now, walking to a Las Vegas hotel carrying a ten-inch knife and an axe to plug 'Jack the Ripper', and being arrested at Orly airport in Paris for wearing 'panther-skin gladiator trunks and a floating green velvet cloak'. In

1966 the band were in Italy during England's World Cup triumph – and got arrested for throwing girls into Rome's Trevi Fountain in celebration.

His other main publicity coup during this period was marriage – or at least the announcement of it – a characteristically indeterminate affair that would set the tone for thirty years of relationships with the opposite sex.

Sutch met singer, actress and model Sue Hunt in May 1966 when they were both signing autographs on the *New Musical Express* stand at the Star Gala in Battersea Park, an event with an eclectic bill that included Trini Lopez, Max Bygraves, and The Pretty Things. The two were with the same label, CBS, and nineteen-year-old Sue – who recorded as Geneveve – was enjoying a minor hit with her single, 'Once', which reached number twenty-three in the charts for a couple of weeks. The *Guinness Book of Hit Singles* later described her as French, although she actually grew up on a fruit farm in Sussex. Sutch, too, had a CBS single to promote – 'The Cheat', his stab at psychedelia, and perhaps (for me, anyway) his best recording of all. The B-side, 'All Black and Hairy' – 'Last night I was digging in the cemetery / Up jumped a man, all black and hairy' – remained a hilarious staple of his live act for many years.

Before the end of May Sutch and Sue Hunt were announcing that they were to wed. 'I don't care what people say about her career being marred by being married to me,' declared an apparently besotted Sutch. 'We are definitely getting married on Wednesday, 13 July at Wembley Park.' So in love was he that he had 'shorn his shoulder-length locks, and junked that leopardskin for a Carnaby suit', a Cambridge blue item costing thirty-five quid, and teamed with a lace-fronted dress shirt with frilled cuffs (£8). He had dyed his hair black. He was even prepared to ditch his most recognised trademarks: 'Rock 'n' roll and that Jack the Ripper stuff is out.' The *Sun* reported that Sutch had given his bride-to-be 'a golden cameo ring, an heirloom from his great-grandmother', and had also ordered a diamond ring. Geneveve was to be known as 'Lady Sutch', the *Evening Standard* informed readers. 'Not only that. Any children they have will be called "baron" or "baroness".' The *Daily Mirror* reported an announcement that was to become familiar over the years: 'I am having my name changed to Lord Sutch by deed poll.'

It seemed set to be the wedding of the year, but on 27 May the *Daily Express* ran the sensational headline: 'GENEVEVE BREAKS IT OFF – AFTER ONE DAY'. This will-they-won't-they teasing of the tabloids pre-dates the likes of Peter Andre and Jordan or Hugh Grant and Liz Hurley by three decades or more.

Geneveve is now Sue Tacker, living in Walnut Creek in California and working as a drama and kindergarten teacher. When I tracked her down she sounded genuinely sad to discover that the man to whom she was once allegedly engaged was dead. 'I have to tell you it wasn't real,' she said. 'In the sixties a lot of things went on – and you just went along with them. I think it was all David's idea, and arranged between our managers. I only met him two or three times. I was in my mid-teens and went along with the whole thing, as I believed it would help my career. I do actually remember David as being very sweet – kind of crazy, but underneath softness and sweetness. I'm really very sorry to hear what happened to him.'

Sutch's relationship with Joe Meek, who had not produced his last single, hit the rocks for good that September, when he announced – to a newspaper, of course – that he was to sue Meek for unpaid royalties. 'I've suffered very much through the story,' complained a cash-strapped Meek to his solicitor in a letter that showed he sympathised with his artist. 'Lord Sutch was in his rights to expect what was his, and it was my wish and instructions that this should be done ... I feel that Lord Sutch should be paid as I'm shure it not to great an amount [sic].'

This row would not be sorted out until years after Meek's death when in 1991 the High Court gave Meek's artists the rights to their master tapes.

In February 1967, on the eighth anniversary of the death of Buddy Holly, a paranoid and mentally ill Joe Meek, obsessed with morbid, occult thoughts and in severe financial difficulties, fatally shot his landlady Mrs Violet Shenton at his flat in Holloway Road, before turning the gun on himself.

Sutch's reaction to the death of this troubled man pre-empted the reaction of many, more than thirty years later, when they learned of his own suicide: 'I was amazed as well as shocked and sad when I heard all this, as I had always thought of him as a fabulously successful producer, and it never occurred to me he had no money and only rented his flat. He was a great man and is much missed.'

But he may have felt a pang of guilt. Shortly before Meek's suicide, writes his biographer John Repsch, 'there was at least £15,000 to be found from bank accounts holding only a few hundred, and with Messrs Shanks, Sutch, Burt and LaVern all bearing down on him like the Four Horsemen of the Apocalypse, it could be many months before he was out of debt.'

chapter six

Turning the Page

'He seemed to settle for becoming famous for being famous'
— DAVE BERRY

Screaming Lord Sutch had played
at a benefit concert for the widow of the rock 'n'
roll singer Johnny Kidd — the frontman of The
Pirates — who'd been killed in a car crash in October 1966. Taking to
the stage in a chariot, and clad in toga and laurel wreath, Sutch now
billed himself as Caesar Sutch and his Roman Empire — Ritchie
Blackmore, Carlo Little, Tony Dangerfield and Matthew Fisher were
his cohorts. The new incarnation lasted until April 1967, when all but
Fisher announced their departure. With the Roman Empire having
fallen, there was nothing to keep Sutch in the country, so when an
opportunity to tour the States (which he had first visited in July 1965,
promoting 'The Train Kept A-Rollin'), make money and play to a new
audience presented itself, he jumped at it.

He travelled to New York at the beginning of 1968 on the *Queen
Elizabeth*, taking with him his 1955 Union-Jack-painted Rolls Royce
Silver Wraith. 'I'd bought it from an undertakers as a sure way of
getting a car that hadn't been thrashed to death,' he said. A contemporary
press release announces that he is to be driven around the US by
'chauffeur-valet Horace the Butler'. Sutch would later explain that his
visit to the States was part of the Backing Britain campaign, publicising
Carnaby Street fashion: 'That was to teach people to be proud of
Britain. To be "Backing Britain" was to buy stuff that was made in Great

Britain. So we all had these stickers made of the Union Jack – that was how I launched that tour when I went over there. It was a tour of America, playing gigs and in the afternoons I would do big shops – Macy's and them kind of shops and display all this Union Jack stuff – there was suits, those psychedelic kind of suits – it was at the time of Hendrix and The Who with their Union Jack jackets and shirts.' He was also, according to his press release, promoting Marshall amplifiers. Travelling in such flamboyant style, one would imagine that Sutch was at least being subsidised, if not handsomely rewarded by a benevolent sponsor, but there is no evidence that he was.

He would spend nearly two years in the US, criss-crossing the country, playing gigs and making numerous PR appearances at a going rate of $100 a day. He started off with a series of gigs (the Scene, Cheetah and Hullabaloo clubs) in New York and New England, and also appeared on the Merv Griffin, Johnny Carson and Dick Clarke TV shows. The Merv Griffin show in particular was a lucrative earner: $265 for a one-hour appearance in early February.

In April, handsomely bedecked in a gold satin waistcoat, a jewelled cravat, Beatle-style black boots and an eighteenth-century coat, he appeared at the International Photography and Travel Fair at the New York Coliseum. In July, Sutch would meet the mother of his child, Thann, but a couple of months earlier, she would later tell me, a seminal incident in his life took place. Sutch had been invited to a party in New York where he had the experience which set him firmly against recreational drugs – 'the punch was spiked with acid', revealed Thann. 'He had a bad trip, but he didn't know about it – he said the sidewalks were moving – he was freaking out, and that set him really against drugs.'

June saw him in New York, New Jersey, Cleveland, Milwaukee and Chicago. July it was Minneapolis, San Francisco, which he didn't like much – 'I was not really into the hippy thing' – and Los Angeles, which he did. On 24 August, his involvement with the 'Backing Britain' campaign saw a personal appearance at 'Capwell's New "Have-a-dashery" Teen Shop' in Oakland, California.

In Las Vegas Sutch saw Elvis Presley's August 1969 International Hotel performance, a midnight show, blagging press tickets on the pretext of being British Ambassador for Rock 'n' Roll, which enabled him to witness 'the greatest performance I had ever seen'. Afterwards he got to meet the King. According to his press biography (compiled by John Tempest), 'Sutch tried to persuade Presley's manager, Colonel Tom Parker, to bring his star to England for a guaranteed £1 million to appear at Wembley Stadium … D.A. Pennebaker, Bob Dylan's film producer, wanted to film the event, but this was not in accord with the wishes of Parker. Sadly the Presley visit never took place.'

Who knows how much of this really happened, and how much was mere wishful thinking or the exaggeration of a snatched word or two? As with so much of David's life and supposed achievements, the evidence is ambiguous and contradictory. One of Sutch's musicians, Mike Crawford, later told me Sutch had admitted he had gate-crashed Presley's press conference, and made his '£1 million offer' to the 'King' on impulse. But Sid Shaw, who runs Elvisly Yours, the famous Elvis memorabilia shop in London, is convinced that Sutch came very close to the unparalleled coup of getting Elvis to play in England: 'Every Elvis fan in Britain should be indebted to David Sutch. He went to visit Elvis and the Colonel three times and spent £2,000 of his own money to try and get Elvis to come to England. He organised backers in England, but the Colonel would not give film rights to the British businessmen so the deal fell through.' For what it's worth, I remember Sutch telling me once that he had been at a remote Scottish airport the one and only time Elvis made a secret, literally flying visit to Britain.

In September 1969, Sutch appeared at what *Rolling Stone* magazine extravagantly trailed as 'the second most important event in rock 'n' roll history' – the huge Rock 'n' Roll Revival festival at the University of Toronto's Varsity Stadium. It was headlined by The Doors, but even more significant was the presence of John Lennon and Yoko Ono, who performed as John Lennon and The Plastic Ono Band and who were introduced (again, in the case of John) to Sutch by Rodney Bingenheimer. Also on the bill were all the great names of rock 'n' roll: Chuck Berry; Little Richard; Jerry Lee Lewis; Gene Vincent; Bo Diddley; Junior Walker; Alice Cooper; Tony Joe White and … Sutch.

'This guy was wild,' enthused Canadian rock aficionado Richard Maxwell, 'diving right off the stage and into the crowd. He had really long hair, wore a frilly lace shirt and Lord Fauntleroy jacket, and screamed like a maniac. Part of his set he was in the crowd with a long microphone cable getting his shirt ripped by fans. I had never heard of him before, nor ever again, but I'll never forget that wild man's chaotic performance.'

In his *NME* review, accompanied by a picture of Sutch with Jim Morrison, Roy Carr wrote: 'As dusk descended and the stadium lights were switched on, our very own Screamin' Lord Sutch in gold brocade suit worked his way through "Roll Over Beethoven" and "Good Golly Miss Molly" along with [band] Whisky Howl.'

What Jerry Lee Lewis thought of Sutch's performance in Toronto we don't know, but Chas Hodges of Chas and Dave would remember a tour on which he was backing the Killer, and Sutch was the supporting act: 'I've never known Jerry Lee Lewis come out of his dressing room to watch an act by the side of the stage – the only one he's ever done that to was Screaming Lord Sutch. He'd just see the humour, see the fun, see the rock 'n' roll.'

Just how cool must Sutch have been at this point? About to turn twenty-nine, a young, good-looking fashion icon at the centre of the US and British rock scenes, he was known to, and hanging out with, everyone from The Rolling Stones to The Beatles and Jim Morrison. 'I used to go clubbing with Jim,' Sutch recollected, 'although I couldn't keep up with him, he was so totally gross.'

It was through Jerry Lee Lewis that Sutch met his good friend Ron Kellerman, who was vice-president of the Jerry Lee Lewis international fan club. The pair had begun to correspond and in 1965 it was Ron who had invited David over for his first visit to the States. 'David and Ron seemed to have a great deal in common,' revealed Kellerman's sister, Denise Kelly. 'Both had been brought up without the presence of a father, both loved being the centre of attention, and both were great collectors. My brother often collected multiple copies of photos, videos, magazine articles and other memorabilia. That's the way David was, too. I remember once going to England and visiting David's house and seeing his room, which was dark and piled high with things he'd collected. I wonder about that – it's as though neither of them ever wanted to let go of anything they had coveted and then collected, unless it was to friends, to whom they were invariably generous.'

Three years after this first visit Sutch caused a stir when he parked his Union Jack Rolls Royce outside Kellerman's modest home in New

Jersey. 'We lived in a blue-collar neighbourhood,' says Denise, 'where the sight of a Rolls Royce painted with a British flag was, to say the least, a rare occurrence. It brought out a lot of curious locals.'

On this trip some of his gigs were in incongruous surroundings. 'One show up in the Catskills,' recalled Denise, 'was at a prime family holiday resort that was frequented by elderly Jewish people. This was a highly conservative and unlikely venue for *any* rock 'n' roll star, let alone one dressed in leather and lace, with hair swinging past his shoulders, and who began his act by popping out of a coffin with an axe! They must have been ashen-faced.'

Denise's mother Belle became a kind of 'surrogate American mom to David,' Denise revealed. 'They got on very well from the start – he once bought her a gold key about two feet long – not my taste, but she loved it and put it up in the living room foyer. They both had garish tastes. She was a dressmaker, and designed David outfits of colourful brocade, gold lamé and other flamboyant materials. She loved it when he wore her gear on stage.' Interestingly Denise also saw the two sides of David Sutch, which were to cause him such anguish later in life: 'He had all the mechanisms in place to make people believe in an image – he was always ready to go into the role of Screaming Lord Sutch – but it is difficult to know whether or not it was real.'

In late October 1968, Sutch was with Ron Kellerman in New York to see Led Zeppelin, by then the hottest live act in the States. The pair of them had spent most of the previous night and that morning with Jimmy Page at Kellerman's home in Perth Amboy. Page, of course, had briefly passed through Sutch's Savages in the early 1960s – but on this occasion it was Kellerman (who would sadly die within a fortnight of 9/11) who seems to have impressed the guitar hero first: 'I over-whelmed Jimmy with my massive army of recorded music. He asked to see some of my personal items concerning Jerry Lee Lewis. I showed him a letter that I had from the Killer. Lord Sutch and Jimmy later got into a discussion of the early days in England. One thing not on the agenda was sleep, although somewhere around 4 a.m. the attempt was made. All I remember was being half asleep on the couch and hearing the delightful chatter of this gig and that gig and this session and that session in two British accents. It was about 10 a.m. when I awoke. Jimmy and Dave were already up and having coffee. My mom offered us breakfast. Jimmy gathered up some of the records I gave him and goodbyes were exchanged. Later that evening Dave and I were among an audience of thousands watching Jimmy and the mighty Led Zeppelin once again roar onstage.'

Apparently inspired by his meeting with Page, Sutch had a burst of creative energy on his birthday in 1968, writing several of the tracks which would appear on his first album.

Many people have wondered why even as late as the end of the 1960s Sutch had never produced an LP, despite having quality musicians aplenty in The Savages. By 1968 The Beatles had already released *Sergeant Pepper*, and The Rolling Stones *Beggar's Banquet*. 'Carlo and I were idiots not to have made albums with the line-ups we had,' Sutch admitted in an interview with former Savage Alan Clayson in 1999, 'but there's not much time to record when you're working seven nights a week, sometimes afternoons, too. We never gave records a thought. We were more of a visual experience.' Now, however, it was at last time. Sutch relocated to Los Angeles, and took Led Zeppelin's John Bonham and Jimmy Page into the Mystic Sound studio in LA. Between 24 April and 4 May 1969 they worked on what would become *Lord Sutch and Heavy Friends*. Bonham and Page were impressed with the facilities: 'They liked the sound so much,' said Sutch, 'that they decided to use it for some of *Led Zeppelin II*.'

It had been nearly four years since Sutch had made a record. *Lord Sutch and Heavy Friends* was released in May 1970 on Atlantic in Britain and a little earlier on the Cotillion label in the US. The 'Heavy Friends' were an impressive roster: Jimmy Page and John Bonham of Led Zeppelin (Bonham had owned up to cycling to Stratford as a kid in 1963 to get Sutch's autograph when he stood for Parliament); Jeff Beck; Noel Redding, bass player in *The Jimi Hendrix Experience*; Nicky Hopkins; Carlo Little and top session guitarist Kent Henrey. Sutch had roped in a number of these Friends after jamming with them at a gig at Thee Experience in Los Angeles. 'The only snag with making the album,' said Sutch later, 'was not having the cash to pay for the recording sessions upfront'– but, *voilà*, 'the American answer was to tell me I could pay the bills after the record had been released and made some money – which I subsequently did.'

The album – whose cover features Sutch's name thirty-seven times

– is unashamed heavy rock, guitars to the fore, with a couple of stand-out quasi-psychedelic tracks both mysteriously credited to one Jay Cee as writer. The self-penned lyrics of the other tracks, however, betray Sutch's limited vocabulary and rhyming ability. But there is no horror content, no gore, no monster references. This is an all-out attempt to target the contemporary rock market. The twelve tracks were: 'Wailing Sounds'; 'Cause I Love You' (released as a single); 'Flashing Lights'; 'Gutty Guitar'; 'Would You Believe'; 'Smoke and Fire'; 'Thumping Beat'; 'Union Jack Car'; 'One For You Baby'; 'L.O.N.D.O.N.'; 'Brightest Light'; 'Baby Come Back'. I later discovered lyrics to a track, 'In Only a Week', recorded at the sessions but never released:

> I went to Piccadilly, the famous tourist attraction,
> To chat up the birds, but I got no reactions.
> With eyes that were bulging out of my head
> I went to a strip club, and now I'm feeling dead.

Sutch would claim that the album became his first ever chart hit, reaching number forty-eight on the *Billboard* listings. I am delighted to confirm that the album was indeed listed in the Top 100 by three separate US charts – Billboard, Cashbox and 'RW' – at numbers 98, 100 and 86 respectively, in March 1970. In two interviews at the time with *Disc* and *Melody Maker* Sutch claimed the album had sold 70,000 copies in one month in the States. To judge by the large number of copies which consistently crop up in second-hand shops and on Internet auction sites that figure may well be accurate. But its chances of achieving that elusive breakthrough were damned when influential *Rolling Stone* magazine described the front man as 'absolutely terrible'. 'The best two tracks,' said *Disc*, 'are the ones they [Sutch/Page] didn't write. It's no musical progression but jolly jiving stuff. It could have been made ten years ago except for the playing of the lead guitarists.'

More serious, however, was the subsequent controversy concerning the true nature of Jimmy Page's contribution to the album, which would sour the relationship between him and Sutch. According to Steve Sauer, of LZHistory.com, Page 'said that he'd been duped as to exactly what the album would be like. Five of the songs were credited to Page and others, but the guitarist insisted he wasn't involved in any song-writing.'

The original typewritten song lyrics support Page's contention. On the album 'Cause I Love You'; 'Thumping Beat'; 'Union Jack Car' and 'Flashing Lights' are all credited to 'Lord Sutch and Jimmy Page', but the originals state: 'Following words and music by Lord David Sutch'. Interviewed in *Rock Magazine* in October 1970, Page denied point-blank that he had played any of the guitar solos on the record:

> It was all fixed that I'd go down there and just do a bit, so we went down and played, and I just did some backing tracks to numbers like 'Good Golly Miss Molly' and 'Roll Over Beethoven'... To cut a long story short [Sutch] rewrote all the tunes. I didn't do any solos – no solos at all. I did a little bit of wah-wah on one track – 'Baby Come Back' [later described as a 'transposed remake of Roy Head's "Treat Her Right"'] – but I didn't do the solo in the middle, which isn't a wah-wah thing; somebody else put that on.
>
> But – and this is where the criminal side of it comes in – he didn't put 'extra guitar: so-and-so' or 'lead guitar played by so-and-so', he put 'Guitar: Jimmy Page', so everybody thought, 'Oh, Jimmy Page played that heap of crap' and it became more than an embarrassment.
>
> He also wrote me in as producer, which was very nice of him. I wasn't interested in that. I just went down to have a laugh, playing some old rock 'n' roll, a bit of a send-up. The whole joke sort of reversed itself and became ugly.

It was the same kind of trick – if Page's memory is accurate – as Sutch had played with the photo of Harold Wilson, the self-aggrandising publicity justifying the shameless means, but it is also perhaps a musical watershed in Sutch's career. The moment of his most important musical collaboration is also possibly that of his most tawdry deception.

The original LP sleeve endeavours to persuade listeners that 'watching Lord Sutch perform is like watching Arthur Brown, Jerry Lee Lewis and James Brown all rolled into one'. Since Sutch's death the album has subsequently been re-issued on CD by the Magnum Force label under the new title of *Smoke and Fire*. Sutch would have been mortified to discover that his presence has been ruthlessly excised from the front cover, which now just features the names of the illustrious band members, the most illustrious of whom apparently has no desire whatsoever to be associated with the project.

chapter seven

Handing it to Wembley

'Larger than life, he was an honest extrovert. He never offended anyone and came across as an intelligent person who just loved to be outrageous. Nothing wrong with that'
— Sir Jimmy Savile OBE KCSG

The *Lord Sutch and Heavy Friends* album cover heralded the genesis of a new Sutch. Gone were the horror trappings, the outlandish gear. Instead, here was a stylish Regency beau, parading in splendid, crimson, three-quarter-length frock coat and other sumptuously regal, foppish clothes, with jewellery a-plenty – a forerunner of Adam Ant's dandy highwayman or even Austin Powers. His hair was blond, and there was a faint six o'clock shadow lurking on his ruggedly good-looking face. He leaned against his Rolls Royce, the very epitome of Swinging Sixties London. For the first time Screaming Lord Sutch could pass muster as a rock star!

With the album bestowing on him some musical respectability, Sutch at last had a chance to move away from being a novelty sideline on the lunatic fringe and gain a mainstream rock audience. In April 1970, therefore, he appeared at the Country Club in Hampstead in a high-profile comeback show trumpeted as his 'first British gig' in four years (it wasn't), with a band billed as Lord Sutch and his Heavy Friends (they weren't). In fact, the line-up was remarkably similar to the one he had put together for a rather lower-profile appearance in Southall a few months earlier where he had recorded parts of the show for possible release. Caroline Boucher covered the Country Club show for *Disc*:

> It was a strange evening. His Lordship took the stage just after nine. The club was bulging at the seams with the hairiest of hairy trendies unwillingly rubbing shoulders with an incredible selection of rockers. The entrance lobby was lined with Hell's Angels, and piled with recording equipment.
>
> The band was Brian Keith of Plastic Penny on trombone, Sid Berry (ex Cliff Bennett) on sax, Spencer Davis on guitar, Ritchie Blackmore and Nick Simper, with Matthew Fisher on organ and Carlo Little on drums. Periodic accompaniment was provided by Keith Moon.
>
> As for Sutch – well, he's not a good singer, and doesn't pretend to be, but he won over an overcrowded and testy audience by sheer willpower. After two hours of old rock numbers interspersed with a great deal of Sutch chat he got a certain rapport going with his audience – although a good few true-blue rockers had walked out.

It seems odd that Sutch would not have played the *Heavy Friends* set in order to promote its imminent British release, nor its introductory single – 'Cause I Love You' – which was already out, but he clearly had no intention of running an expensive band of 'Heavy Friends' quality for live shows following this one-off. Those who attended future gigs hoping to see the star names from his albums, however, may not have been best pleased. 'People turned up in droves,' wrote Nick Hamlyn in his *Penguin Price Guide for Record and CD Collectors*, 'to watch Sutch chase members of an anonymous backing group around the stage with a mop!'

'I remember once Sutch introduced some guy from the Midlands as being a member of Vanilla Fudge,' adds Nick Simper, who really did play with Deep Purple. 'The accent was a bit of a giveaway!'

Sutch was already looking towards the follow-up album that would emerge out of the Country Club gig, for the show was, like the earlier one, recorded – although he apparently neglected to mention the fact to many of the participants.

But he was still in demand as a live draw, in May 1970 joining major acts like Black Sabbath, Mungo Jerry, The Grateful Dead and Alice Cooper for Newcastle-under-Lyme's Hollywood Festival. *NME*'s Richard Green called Sutch 'a surprise hit ...[He] lit a fire and almost ignited a giant structure which had been inflated in front of the stage. He also had smoke bombs let off in the audience which caused a minor stampede.'

'If only he could sing,' complained *Music Now*, while acknowledging 'that as an entertainer and professional he is second to none.'

Backing him that day were Angela Wayne and Renee Horshkowitz – better known as the Wah Wah girls. 'We would be dressed up as schoolgirls,' Angela said: 'playing tennis rackets and throwing things to the crowd, and Sutch would chase us with a long stick he called the Minge Pole. He was a lunatic, really weird – I went to his house once, it was ghastly. His mother was there and he sat watching two televisions at the same time – one with the sound up and another with the sound down, but on another channel.' Around this time the *Daily Mirror* informed readers that Sutch 'put a topless girl into his group, but she quit after getting her bosom meshed up in the guitar strings one night.'

When *Melody Maker* invited him to discuss a selection of new records in their 'Blind Date' column, Sutch ranged impressively far and wide. Of The Who he remembered: 'I played with them at a British exhibition in Lyons. The organisers wanted two typical English groups and they got The Who breaking up their guitars and me setting fire to the stage ... If I had a voice as good as Otis [Redding], with my mind for publicity and my knowledge of the business, then ... Alas, you can't have everything.'

In June 1970, after four years in abeyance, Sutch resumed his political career for the general election. He reportedly handed in his nomination papers wearing swimming trunks.

Atlantic released his tie-in single 'Election Fever', with Sutch's deathless self-penned lyrics inspired by one of Harold Wilson's most notorious soundbites:

Election fever is all around
Election fever will get you down

The pound in your pocket will never vary
Whoever said that, he must be a fairy.

He stood in the City of London and Westminster constituency for the Young Ideas Party (not, as claimed in his autobiography, the Go To Blazes Party), on a platform of building council flats in the garden of Buckingham Palace to help Royal finances, and calling for the pedestrianisation of Carnaby Street, where he canvassed from the back of a lorry with a band and 'go-go girls', causing 'considerable traffic confusion'. (Pedestrianisation of Carnaby Street would, like so many of his off-the-wall policies, eventually come to pass.) Other manifesto pledges included the establishment of a Rock College, in which Mick Jagger and Eric Clapton were said to be interested, and the reintroduction of National Service – not, however, of the kind he had avoided experiencing, but rather an institution in which 'fighting would be forbidden' along with 'saluting, shouting' and 'short back and sides' haircuts. Down at the bottom of the list of proto-Loony suggestions was one which seemed strangely out of place amongst all the jocosity: a call for 'more money to be spent on mental hospitals'. No explanation, no elucidation. Could it be that Sutch had already noticed early signs of the distressing condition which would lead to his death? This time he gathered only 142 votes.

The next two years are a chronicle of Sutch's continuing, indefatigable and successful efforts to keep himself in the public eye, and also see him reverting to the rock 'n' roll fare he knew and could rely on. In 1970 he was photographed clowning about in a boxing ring with Muhammad Ali. In 1972, under a newspaper picture of Sutch feeding a bear with milk from a baby's bottle, there were reports of a new interest: his own zoo. The seven-month-old Himalayan bear had apparently cost him the then-substantial sum of £200, and he claimed also to have already acquired 'an African Grey parrot, two Macaws, a black-billed Jamaican parrot, a cat, a dog, and this bear, Howling Booboo. I love animals, and I use them in my act.'

Presumably it was Howling Booboo that, according to a 1976 interview, Sutch took along to a gig one night 'and had one of my team lead him on stage while I was singing the old Elvis hit, "Teddy Bear".

The only trouble was, nobody would believe he was real. One of the teddy boys tripped him and, of course, the bear got narked. He picked himself up, swung round and ripped a girl's leg with his paw. Finally, everybody got the message that the bear was genuine, and bolted for the doors. Unfortunately the bear decided to scarper, dived out of the back door, climbed over a wall and ran out into the night. It took a score of us two hours to find him.'

Ken Fagan, whose father ran the Fishmongers Arms in Wood Green pub where Sutch regularly played, confirms that the tale is not apocryphal: 'He used the bear for a Teddy Boys versus Teddy Bear act. The bear was later shut into a corner of the back yard and escaped. Police were called by some poor drunk who had shut himself in the phone box. The area was sealed off until the bear was recaptured.'

Meanwhile, the Heavy Friends were replaced by a new rock 'n' roll band known as The House Shakers, who set off for a two-week tour of France with the legendary rock 'n' roller Gene Vincent. Sutch did return to the US in late 1971 and played a number of gigs with the former Bonzo Dog Doo Dah Band frontman, Viv Stanshall, as well as headlining at North Hollywood's Whisky-A-Go-Go, where he was introduced by the maverick pop svengali Kim Fowley and supported by the garage band of the moment, The Flamin' Groovies, who had recently released their seminal *Teenage Head* album. But, home in the UK, a review of his bill-topping appearance at the Carshalton Park Rock 'n' Roll Festival confirms it was back to the mixture-as-before, albeit as spectacular as ever:

> It was dark and a chilly wind blew. The crowd stirred as the Rock 'n' Roll All Stars struck up the Death March and howled ghoulishly into their microphones.
>
> Suddenly a green light appeared in the distance and down the hillside came a procession of hooded monks, bearing a black coffin, lit by two flaming torches.
>
> Excitement rose as the pall-bearers made their way among the crowd and the music came to a climax as the coffin was put on the stage. Three spine-chilling screams were emitted from within, and, in true Sutch style, a headless, bloody body, with grotesque hands, emerged.

The follow-up album to *Heavy Friends*; his last for eight years, was *Hands of Jack the Ripper*, but the only similarity to its hard-rocking predecessor was the presence of big names on the cover: Matthew Fisher; Ritchie Blackmore; Noel Redding; Nick Simper (referred to as Simpler); Keith Moon; Brian Keith; Sid Phillips; and Annette and Victor Brox. It was co-produced by the late Vic Maile, who would later become the highly-rated producer of bands like Dr Feelgood, and was based around Sutch's 1970 Country Club comeback gig, which had been secretly taped. Released in July 1972, it was a repeat of the debacle with Jimmy Page.

Tony Fletcher's biography of Keith Moon, *Dear Boy*, reports Moon as being 'embarrassed', and even Carlo Little was 'chagrined' that the album featured their names 'prominently on the sleeve'. The upshot of it all was that, having put himself on the cusp of breaking out of his established rock 'n' roll identity to a more cutting-edge presence on the heavy rock scene, the momentum of Sutch's musical career would from this point begin to fall away.

This time around Sutch had reverted to type: the album combined time-honoured classics like 'Roll Over Beethoven', 'Good Golly Miss Molly' and 'Great Balls of Fire' with purportedly original numbers like 'Gotta Keep A-Rocking' – though this last was a cheeky clone of 'Don't You Just Know It', and 'Country Club' little more than an instrumental topped and tailed with derivative vocals owing much to 'Honey Hush'.

And there was the title track, 'Hands of Jack the Ripper', nine minutes and fifteen seconds long and written by Sutch. Matthew Fisher, who played on the album, even suggests that it *was* a rendition of 'Jack the Ripper', but extensively over-dubbed so that Sutch could claim authorship of it. But this Sutch version differs from the original in that the victim is Mary Clark rather than Mary Kelly, and its repeated refrain, 'I'm looking for Mary Clark', is almost a direct lift from the 1959 British film *Jack the Ripper*, notable for a climactic sequence in which the black-and-white film suddenly bursts into colour as blood oozes through the floorboards. When it was released Sutch would have been an impressionable eighteen-year-old. The song features more screams, screeches and orgasmic moans than you can shake a freshly sharpened knife at, as Sutch prowls the streets, noting 'blood on the pavement beneath my feet, the girls in the town never sleep' before launching into a frenzy of howls and demonic laughs as he goes about his blood-soaked business, and warning 'all you evil women better watch your step – he might be right behind you, reaching for your neck'. Thann Rendessy did the screaming.

Nigel Molden was working for WEA Records' Promotions Department when the *Hands* album was released: 'Nobody in the company had any idea what to do with a Lord Sutch album which was only scheduled for release as an import item. None of this stopped Sutch coming into the office to make sure that everyone was aware of the album. I particularly remember a conversation in which he said that he would guarantee the front page of every Sunday newspaper in the country prior to his forthcoming performance at the London Rock 'n' Roll Show at Wembley Stadium. His first step was to invite the prime minister, Edward Heath, a noted classical pianist, to appear as a guest artist. The second was a master-stroke, turning up at Downing Street on Saturday afternoon with a bevy of topless models, issuing the invitation to the PM personally.'

Before he got to Downing Street though, Sutch (who had dyed his hair green) paraded through London in a red double-decker bus, waving a football rattle. His 'nude nubiles' had stickers attached to 'various parts of their bodies' advertising the upcoming Wembley concert on 5 August. According to a newspaper report, Sutch then 'rushed to the door of Number 10, and pushed aside a group of six children having their photo taken'. Worse followed. Sutch 'refused to go away' when requested so to do by a policeman and, appearing in full football kit, was subsequently remanded on bail. Sutch turned up for his court appearance at Bow Street in prison garb with a ball and chain attached to his leg, though he then changed into a blue suit (his hair remained green). He told the court it had been his intention to invite the Prime Minister to the concert and was found not guilty of insulting behaviour. However, the four young ladies were each fined £20 – which just happened to be the amount they had been paid.

The London Rock 'n' Roll Show at Wembley was to be Sutch's last stadium gig, and one of the highlights of his whole performing career. More publicity for it included a photo-call of Sutch, decked out in frock-coated finery and sporting a parrot on his shoulder, kicking a ball about on the famous Wembley turf with a somewhat baffled-looking Little Richard, who was stripped to the waist. The bill was a stellar line-up that also featured Chuck Berry, Bill Haley, Jerry Lee Lewis, Bo Diddley and Heinz. On the night, the crowd was (optimistically) reported to be not far short of a 100,000 full house. Sutch later claimed that Johnny Rotten had been at Wembley that day selling Sutch T-shirts and badges. Apparently Rotten's sales spiel went: 'You buy 'em or I'll punch you in the face.'

Screaming Lord Sutch was fourth on the bill. He had plastered his face in white make-up, his hair was still green, and he was resplendent in a flowing gold cape. Dressing his gyrating backing singers in skimpy bikinis – even the band members stripped off their tops – instantly guaranteed him publicity far exceeding his role in the show. But his performance was also one of his most effective. His white coffin was carried on by four scantily clad females, and as he emerged from it, precariously balancing on his head a stovepipe top hat almost as tall as Marge Simpson's hair-do, hundreds of pigeons were released into the skies above Wembley. Red smoke swirled around him as he sang 'Till the Following Night'. Later he romped through a medley of 'Jack the Ripper/Hands of the Ripper', before introducing 'Alice Cooper', with whom he was conducting a public argument at the time. This 'Alice Cooper' turned out to be a tall girl who proceeded to strip off her black dress and underwear.

As it happened, the real Alice Cooper was also in London to play Wembley's Empire Pool. Sutch had made headlines in the *Record Mirror* by accusing the American of stealing his act and calling him out for fisticuffs. 'I can beat him and Iggy Stooge in a tag match with one hand tied behind my back,' he claimed. In support of Sutch's claims was the fact that an unknown Cooper had been down the bill back in 1969 when Sutch played the Toronto Festival.

In July the *NME* went in to bat on Sutch's behalf: 'For all his outrageous make-up, theatrics and carrying on, Alice Cooper is really second in line, because for folks old enough to remember, Lord Sutch was the original mad man.'

'I was wearing white powder and black around my eyes in 1959,' Sutch boasted. 'I've lasted because I've built up a reputation as a visual act. We're like a Marx Brothers film put to music.'

Cooper, though, was at the height of his popularity. 'School's Out' topped the charts that summer and it was probably Cooper's fame which ensured that yet another of Sutch's outbursts was granted front-page status in the *RM* when he challenged Alice to a 'battle of the bands' showdown. In August, the *RM* ran a risible front-page story, headed 'COOPER SHOWDOWN', in which they tried to convince readers that Sutch had flown to LA 'to have it out with Cooper once and for all'. 'This queen pinched my act,' ranted his Lordship, 'and I'm determined to prove once and for all who is really the king of horror rock.' It must have been a brief stay in LA, as by the end of the month Sutch was playing the Dorchester Tavern, and two days later was in Gloucester at the Sharpness Hotel.

No more was heard of Sutch's spat with his American rival until November, when *Record Mirror* ran an interview with Cooper in which Charles Webster, who had been instrumental in whipping up the whole artificial furore, wrote: 'A lot of people consider [Sutch] to be a jerk.'

'Is he still alive?' responded Cooper, reasonably adding, 'He copped his act from Screamin' Jay Hawkins.' He then killed a spider, pulled its legs off and declared that was what he'd like to do to Sutch.

Sutch would have loved stirring up this media 'handbags' controversy, happily wallowing in the cheap publicity, but probably only too aware, deep down, that although he had definitely once been leader of the pack, he was now playing catch-up.

But there was a further moral to be drawn from Sutch's manufactured row with Alice Cooper and the comparison of their two acts, which the American himself perceptively articulated in 2003:

> People who have tried to live their character have died trying to do it. Jim Morrison, Janis Joplin and Keith Moon. All these people were larger than life off-stage – I knew them all – and they burned out, fast. So I separated Alice and myself a long time ago. When I'm becoming Alice for a show I really look forward to it. But don't expect to see that character walking down New Bond Street if I'm out shopping.

David Sutch, on the other hand, found it almost impossible to deny his other half, and it was to destroy him.

chapter eight

Wife Not

'He was a genius, I believe – just in a different way'
— THANN RENDESSY, EX-PARTNER

t was while he was still in Los Angeles, mid-July 1968, that Sutch had met Rodney Bingenheimer, the DJ and socialite who styled himself 'Mayor of Sunset Strip'. Sutch partied enthusiastically with Bingenheimer, who one day brought along to the studios in Hollywood where Sutch was recording *Heavy Friends*, a teenage friend of his, 'one of LA's top models', Texan girl, Thann Rendessy. According to the smitten Englishman, Thann had the cheekbones of an angel 'and the most perfect figure I had ever seen'. She was at least a dozen years younger than Sutch.

Within a week of their introduction they were living together. By this time Sutch had acquired a 'handy apartment off Sunset Boulevard with a pool and lock-up for the Roller'. (This proved not to be as secure as he would have liked: the Rolls Royce was stolen, never to reappear, despite a $10,000 reward.) Thann taught Sutch to surf.

Thann, estranged from her most recent husband, now lives near a lake in Dallas, and her son Tristan lives nearby. These days she still looks the part in a rock-lady kind of way – slim, blonde, be-jeaned and accessorised with several splashes of leopardskin. She claims no credit for Sutch's leopardskin obsession: 'He was already into it when I met him.' Back in 1968 'we hit it off', she says, 'and stayed together eight years'.

But even in the early stages of their relationship Sutch's commitment appears to have been equivocal. In December 1969, for instance, Thann wrote to him at the New York address where he had been temporarily living, only to discover he had already returned to 'White Lodge' in Harrow without telling her. In the letter (which eventually made its way to England) Thann reveals that a friend had told her she was acting 'like I'm married, very married'. In fact, despite Sutch's boast in his autobiography that Thann 'became my wife', they never made their union legal.

It seems possible that their already troubled relationship had been uppermost in Sutch's mind when he penned the lyrics to 'Baby Come Back' for the *Heavy Friends* album:

> *Let me tell you 'bout my girlfriend — she's a doll*
> *She's so good-looking that there's nothing wrong.*
> *She can be awkward, as awkward as can be*
> *She can be mean, just as mean as can be.*
> *I'm afraid I still love her with my heart and my soul*
> *I love her so much.*
> *Why do you keep doing this to me?*
> *Why do you keep torturing me?*
> *Why don't you, girl, tell the truth?*
> *Don't keep lying to me*
> *Baby come back, baby come back, baby come back to me.*

However, Sutch later told Val Bird, his occasional girlfriend for some years, that this was 'our song', so who originally inspired it remains unclear.

In the early 1970s, and still a teenager, Thann moved to England. She does not look back on her early days in Britain with much affection. 'When I first got here we stayed at his mother's for six weeks, starting off on the couch downstairs.' Sutch's close relationship with his mother was from the beginning a source of tension. Even when they moved out of the family home, other problems surfaced. 'He bought the house at Petts Hill [on the borders of South Harrow and Northolt]. I was only nineteen – I didn't know anyone. The five years I was here we did not socialise. I never really met Carlo or anybody – we did gigs, clubs, did more gigs.'

In 1972 Sutch confided to his diary that he was dyslexic and had word blindness. 'He was bothered by the fact that he couldn't spell or read that well,' says Thann. 'I had to spell everything for him when he was writing anything down – when contracts would come in he didn't trust anybody because he couldn't comprehend everything. He wouldn't tell anyone, but I knew for a long time and always had to take care of business for him. Even though he was smart he just couldn't do that part, and that bothered him a lot. He was a genius, I believe – just in a different way.'

In October, Sutch went public with his wish to marry Thann. 'I am keen to get married,' he told *Record Mirror*. 'More than anything I dream of an heir to carry on the act.' But by the following February the *Sunday Mirror* was running the headline 'THE POP STAR WHO CAN'T BE A POPPA' with the following story:

Screaming Lord Sutch has called off his wedding tomorrow to model Thann Rendessy. The reason, he says, is that doctors have told him he is sterile and he feels it is unfair to deprive Thann of children. The four-year romance will continue, however, while Sutch seeks a cure. Sutch said, 'We are bitterly disappointed. I feel like I am only half a man. Thann wants children. I don't want to get married and not give her children. It's not fair to her.'

Honey-blonde Thann, a twenty-year-old fashion model, broke the news to him on Tuesday about being sterile. 'I expected it, more or less, but I still feel shattered.'

After describing how he and Thann underwent fertility tests, Sutch said, 'We have tried for quite a while for a baby. We discovered the times when Thann was most fertile and stayed in bed all that day. I have always led a very healthy sex life. I have never used contraception and have never made anyone pregnant. It seemed very strange.

Sutch, who lives in Craven Close, Hayes End [not one of Sutch's recognised addresses], and says he earns £1000 a week, said it was important to him to have a son – 'I'd like a son to take over my rock 'n' roll horror act in which I rise from a coffin.'

The *Mirror* story was accompanied by a photo of Thann, looking for all the world like the archetypal rock chick, from the long hair to the long fingernails, standing behind a seated Sutch with long hair and neck-chain.

The story certainly reads like a thoroughly modern tabloid confection, of the sort that, planted by savvy PRs, nowadays keeps countless soap stars and pop celebrities continually in the public eye. But it did mark the beginning of the ongoing rumours about the paternity of Tristan, who would be born to Thann in 1975. In any event, the wedding was never rescheduled. According to Thann, it was not true that he wasn't able to have children: 'It was strictly for publicity – after all, he had Tristan, didn't he?' The intended marriage was media bait, too: 'David and I never married. He had a fear of marriage – he was convinced a wife would take all his possessions. In fact, not only did we never marry: he never even asked me to marry him.'

The music business, in the meantime, was by now dominated by ostentatious and sophisticated progressive rock – bands like Pink Floyd, Yes, Emerson Lake and Palmer, and Supertramp, with their ambitious double-LP concept albums sold in gatefold sleeves with illustrations by Roger Dean and Hipgnosis. Sutch simply continued to plough his own furrow – a wide one, but not very deep.

In October 1973 he opened his own rock 'n' roll club at the Railway Hotel in Wealdstone, and advertised for 'authentic rock 'n' roll bands to appear'. On the opening night the rookie promoter played safe by booking a band he knew well: Screaming Lord Sutch and The Savages. One member of the audience at those first club nights sheds an interesting light on Sutch at this time. According to Bob Bassil, during the riotous weeks which followed, Sutch would be 'so drunk he'd almost fall off the stage'. This was the first eyewitness account to back up Sutch's own boastful stories of his early heavy drinking. But Bob never saw him knocking back scotches: 'In those days just about everyone, including the women, drank ale. I was about nineteen. Sutch would attract audiences of bikers and teddy boys. He would wear drape suits, often with velvet collars, and his hair was DA-ed with dollops of Brylcreem and would have to be combed back every few minutes. He was knowledgeable about the music and knew how to put together a good set of records and how to pace an evening – although his play-list would usually be much the same each time. He didn't play his own stuff – we wouldn't have let him get away with that!'

Martin Newell tells of a Sutch gig in Braintree in the mid-seventies: 'Sutch jumped off the stage towards a girl in the audience, shouting at her – whereupon she fainted. Her boyfriend, a great lump, didn't bat an eyelid – he turned to Sutch, grabbed him, called him a c— and punched him straight in the face, knocking him out. The gig was cancelled.'

Around this time, too, he was booked by old friend Paul Barrett to play at a plush function along with Barrett's current star client, Shakin' Stevens, in the barn of a luxury farm in Cambridgeshire. Barrett recalled: 'All went well until Sutch decided to do "Great Balls of Fire", featuring fire in a bucket which inevitably caught the hay in the barn alight. We saved the house, largely due to a chain of buckets – the fire-brigade took ages to get there, it was the middle of the night in the middle of nowhere. There was much distress and many concerned people looking for Sutch, perhaps not to congratulate him on his performance.

'As dawn broke we were preparing to leave, and as we got into our Transit I spotted a very faint glow coming from what I could see was a big old car parked on the edge of a field. There was a figure huddled inside, wearing a Superman T-shirt. It was Sutch, smoking a joint for the first time I'd known him do so. He wound down the window – "Is everything alright, man?"'

The young rocker who at the start of the 1960s had been far ahead of his time and set the fashion was now, ten years later, very much niche market. In 1974 he stayed very active out on the road, with gigs from February throughout the year in pubs, polys, rugby clubs, ballrooms, halls, cinemas and hotels. Contracts show his fees varying from £250, the highest, for a show at the Polytechnic in Sunderland, to fifty quid, the lowest, for Scamps in Croydon; the average was £200, sometimes including accommodation for him and the band. There were to be two general elections that year, but in the first of them on 28 February, when Edward Heath went to the country in the aftermath of the miners' strike and the three-day week, Sutch took no part. Instead, eight days before the election, he found himself in Copenhagen recording 'Shake Your Moneymaker' with a Danish group, The Zig Zag Band, for the B-side of their new single.

Dave Berry is a real rock 'n' roll survivor – when we spoke in May 2003 he was looking forward to a three-week trip to play in Australia. He remembered David Sutch with clear affection but, refreshingly, without the uncritical overview which so many of his musical cronies applied to their memories. 'When I first met him in the very early sixties when he came up to the Sheffield area they were one of my favourite groups – and David had perhaps the best British band I've ever seen behind him, with the likes of Carlo Little and his guitarist, "Strawberry" – yet he was never to reach his full potential, and too often in later years he would settle for pick-up bands or inferior musicians, and let himself down with poor time-keeping or inadequate rehearsals. It was as if he was going through the motions. Apart from his initial period of five years or so from the late fifties he seemed to settle for becoming famous for being famous.'

The two Davids' paths would intersect frequently and they became friendly, albeit on a superficial level – 'He really didn't have much to say once we'd exhausted all the usual chat about music and gigs. I had the feeling that there was not really much there, not a great deal of depth. In my long acquaintance with Sutch I never had what you might call a proper conversation with him.' Berry also saw evidence of Sutch's – almost touching – devotion to the cause of fame for its own sake. 'He was opening a village fete in North Devon, but it was a grotty day and almost no-one turned up – yet Sutch still went round the edge of the field as though there were almost a thousand spectators instead of two kids and a dog. Anybody else would just have said, let's stunt up a photo for the local paper and get out of the rain, but he did the whole bit, even waving to the non-existent crowd.' You get the impression that Dave Berry is nobody's fool, and that, without denigrating Sutch, he detected a sense of Emperor's New Clothes in many people's reactions to him.

Sutch's hectic schedule evidently admitted some time for him to devote to Thann, because towards the end of the year Sutch was eagerly anticipating becoming a father. Once again he indulged in his favourite sport of misleading the media. A newspaper report on 10 June read: 'Another spliced couple may well honeymoon in Transylvania – Screaming Lord Sutch MP (failed), hitched to Thann Rendessy only after he was sure they could have children.'

When Harold Wilson, whose Labour Party had defeated Heath's Conservatives in the first election of 1974, called another for 10 October, in the hope of securing an overall majority in the Commons, Sutch bounced back onto the political stage, standing for the GB – Go To Blazes – Party (not, as he claimed in his autobiography, for the Ban the Old Fogeys Party) in Stafford and Stone. Around this time he delivered himself of one of his most famous soundbites: 'Why is there only one Monopolies Commission?' He also introduced to the world his long-lasting (and perhaps prophetic) party slogan: 'Vote For Insanity: You Know It Makes Sense.'

Sutch managed 351 votes.

Towards the end of 1974, a pregnant Thann was driving David mad with a craving for radishes, as she recalls: 'I remember one Sunday when most places were shut and I'd run out of radishes. I made him take me out to search for an Indian shop so that I could get a new supply.' Sutch, of course, was making sure that the imminent birth of his first child would be a publicity opportunity, already pledging – in public at least – to take the advice of his fellow Harrovians in the naming of his offspring. 'Sutch and the *Post* got together to run a competition to choose a name for the baby,' recalls Sandy Guthrie, a *Harrow Post* reporter at the time. 'The winning name was Royal Highness Earl Duke Plantaganet Sutch.'

On 4 January 1975 at Northwick Park Hospital David Sutch became a father. How must the man whose own father died before he was a year old feel at becoming a father himself? Whatever his inner thoughts, in public even this undeniably profound addition to his life became the stage for a mugging photo-opportunity, with the newborn son posed in his mother's arms in hospital wearing, like his father alongside, a miniature top hat.

Despite the *Post* competition, the baby boy was registered as Tristan Lord Gwynne Sutch. In his autobiography David omits the 'Gwynne', which is Thann's middle name, apparently deriving from a Welsh king. 'David wanted to give him twenty-five names to get him in the *Guinness Book of Records*,' adds Thann. 'I said, "It's not going to happen."'

*

On 15 June Sutch cut a story out of the *Sunday Mirror* and sellotaped it to the front of a folder in which he kept bills relating to his home at Petts Hill. It read: 'A country squire said to have shot himself over money worries left £463,000 in his will. Major Morey John Starkey, 58, was found dead on the lawn at his parents' home Radway Grange in Kineton, Warwickshire, in January.'

Given that Sutch would be found dead by his own hand at his mum's home at the age of fifty-eight, leaving much the same amount, one wonders what was going through his mind even then.

In January 1976, the month of Tristan's first birthday, Sutch performed at the Ash Tree in Chatham dressed, according to *Melody Maker*, 'in a shabby gold lamé cape and trousers which appeared to have been tailored for a midget with curious anatomical defects.' Perhaps this is the point at which he realised his heart-throb days were over and the quality of his costumes began to deteriorate. Thann appeared as the Ripper's victim Mary Kelly, 'dressed in a pair of hot pants and see-through blouse. She informs me that she has frequently been stabbed by her occasionally over-zealous husband,' added the paper, 'but "it's OK, the knife is blunt, I didn't get cut up, just bruised."' Tristan's where-abouts were not mentioned.

As the year went on Thann became increasingly disillusioned with her relationship with Sutch. Glamorous it wasn't. They rarely socialised outside of gigs, and she now had a baby to cope with in an environment not conducive to children. Sutch was prone to disappearing for hours at a time to his mother's house and, more serious still, was filling every available space with his now familiar 'stuff'.

The problem – which Sutch would never conquer – may well have had its roots in his upbringing, in what we would now call a deprived environment, with precious little money for life's essentials and none for luxuries. It would have taught him – to a fault – the value of money and the desirability of possessions, both of which he would covet to extremes when they became available to him as he grew up. In a notebook Sutch was using shortly before his death he wrote: 'You may think money will give you the chance of freedom, but it does not. But if I had to choose money or no money, money it is.'

Sutch's next-door neighbour for many years in Parkfield Road, Ray Wade, tells an amusing story about David banging on his door once to tell him that nearby South Harrow tube station was being refurbished, with the result that there was 'loads of free wood' available. '"You could partition the house with it for nothing," he said. Well, yeah, Dave, but I really don't want to partition my house. "But it's free."'

But by the time he and Thann set up house together Sutch's habit had already become obsessive. 'He had filled the house up,' Thann said. 'The workshop was filled with stuff, the front room was a big, big room but packed with stuff. There was no spare bedroom – it was full up. The attic was full. He got stuff that people would leave behind because they didn't want to move it. He'd pick it up, take it home. Tristan was crawling, but it became dangerous with boxes piled up everywhere.' Sutch had filled every nook and cranny at his mother's place, too, including a garage and shed. 'Her bedrooms got full; then her living room. There was nowhere else – it was all full up. He couldn't get rid of stuff – he just couldn't do it. He kept every bill, every electric bill, phone bill – from the fifties onwards. He would not even throw a piece of paper away – he'd just put 'em in a box.' Thann herself never dared to try removing articles, for fear of the consequences. 'I never did, just didn't do it – because he was so obsessive.'

I asked Thann what had happened to all the Sutch memorabilia she must have inherited after his death. "Everything passed to Tristan. Most of David's stuff in Parkfield Road was charity-shop stuff – we gave it back to them and to boot sales. I think the obsessive collecting was a symptom of his illness. He was trying to do something about it – there were signs in the house saying "Sell, sell, sell".'

Though reports vary as to whether it was later that same year or, as Thann maintains, not until 1977, eventually she returned to America with Tristan. 'I told him I believed it was an unsafe environment in which to bring up a child and I left.' In his autobiography Sutch would subsequently suggest that she left because she 'suffered badly from post-natal depression and did not like the food or the weather here'. And in an article in *Titbits* that autumn, Sutch gave a robust report on marriage and fatherhood:

Married? I'm not that much of a nutter. I leave marriage to the real cases. Thann and I live together for a while, then we part for a while. That way we don't have blazing rows and punch-ups. We don't get bored with each other.

I think I'm a good dad and I think the world of the boy and that's all that matters. I think marriage is out of date and I can't think of a pair of my friends who are happily married.

Back in the summer of 1976 Sutch had met the French costume jewellery designer and antique collector, Giselle Menhennet, with whom he would share a lengthy and occasionally tempestuous relationship. Thann and Giselle would become friends: 'David brought Giselle over to America. They really didn't have a lot in common – although they were both night people. What kept them together, according to both of them, was the fact that she'd be gone for half the year, so they'd only be together part of the time.'

In March 1977 a quite extraordinary story appeared in the *Daily Express*. Headlined, 'NO SUTCH LUCK – AS GAIL IS LEFT HOLDING THE POP BABY', it was accompanied by a large picture of a girl with a pushchair, in which sat two-year-old Tristan Sutch. They had just arrived at Heathrow Airport. '[Sutch's] ex-girlfriend, American dancer Thann Rendessy,' ran the story, 'took [Tristan] to Los Angeles Airport, put him on a flight to London and phoned to tell Sutch, "It's about time you looked after him."'

Twenty-two-year-old American Gail Wexler had been roped in to see Tristan safely across the Atlantic. The airline would not have allowed him to fly alone.

'A woman came up to me while I was checking in and said, "How would you like to earn yourself a hundred dollars?" said Gail. 'She said all I had to do was take the baby to London where his father would be waiting. I don't know how anyone could be so heartless as to dump a baby on a total stranger.'

Sutch was duly on hand to pay Gail her money and take delivery of Tristan. 'I had a call from Thann to say that she had decided to send him back to me because she wanted to get on with her career and it was my turn to look after him. The young lady told me she had been offered one hundred dollars, so I paid up. I expect I shall look after him for eighteen months – and then I'll send him back to Thann. He's flown on his own once, so I'm sure he can do it again.'

Sutch later told *OK!* magazine: 'Tristan was barely a year old when my ex-wife said, "It's your turn to look after the kid"' – not the most flattering way to refer to his own two-year-old son. Thann does not dispute sending Tristan back.

How pleased David was to have Tristan and how committed he was to bringing the boy up himself are moot points. By August he was back in Germany for his second mini-tour of the year. Drummer Mike Crawford remembered the band pulling up outside Sutch's home at the end of the tour, to hear his phone ringing indoors: 'We started unloading the gear as he went in to take the call. Minutes later he came running out, shouting, "Put it all back, we've got a gig." We certainly did have – it was on the Isle of Man, and when we got on the ferry there was a force nine gale blowing.' Wouldn't you have thought that Sutch would have been rather more keen to see his girlfriend – by this time, Giselle – and son than to head off again so immediately?

Tristan stayed in England for 'three or four years', said Sutch, presumably being passed between Giselle and David's mother. When Thann did ask for the return of their son, Sutch does not seem to have put up much of a fight. Giselle, he said in 1995, had been a 'fantastic' surrogate mother to Tristan who, he said, 'in a way, has got two mothers', but 'I was always on the road, working, so I agreed that maybe he would be better off with a mother who was there all the time than with a father who wasn't.' But Sutch's mother was devastated: 'I've only seen Tristan six times since [he went back to the States],' she declared in April 1995, 'and I miss him terribly.' Was David once again failing to face up to his responsibilities, or was he genuinely doing what he thought best for Tristan's long-term good? Tristan would never again live with his father for any length of time.

On 19 November 1981, David received a letter from Thann:

> Thank you for the money order – Tristan will appreciate it. I've already bought a lot of toys for Christmas, but like all kids he wants everything he sees on TV.
>
> When will you know if you're coming over at Christmas? We only get one day off work then, too bad for us …
>
> Hope you had a happy birthday, guess we're all getting older – I'll be thirty next year.

It seems baffling that a man who had grown up without a father, and who must have felt the emotional and practical absence of a father's influence, could permit his own son to experience the same sense of deprivation. Perhaps therein lies the answer: what he learnt from his childhood was that if fathers are absent, children must learn to make do without them. Certainly David's lifestyle was not conducive to traditional parenting – so why have a child in the first place? No question that David and Thann's relationship broke down, and in such circumstances blame is always impossible to apportion, but Sutch seems to have made little effort to maintain contact with Thann, and he appears to have made even less effort to retain close contact with his son, either before Thann returned him to England or when she then called him back to America.

After her split from Sutch in 1976, Thann had several relationships and marriages, some of them tumultuous. The most violent ended with her being charged with the murder of her husband David Benavidez in Texas in 1996. She was found guilty of murder in self-defence and sentenced to five years probation. My early efforts to contact her produced a thought-provoking response from the editor of a Texas website, John Troesser: 'Texans are very reluctant to talk about any sort of scandal when it involves their neighbors, [because] anyone … can shoot them after the article is published.' Fair enough.

David was a parent who – for whatever, and however justifiable, reasons – failed his son. Was there a deeply buried element of 'why should he get the normal childhood denied me?' in his attitude to and relationship with his son? During my first conversation with Tristan – at 5 a.m. Texas time; he was working the night shift – he made little mention of his infant days. I detected a real affection for his father, and a sense of regret that they had not enjoyed a closer relationship. Asked what his favourite memory of his dad might be he replied unexpectedly, 'It was when he came over once and we sat up late into the night playing Monopoly.' He saw his father perform when he was in Britain and said he is, and always will be, proud of him. Having an American passport, despite being born in England, means he still gets a nod of recognition from immigration officials when they spot the 'Lord Sutch' part of his name. I asked him whether he had any thoughts on my idea of a permanent memorial of some sort to his father.

'I'd love him to have a wax model at Madame Tussaud's,' he said. 'It would have to be in the Chamber of Horrors, of course. He took me there once – more people wanted their picture taken with him than with the exhibits. He was always being stopped and asked for autographs when I was with him, and he loved that.'

chapter nine

French Bred

'A kind of Zelig figure, who might be mistaken for Chauncey
Gardner in a bad light'

— ALWYN W. TURNER

In February 1976, Sutch played a Valentine's Dance at High Wycombe College in Buckinghamshire, supported by a little-known band called The Sex Pistols. While The Pistols were playing, lead singer Johnny Rotten's microphone went dead, 'so he started to smash it up,' recalled Sutch. 'The silly buggers wrecked the stage and all my mikes. I did about five gigs with them as my support band – and they'd start smashing up the PA, putting the mikes through the speakers 'cos the crowd was booing 'em, so they went berserk. I thought it was quite exciting, a good effect, until someone said to me, "I don't know what you're laughing at – that's your PA!" I slung 'em off the tour – they didn't have no money, so I never got a penny from them.'

Reportedly Sutch came to blows with the punks over his damaged microphones, and Malcolm McLaren, The Pistols' manager, who happened to have known Sutch for several years, had to break up the fisticuffs and smooth matters over by promising to reimburse him.

By the mid-1970s Britain and the US were witnessing a musical revolution. In reaction against the vast stadium gigs and overblown concept albums of groups like Led Zeppelin and Pink Floyd, live music was going back to the pubs and clubs, and re-discovering the roots of rock 'n' roll in a no-nonsense, high-energy, kinetic music called punk rock. In

New York bands like The Ramones concentrated on extreme speed and short, cartoonish songs; in London, at venues like the Roxy Club, the Hope and Anchor and Dingwalls, groups like The Sex Pistols had something of the early Stones' fury, Siouxsee and The Banshees played and dressed in a Gothic manner while The Damned, with their vampirish singer and, in Captain Sensible, a bass-player who would take the stage clad in anything from ballet tutu to gorilla suit, were modern vaudevillians. In the wider 'New Wave' of bands that found a live audience in the pub and club venues springing up all over the UK, even classic rock 'n' roll acts like Darts became popular, and straight rhythm and blues bands like Dr Feelgood, who had risen on the pub-rock circuit, built a massive following. Though all the punk bands quickly began releasing singles and albums, live performance was where they made their reputations – this and notoriety. The Sex Pistols created a furore by swearing and cursing on live television; their 'Anarchy in the UK' tour with The Damned and The Clash was swiftly curtailed as council venues across the country pulled out of bookings. In many ways punk was a re-run of Screaming Lord Sutch's rise to fame fifteen years earlier.

Sutch was grudgingly impressed by The Pistols. They were talking his language. 'My band said, "What an amateur lot of useless bastards they are." I said, "But look at all the bands who have supported us. How many of them do you remember? They created something that night."' Compare a 1977 Sutch gig at the Bedford Corn Exchange. 'The hall manager expressed concerns,' remembers the promoter, Keith Rothesay, 'as he had heard that Dave used fire in his shows and the hall had just been refurbished. I reassured him that Dave was very professional and extremely careful. During "Great Balls of Fire" Dave came on stage waving a flaming trident. Some burning liquid splashed off it and set fire to the brand-new valance around the stage. One of my bouncers grabbed a fire extinguisher and put out the flames, but not before a three-foot hole had appeared.'

During this period Sutch was also supported by The Damned, who used to carry his coffin on stage – his then-bass player, Jerry Chapman, remembers those gigs as 'a sea of fishnet and leather'. Sutch also played with both The Stray Cats and The Cramps. Later, and perhaps inevitably, Sutch would claim for himself the title 'grandfather of punk'.

Why didn't punk facilitate a revival in Screaming Lord Sutch's career? According to Jack Irving of The Savages, both The Stray Cats and The Cramps offered Sutch the opportunity to tour the States with them – but he turned them down. 'Perhaps it was because the money wasn't good enough,' muses Irving. 'Perhaps because he didn't want to be away from his mother for that long.' It could have been that Sutch was already too much of an elder statesman (albeit only in his mid-thirties) in a scene that was galvanising young people into seeing live music every night. Perhaps he just didn't have enough of a game plan, or, of course, the material – maybe he just wasn't savvy enough.

Sutch even occasionally teamed up with bands more used to playing hard or heavy rock – which did not always go down well with the rock 'n' rollers. Keith Rothesay, also a long-standing fan, remembers a Sutch gig at the Edwardian Club in Brixton: 'Inevitably the "heavy music" upset many of the audience and after the show we were obliged to position ourselves between the small dressing area and the baying mob. More by luck than judgement, the incident passed without injury. This started an unofficial campaign to persuade Dave to use established rock 'n' roll bands whenever he worked the rock 'n' roll circuit where most of his fan base was.'

He had three singles out in 1976, although he came no nearer to breaking his chart duck. The first, 'Monster Ball', was three minutes and thirty-eight seconds of sound effects and what seems to be a primitive attempt at rapping, bristling with typical cod horror references; it was followed a couple of months later by 'I Drink To Your Health, Marie', parts one and two, and then a re-recorded, re-arranged version of, yet again, 'Jack the Ripper'.

Later in life Sutch would be plagued by severe headaches. A contributory factor may have been a silly accident that occurred around this time. 'It happened, inevitably, during a performance of "Jack the Ripper",' he remembered in a 1995 interview. 'All was going well until I came out of the coffin, pushed the lid up – and it fell back on my face and busted my nose. My nose was pouring with blood and I couldn't breathe properly. I'm not a panicker or a hypochondriac, but I was sure there was something seriously wrong.' He underwent an operation, but 'had twinges of pain in my head for at least a month afterwards'.

*

In August 1976 Sutch met Giselle Menhennet. It was to prove a significant relationship. 'Something happened when I fell in love with her,' Sutch later told the celebrity magazine *OK!*. 'I knew deep down inside it was time to stay with one steady girlfriend. I became a changed man.' It was as if Giselle awoke a different Sutch, one who sounded uncharacteristically romantic: 'She's made me appreciate flowers and birds and the simple things in life ... made me realise that all work and no play make Jack a dull boy, but also leads him by the hand to an early grave.'

Previously married to an Irishman, Giselle came from a wealthy background. Her family, the Chanceliers, owned apartment blocks, hotels and garages, and she was sent to England to be educated and to learn English. Her boutique in Rue Bonaparte, L'Heure du Bijou, was reportedly frequented by the likes of Barbra Streisand, Brigitte Bardot, Rod Stewart, Catherine Deneuve and Gerard Depardieu. She also owned an eighteenth-century house in Paris, with louvred shutters and vine-covered walls, which is where the *OK!* interview took place in 1994. The magazine thought them 'on paper, at least, an ill-matched pair'.

When I went to meet Giselle, who had agreed to speak about Sutch for the first time since his death, I found an elegantly dressed woman in tinted glasses, living in Notting Hill among flamboyant furniture and mirrors (one 1991 interviewer described the house she shared with Sutch as 'a cross between Miss Havisham's cobwebbed drawing room and a ready-made setting for the Mad Hatter's Tea Party'), whose well-connected social circle includes friendships with Vivienne Westwood and Ivan Massow. Her table was laid with leopardskin serviettes.

How had two such disparate characters met in the first place? According to Giselle it was at a showbiz party given by a mutual acquaintance, where they got talking after Sutch informed her that there was a queue for the bathroom. She rang him soon afterwards and a relationship began. She had had no idea of his notoriety, and – remarkably, given the 'horrible old van' in which he had given her a lift home that first evening – believed he was genuinely upper-class and ennobled. But he made an instant impression on her: 'David did not look English – he looked a little like a gipsy, especially in his earlier days. He was very dark.' On their first date he took her to see AC/DC, which she thought 'fantastic'.

It seems to have been Sutch's showmanship that made the earliest impression on Giselle. He was very nervous, she told me, about letting her come to see him live, but 'he was *brilliant*! It was like he *was* Jack the Ripper – he *became* Jack the Ripper. I was very impressed. It was fun, that show ... It was not sophisticated, but it was so good. It looked like an old film – like *King Kong*. Today they make new versions, but the new ones are not so good as the old – sometimes simple effects work better.'

His favourite film, she said, was *Frankenstein* – 'the old one, black and white with all those shadows – very theatrical. He had a great sense of theatre.' He also, she says, liked *The Texas Chainsaw Massacre*. Giselle's favourite Sutch track was 'All Black and Hairy': 'I love that song. The ending is terrible' – the scream at the end – 'it makes you sick! You'd think he was being strangled!' It will surprise some of Sutch's musician friends, who believed Giselle was no great fan of his live appearances, that her enthusiasm even extended to joining him on stage: 'Once at Hammersmith I was the widow behind the coffin.'

Some may feel Giselle invests Sutch with abilities few others could discern. She insists that 'he was creative. He was innovative – that's the sign of a great talent. When someone does that in any other field they are celebrated. Unfortunately there was a misunderstanding in how people viewed him. People only picked up on the gimmicky things. Maybe it was partly his fault – he was not sure enough of himself, and I could never make him see it. He was much greater than anybody would admit. He had an amazing talent, David, but he did not exert it to its utmost. We had an artistic world that we created together. When he took himself off from there it was fatal.'

A constant theme in our conversation was the fact that Sutch 'did not like to spend'. His parsimony revealed itself early on in their relationship when they were in the States, and she wanted him to lend her the money to buy a collection of jewellery she was confident would prove a good investment. 'But David did not want to spend the money, even though he would get it back. In the end the woman selling the stuff, who could see how determined I was to have it, let me have it on trust. We never spoke about it again.' She had also tried to persuade him that, had he been able to keep together the best musicians he had ever worked with, he would be enjoying massive success: 'It wasn't very clear to me why he could not do it. I think originally it was a matter of money — unfortunately, because of his background, he wanted to save every penny.'

Giselle also told me the truth behind a sensational story I had come across in the *Sun,* of how, during the 1980 Notting Hill Carnival, a gang of forty youths 'ransacked' Giselle's house. The two of them had been sitting playing cards that night, she said, when the door was kicked in and in rushed a group of men. Giselle fetched a box of jewellery, and tried to convince them that it was worth taking, but 'they wanted money. I knew we had some upstairs in a yellow packet and David suddenly ran up there. I thought he would bring the money down to persuade them to leave. Instead, he hid it.' The robbers took the jewellery, but Sutch ended up with a knife gash on the arm and Giselle was punched in the face.

According to Giselle, getting married was never on the agenda for them: 'I did not suggest marriage. I'd been married before. I think he was thinking of it. I think in the end it would have been his safeguard in a way, but I did not realise that. But we did want to start a family together — he said to have a child together would be fantastic.'

When Tristan arrived in England they began seriously to consider it: 'I realised how much I did like children when I had Tristan. I did not know that before. Because he was so irresistible, Tristan. He was not easy, but he was fun. Tristan was like David as a young boy — very bossy. He's not like that any more. I think it was in the genes — David used to call Tristan "Bossy Boots". Tristan used to order me about … It was so funny.'

However, Giselle found out she was unable to have children. I wondered if she would have felt better about their long relationship had she and David produced a half-brother or -sister for Tristan. They had considered adoption, she later confided, but 'that was not really what he wanted. David was very secretive. He did not actually talk about his most important feelings. It should not be like that — it's not healthy. His mother used to say, "He keeps it all bottled up."'

Giselle, it seems, was not the greatest fan of David's mother — and the feeling appears to have been mutual. Whenever she visited Mrs Sutch's house in Harrow, she admitted, she would feel a huge cloud oppressing her, and 'when we were driving back it was like coming back to civilisation'.

Living with Sutch was not easy, she said, because of the nature of his work and his ongoing battle with depression. Sutch sometimes suffered depressive episodes so bad that he was unable to talk intelligibly. Thann told me that David suffered a nervous breakdown in 1985: 'only a handful of people have ever known. He made them swear never to talk about it.' As he got older these episodes became more frequent. Giselle admits that they split up on occasions – once for eleven months, during which time he moved in with Cynthia Payne (they were reunited when Giselle had her handbag stolen in Camden Market and rang Sutch for help – 'he arrived like a knight in shining armour. It was like we were before'). As I understand it, Giselle feels that he was finally lured away from her for good on the pretence that his depression could be cured.

The *OK!* magazine article, written by Ian Woodward in 1994, was, Giselle revealed, a poignant example of the hidden reality beneath Sutch's cheery exterior. It was accompanied by some priceless photos: in one, a petite and chic Giselle is dropping just-picked grapes into a basket held by a very domesticated-looking David. It could be a scene from *The Good Life*. Sutch made no bones about his feelings for Giselle: 'I love her madly.' Yet even in the course of the interview his old ambivalence about marriage asserted itself. 'I think if we could have had children we would have got married, simple as that,' he claimed – but of course Giselle had 'blocked tubes': an echo of his old excuse for not marrying Thann. And later in the article he was declaring, 'Marriage can be complicated. If it doesn't work out you argue about who gets what. If you don't go into it you don't have that sort of bust-up.' He added, 'Marriage kind of puts the mockers on some people's relationships.' This seems a more accurate representation of his true feelings.

But then Sutch made a rare and telling revelation: that seven years earlier he had collapsed from exhaustion. 'I was as close to a nervous breakdown as damn it. I was suffering from the classic stress syndrome of people who try to pack too much into every day of their lives. When I realised I was on the verge of a breakdown from stress and when Giselle told me how I was becoming somebody she hardly recognised – somebody tense and snappy – I stepped to one side and took stock of my life.' Then he made a prescient comment: 'I now have to cut back on things, pace myself, or I'm going to end up in a coffin' (as if he hadn't already spent much of his working life in one) and denied having entered a clinic to cure his problems: 'I had to do it the long, lonely, hard way, by my own self-discipline.'

If Sutch seemed more vulnerable and revealing than usual in this interview, it is perhaps because he was at a low ebb when it took place. At the time of the interview, Giselle told me, their relationship was almost over. 'He was already very bad then. After that we finished. I think he was pushing himself that day. Normally he would have loved it, but he was reluctant to do it.' Most people, of course, would simply have cancelled it. Sutch, however, while understandably 'reluctant', still went ahead.

'You've got to remember,' he told Woodward, 'that Elvis Presley, my hero, was dead at forty-two from excesses of every kind. I never forget that, ever.' Presley died in August 1977, a year after Sutch had met Giselle. Jimi Hendrix, whose bass player, Noel Redding, and drummer, Mitch Mitchell, had both played with Sutch, and Jim Morrison were already dead. A year later, in September 1978, the world would lose Keith Moon to a drug overdose. Of all his fellow musicians who had gone, Sutch would write in his autobiography, Moon was the one he felt saddest about. In September 1980 there was yet another untimely death of one of his musical colleagues, as Led Zeppelin drummer John Bonham, who had played on *Heavy Friends*, choked on his own vomit at the age of thirty-two. All these early deaths can only have strengthened Sutch's anti-drugs and apparently teetotal stance.

Giselle and I talked in the London home that she and David shared, and I asked her about the last time she spoke to David: 'I think he phoned me about five minutes before [killing himself]. He said, "There is nothing you did wrong at all – nothing. You have done nothing wrong, ever." I was in France. I was totally speechless. I'd never heard him say that.'

The connection was cut off, so she rang back.

'I heard a sort of strange noise.' She gave a harsh, throaty sound. 'I said, "David, what is wrong? You cannot talk?" 'He said, "No." So I thought, maybe he is with people, so I said, "You are not alone then?" So he said, "No." So I said, "I will call later." And that was about when he killed himself. He could not have committed suicide in this house because we had been too happy here.'

Just then Giselle looked over my shoulder and noticed that one of the candles burning in a holder on a table in the front room had fallen

on to the tablecloth, which was beginning to blaze. She walked briskly
to place a plate over the offending flames. It didn't extinguish them, so
she flung water over them.

'That has never happened before,' said Giselle quietly. 'That has
never happened before.'

chapter ten

Loony Birth

'You felt you hadn't really fought a by-election unless Lord Sutch
was on the ballot'

— NIGEL EVANS, CONSERVATIVE MP

'**Politically the seventies** were my
wilderness years,' Sutch once admitted. For eleven
years he had trooped around the by-elections and
general elections alone, picking up a couple of hundred votes here, a
few paragraphs in the local paper there. He had regularly changed the
name of the party he was standing for, made things up as he went along.
But his political life lacked a focus: he had been a virtual one-man band
and it must have been exhausting to organise. At the start of the
eighties, however, he struck publicity paydirt.

From the first, the Official Monster Raving Loony Party (OMRLP)
was media-friendly and, unlike his earlier political incarnations, this time
other people were involved with him in the formation of the party,
including Alan Hope whom Sutch first met on the circuit when Hope was
Kerry Rapid. They lost touch until one day in the early 1980s when Sutch
was playing a local gig and they got together, coming up with the idea of
the Loony Party – with a little help from one or two other friends. Hope
became the co-founder, chairman and deputy leader; also involved were
music business friend Pauline Healy, journalist Russell Newmark (whose
phonecall in order to write a profile of Sutch had been the catalyst, he
claims, to coax Sutch out of semi-retirement), and drummer 'Wild' Bob
Burgos, a heavily-tattooed member of Sutch's Savages at the time.

Sutch had also met student John Lewis, who stood at the autumn 1981 Crosby by-election for the Cambridge University Raving Loony Society. They both appeared on a Terry Wogan TV show about fringe candidates. Sutch suggested, says Lewis, that they team up to form the Official Monster Party. Lewis insisted on a Raving Loony element, and became Sutch's agent until he retired from politics after the 1983 General Election.

In October 1981 Sutch recorded a four-track record, featuring 'Loonabilly Rock 'n' Roll', which, said the sleeve notes, 'was to be the very beginning of what grew to be the Loony Party'. Bob Burgos co-wrote the track, and the sleeve image showed an eerie, skull-clutching, caped Sutch emerging from a primeval swamp, as monk-like, cowled figures walk towards a prophetic illustration of an indistinct figure hanging by the neck from a gibbet.

The Loony Party was a simple but inspired idea, the right joke for the right time, and Sutch's passport to permanent residency in the media spotlight. By the early 1980s the character of Thatcher's Britain was becoming clear: unforgiving, even ruthless policies designed to stabilize the economy and make industry more efficient, but having the effect of large-scale job losses, plant closures and social unrest. Others may have cogitated on such weighty matters. Sutch, though, wanted a route back to public prominence.

The genial, unserious manifesto of the more mature Sutch and his new party struck a chord with the British people, who quickly took him to their hearts as a kind of national institution – anarchic yet harmless, entertaining yet unthreatening. The 'policies' were contrived jokes which endeared Sutch to the average person in the street, even if he or she didn't always feel the need to hand over a vote for him: giving pensioners heated toilet seats, for example, or banning January and February to make winter shorter, and breeding fish in a European Community wine lake so they could be caught ready pickled.

But it was Sutch's willingness to counterpoint the insincere sincerity of conventional politicians with his own patently genuine good humour and lack of self-regard that built the affection with which he came to be ultimately regarded. Trevor Cajiao, the editor of the rock 'n' roll magazine *Now Dig This*, remembers a unique interview he conducted once with Sutch during the mid-eighties when he was in

South Shields for a gig. 'He was staying at the flat of a buddy of mine, and called me asking if I'd like to come over and interview Screaming Lord Sutch. By the time I got over there it was nearing show time, and Dave was in the bath. "No problem," he shouted, "come on in and we'll do it now." So, in a flat in South Shields, I interviewed Screaming Lord Sutch as he sat in the bath scrubbing his back and washing behind his ears – rubber ducks and all!' He would come to be accepted and valued as a true English eccentric, as much of a national treasure as Jimmy Savile, John McCririck or Patrick Moore. (After Sutch's death, Moore vetoed a suggestion that he should himself lead the party, but declared in his autobiography, *80 Not Out*, 'I have a great deal of sympathy with the Loony Party, which differs from all the others in one vitally significant respect – its members *know* that they are loony.')

The fledgling party first stood at one of the most controversial by-elections of the 1980s: the Bermondsey by-election of 24 February 1983, when, after a campaign notorious for its dirty tricks and smear tactics, the Labour candidate, Peter Tatchell (who would go on to become one of the country's leading gay rights activists), was subjected to an unsavoury focus on his private life, and defeated by the Liberal candidate Simon Hughes. Registered as D.E. Sutch, of the Monster Raving Loony Party, and campaigning, among other things, to make voting eligible at sixteen, Sutch won ninety-seven votes, finishing sixth of sixteen candidates. It was not enough to save his deposit – he needed one-eighth of the votes (in 1985 this changed to one-twentieth). Sutch told a journalist that the Loonies had 'only three party workers', and hit out at the proposal to raise the deposit for election candidates from £150 to £1,000 as 'monstrous ... It will affect everybody's democratic right to stand for Parliament'. Television coverage of the declaration included a wonderful moment when Sutch's name was announced and the strait-laced commentator was forced to utter – with great disdain – the word 'Loony'.

Peter Chippindale, as he ghost-wrote Sutch's autobiography, grew 'not just to admire, but actually love' its subject: 'His genuine warmth and consistency in turning up, always polite on the platform while ensuring he got his face in front of the cameras, changed public perception of him as a self-promoting nuisance to an integral, and uniquely British, part of the political scene.' Sutch, he added, was 'an ironic commentary on British politics – a sort of one-man piece of performance art', and believes that underneath he had 'a burning motive, too – a huge and enduring contempt for his political opponents – actors solely in it for themselves and willing to make any promise to gain votes.'

Many politicians patronised Sutch – and after his death blathered on about how he had brought a splash of colour to politics and pricked the pomposity of politicians – but by and large he irritated the hell out of them. They detested having to stand next to him and his gaudy followers during elections and at the count. Tony Benn admitted to me: 'His long campaign through Parliamentary elections was designed to make a point, although as a committed democrat I began feeling hostile towards him.' One or two got the joke and became friends. Harry Greenaway, the former Conservative MP for Ealing North, was the only MP ever to invite Sutch to tea on the famous Commons terrace: 'He was tickled pink. I asked him to come incognito, but he wasn't having any of that. Along he came with his absurd hat and his motley attire. He put a piece of doll's house furniture around my neck complete with drawers, and said, "Let's have a cabinet meeting."'

Nigel Fountain, writing in the *Guardian*, summed up perfectly and perceptively Sutch's role as a public figure: 'Whatever the national crisis, whatever the earnest fatuities of the victorious by-election candidate, there on the edge of the screen would be Sutch, or a sidekick, a Shakespearean antic for the TV age. It was a great joke, but the viewer could never be absolutely certain that Sutch was in on it.'

Here was the eternal crux with David Sutch: you never knew if he understood the impression he created, or if he ever wondered whether people were laughing at or with him. He seemed not to care, just so long as they noticed him.

The annual Loony conference was held for many years at Alan Hope's nineteenth-century Golden Lion inn in Ashburton, Devon. Sutch would always ensconce himself in room six, where Arthur Conan Doyle was said to have stayed on his tours of Dartmoor. When I made my first visit to the conference, I and a number of Loonies and media were in the bar when Sutch appeared and demanded that everyone follow him. We rushed outside and joined the convoy, which set off down narrow lanes and hidden turnings, out into countryside and, eventually, to the foot of a tor, where we parked and climbed expectantly to the top. Sutch raised his hand for quiet and announced: "Ladies and gentlemen, I have brought you here for a summit meeting ..."'

Within a month of Bermondsey, the new party was handed another opportunity to establish itself, at the Darlington by-election on 24 March: when he arrived for the poll by train, the ticket collector asked for his autograph. At the count he sported green hair and a massive rosette. Sutch was rewarded with the party's first three-figure result: 374 votes, coming fourth of eight candidates, and beating all other independents. At William Hill I had resumed my connection with David by becoming a – I think the only – Loony Party sponsor, which meant good media exposure for my company without appearing to show real political bias and perhaps alienating customers. I made a bet with him: £50 on himself to poll over 200 votes. He won enough money to pay for his deposit and counted it a great victory. On the night he played a gig at his election HQ, the Dun Cow pub (a tactic that was to become an integral part of future campaigns), and the local paper reported that 'more people were in the toilets at Sutch's victory party than attended the Social Democrats' rally'. He was blurring the line between his musical and political careers. Previously, he confessed, 'I'd always kept the two strands of my life apart.'

Whilst in Darlington, Sutch met a Radio Stoke DJ called Legendary Lonnie (alias Clive Cook), 6ft 6in and also the owner of a record shop in Stoke-on-Trent. I was surprised to learn from Cook that Sutch was a big fan of George Orwell, and that his favourite book, *Animal Farm*, became a one-man party piece. 'He knew *Animal Farm* from cover to cover,' said Cook. 'He used to perform it when he stayed with me.'

Following the success of the Darlington campaign, Sutch and Pauline Healy convened a meeting of potential Loony candidates at Healy's home in Paddington. Thirty people turned up. The Loonies were on the march.

By the time the general election was called for 9 June Sutch was raring to go and, as he had with Harold Wilson, decided to take on the Prime Minister by standing in Margaret Thatcher's own seat of Finchley. He came up with the novel idea of campaigning while carrying a large tin opener to 'open up the Iron Lady'. The media coverage was sensational. The Prime Minister, however, was less than amused by his antics. 'Thatcher had no sense of humour, and wanted everything kept serious,' says Sutch's guitarist Chris Black, 'but David had Elvis-lookalike Leyton Summers on the stage with him at the count. Alistair Burnett, ITN's venerable election night anchorman, commented that it was a bizarre scene.' Sutch managed 235 votes.

Across the country, the Loonies fielded eleven more candidates, having merged with another fringe group, the Green Chicken Alliance, to boost their strength. The star performer was Wally Welly, who polled 664 in Esher, while Legendary Lonnie managed 504 in Stoke-on-Trent. Only Dick Vero failed to make three figures, finishing one short in Dulwich. Sutch arranged morale-boosting visits to constituencies being contested by Loonies and found himself playing a gig in Bradford backed by a punk band whose members had no knowledge of his repertoire. 'I did four numbers at 200mph with lots of noise and shouting,' he later reported, 'and none of us knowing what we were doing. It was my most embarrassing experience in thirty years on the stage.'

After the general election the *Daily Mirror* commented: 'Many people will say that Mr Sutch and his friends ought not to be allowed to make mock of the electoral system, but they have a right to stand and the people have a right not to vote for them. Except for lunatics, of course, who don't have a vote. Does Mr Sutch realise that?'

By now Sutch was hooked on the adrenalin of political publicity. He contested Cumbria, Penrith and Border on 28 July, arriving two hours before the deadline for nomination. By swapping autographs for nominations he just made it, and won 412 votes – 1.08 per cent of the total cast, and his highest percentage yet. In March 1984, fearing the consequences of raised deposits and standing as the Monster Raving Loony Last Stand Party, he polled 178 votes at the Chesterfield by-election, at which Tony Benn was re-elected to parliament. Sutch finished fifth of a record seventeen candidates. (Benn said: 'At one stage I was afraid Sutch would come out and support me, which would not have helped my cause.') Sutch and Sid Shaw, his 'running-mate', who stood for his own Elvisly Yours Elvis Presley Party, campaigned together and held what Shaw claims to have been the world's first press conference in a fish and chip shop. In the same month Sutch was initially turned away from Russell Newmark's wedding reception when

someone mistook him for a tramp. He failed to make the ballot paper for
the Southgate by-election in December when he insisted on proposing a
dog, Splodge, described as 'Chief Barker of the Votes for Pets Party', as
a candidate alongside himself. 'I think he would have added a bit of colour
and excitement,' a town hall official Maurice Wiggall said later, 'but it is
a serious business and we couldn't treat it as a joke.'

In the summer of 1985, Sutch descended on Wales and picked up
202 votes at the Powys, Brecon and Radnor by-election with a 'Votes
for Sheep' policy ('ewesless'). The winner, Liberal Democrat Richard
Livsey, revealed that his son wore a Vote Sutch sticker during the
campaign. Shortly afterwards, interviewed on the *Terry Wogan Show*,
Sutch sat on Wogan's knee and tried to bully him into becoming a
Loony candidate. That September, Sutch missed the Loony conference: 'Screaming Lord Sutch is tickled pink with the news that his
wife Giselle is pregnant after treatment at the clinic of test tube baby
specialist Dr Patrick Steptoe,' reported the papers. But was this yet
another Sutch publicity stunt? Giselle, who did have fertility treatment,
of course, never gave birth to David's child (and was not his wife).

Nor, that year, did he get around to standing at the Greenwich by-
election (on a platform of replacing Greenwich Mean Time with Sutch
Time), or, more importantly, at the general election in June 1987. Why
not? 'I had been planning to star in Thatcher II in Finchley,' he explained
to a newspaper at the time. 'With my normal sense of timing I reached
the registration office with fifteen minutes to spare before nominations
closed. But my papers were then found to have the signature of a voter,
who, though on the register, was not yet eighteen. It was too late to get
anybody else so I was disbarred and forced to watch from the sidelines.'
Altogether the Loonies fielded five candidates, with Stuart Hughes, an
early stalwart of the party from his 'Fawlty Towers' hotel in the West
Country, notching up a remarkable 747 votes in Honiton. Lord
Tiverton, 'a perfect gentleman of the old school' according to Sutch,
made his debut in Hastings and Rye, and managed 241, and in
Camborne and Redruth, the fire-eating DJ Freddy Zapp, who
campaigned in a hearse dressed as an undertaker, scored 373.

Sutch picked up his relationship with Val Bird again. A rock 'n' roll fan,
Val made her career in the business, promoting shows and setting up

her own record label, Pollytone (the name and logo inspired by Annie Sutch's parrot and her own surname). Sutch's presence is everywhere in the house in Ruislip Manor where she lives today: a postcard from an American holiday, model dogs he bought her, plants he gave her for the garden. 'He often reminds me he's still here,' she told me when I went to see her there: pictures of him would sometimes fall to the floor while she was looking for something else entirely.

She admits to being fifty now, a pleasant lady who obviously has enough business acumen to survive in the predominantly male and notoriously tough record world. She was certainly not out of her teens when she first met Sutch in 1970 at the 6-5 Special and Railway Tavern clubs in Harrow. After her dad had demanded, 'Who's that long-haired yobbo kissing my daughter?' she had to tell him that her new boyfriend was one of Britain's most outrageous pop stars.

Of course, Sutch was ostensibly in a relationship with Thann. 'He had quite a few girlfriends at that time,' says Val, 'but I knew where I stood – and eventually he went back to Thann.' She met Tristan once, one Christmas when they were all invited to a party. 'We set off, but he got lost. Tristan couldn't believe it and said, "What is it with my dad? He never leaves on time, can't find the place he's going to, and always arrives late!"'

Val and Sutch stayed pally over the years – even after their romantic attachment ended. She always made a point of keeping her professional and private relationships with Sutch separate and never released any of Sutch's records on her label: 'Perhaps we were just too close – you shouldn't mix business with pleasure.' (After Sutch's death, however, she leased his track 'Murder in the Graveyard' and added it to a compilation disc she put out.) She booked Sutch for a gig only once. 'He was a nightmare to work with – to him there were no bends or traffic lights in the road, so he'd be sitting at home thinking he didn't have to worry about travelling until shortly before he was due anywhere. I was well aware of his time-keeping and told him he was on five hours earlier than he actually was. He still only made it by fifteen minutes.'

It was October 1987, to be precise, when they got back together, at which time, of course, Sutch was with Giselle. When they had first reunited, she says, Sutch was so depressed that he couldn't even drive. Val hints that he was also on good terms with Kim Roberts during this period. Kim, a singer, was the former partner of early Savages guitarist Dave Wendels, and has since died, but many believe she was the true love of Sutch's life. Val and Kim were good mates. 'We'd often joke that one of us would have the top half of Sutch, the other could have the bottom half. Each time Giselle went back to France he was with either Kim or me – whichever was convenient at the time, I guess.'

But after eighteen months, says Val, 'I told him I wanted some stability in my life. I said, "I'll give you seven days to decide. I want to move on." I was thinking, "Can I have a life, or am I going to be the bit on the side for ever?" He made a decision all right – he buggered off to Devon. Giselle was back on the scene and after I'd been with him through months of depression he was suddenly feeling just perfectly fine.'

Val eventually became firm friends with Annie Sutch. 'When I was going out with him I was her worst enemy; when I wasn't I could be her best friend – she was a possessive mother, but he doted on her.' Val believes Annie had Alzheimer's at the end of her life and she 'helped a lot with the hospital, and taking her up for X-rays'.

Even when Val married, Sutch 'always made a point of letting me know he was around'. Once, she says, he told her, 'I should have married you. You should have been the mother of my children.'

In 1987 the Loony Party appeared to upset all of its strictures by winning a seat. Party chairman Alan Hope was elected to Ashburton Parish Council in Devon, but the party's reputation was somewhat redeemed as he was elected unopposed. The following year the stand-up comedian Bob Winter (then known professionally as The Late Henry Henderson – He's A Dead Man) became a Loony candidate. He and Sutch shared a room for the night a couple of times on the campaign trail, and Winter was struck by Sutch's naivety: 'He would ask the most ridiculous questions in all seriousness. Things you'd think a fellow would know, like, "Is pie and chips fattening?" He had absolutely no idea about exercise, and his physical condition was one of the things which seemed to concern him. He knew I had experienced depression and wanted to know what it had been like ... When I learned how he died I found it incredible, the fact that he even managed to tie a knot in a rope – he was so useless at practical things.'

In the meantime there was no let-up in his publicity-seeking escapades – frequently, however, with genuinely civic or altruistic agendas. In April 1988, the *Sun* ran the headline 'SUTCH TRIES TO RAISE THE DEAD!' over a story reporting Sutch's launch of 'Grave Aid', with the aim of raising £2 million to save Mill Hill East cemetery, where Billy Fury was buried, after it had been sold to developers. Sutch planned a concert to kick off the campaign – featuring The Grateful Dead.

The following month he recorded a live single in Finland, and announced details of a backward walk around the Scilly Isles to raise cash for a children's cancer charity. This walk caused the first rift in the party. In the usual blaze of publicity, Sutch, Cynthia Payne and Lord Tiverton turned up in the Scillies in late November, claiming credit for the fund-raising, but not having actually walked as far as another group, headed by Loony colleague Stuart Hughes, who arrived to find their thunder had been stolen. This 'played a big part' in the breakdown of the Hughes–Sutch relationship, said Stuart, a tireless publicist for Sutch and the party. Another example of Sutch taking help and helpers for granted.

A summer tour of Spain with Jet Harris, Cliff Bennett and Mike Berry that ended in a shambles when the promoter turned out not to have bothered with things like licences, insurance and permits made it into the *Sun*, which reported the unlikely story of how the self-exiled English villain Ronnie Knight 'shelled out thousands to clear the debt and buy air tickets for the stranded stars'.

Cliff Bennett tells the true story: 'Hotel bills were mounting – about two and a half grand was owing – and those of us who did have some money didn't particularly want to settle up the debts. I had to shell out for a first-class ticket via Italy to get home – cost me about four hundred quid. Sutch blagged his way on to a direct British Airways flight by spinning them a yarn about having to get back for a by-election. We got nothing from Ronnie Knight – he only turned up after we'd gone.'

There were several more by-election appearances before the end of the 1980s. Glasgow, Govan (the poll was held on Sutch's birthday) marked the first time a commercial company name was incorporated into that of a legitimate political party when Sutch stood for the Monster Raving Loony I Bet I Will Beat William Hill Party. Result: 174 votes.

In February 1989 the Loonies managed 167 votes to the future Conservative leader William Hague's 19,543 in the North Yorkshire constituency of Richmond, but yielded a great yarn – dreamed up by Sutch and Stuart Hughes – about him having spent two days canvassing in Richmond, London, before realising his mistake and heading up north. (Given Sutch's notorious sense of direction, the story could well have been true: Pat Hellier recalls a gig in Colchester. The Savages were set up and ready to play when Sutch rang to ask them where they were. He had just arrived in Gloucester.)

Two days before almost simultaneous local and national government by-election campaigns in Wales and Devon in May 1989, a delighted Sutch could bask in the glory of a double-page centre spread, liberally illustrated, in Scotland's best-selling paper, the *Daily Record*, headlined 'WHEN I RULE THE WORLD'. 'You can't buy a spread like that,' he enthused. 'The more people read about us, the more join the party.'

But television and video footage of these last campaigns of the 1980s paint an intriguing picture of the nature of his celebrity. In Budleigh-Sidmouth's council elections he stood for the Loony Liberal Headache Party, used Stuart Hughes's Fawlty Towers hotel address to get residential qualification, and went out campaigning with Hughes aboard a three-person tandem of the type once used by TV comics the Goodies, which they struggled to get moving. Poignant footage of the count shows Sutch looking more Lonely than Loony; after the announcement of the result (Sutch 145 votes, last of five runners behind the Tory who won with a landslide 3,081), he completely takes over proceedings, marshalling each candidate's speech before making one of his own: 'I'd like to thank my mother – without her help I wouldn't be here in the first place. I've won my bet with William Hill. God bless.' Clearly in manic mood, he insists on shaking hands with every candidate, calls for donations for a jumble sale to be held in the public hall in which they are assembled, then goes off for another round of handshaking, this time with the volunteers and officials.

'You make it a lot more fun,' declares one elderly Tory voter.

'See you all later,' shouts Sutch.

No one seems to be listening.

For the Vale of Glamorgan by-election Sutch teamed up with Shakin' Stevens band, The Sunsets, whose bassist Dave Goddard took on the role of election agent. His big vote-catcher was a plan to build the other six bridges to complement the Severn Bridge. Another revealing, and somehow pathetic, piece of video footage shot by film students at the pre-vote victory party in a local pub illustrates one of the frequent rituals in Sutch's life: unpacking his gear for a show. One is immediately struck by the complete and utter lack of glamour. It is a scene of dingy subterranean gloom and squalor. Backstage, Sutch is going through his set list with the band. No surprises, even though he has just lied to a keen fan by promising he would play some material from *Heavy Friends* and *Hands of Jack the Ripper*. The fan has bought Sutch vinyl copies for him to sign and tells him that he paid £30 for them. Sutch opens his battered props case and blows up the limp-looking inflatable skeleton which will appear for 'Bony Moronie'. He then gets out the toilet seat for 'I'm a Hog For You Baby', and chats and kisses a couple of female fans.

Out on the campaign trail, further video footage makes for more uncomfortable viewing. A sequence showing Sutch arriving at the studio of Dragon Radio for an interview demonstrates his selfish desire to hog the limelight. He is accompanied for the interview by a party stooge who also gets miked up – only for Sutch to completely dominate the proceedings to the extent of not allowing his sidekick even a single word on air.

Now we join Sutch on the hustings, accompanied by Cynthia Payne. The two of them insinuate themselves within range of television and radio reporters in a desperate attempt to secure air time, and sometimes it seems as though the interviewers decide to go through the motions just to get rid of them. At the count we watch Sutch standing un-noticed and un-elected, clutching a bunch of flowers. Then he spots someone being interviewed and edges over, gradually wheedling his way into the camera's field of vision. That interview over, he urges the unenthusiastic BBC man to line him up next. When this fails, he makes a beeline for the next camera – Granada's – and gets the nod. 'Your red light's not on,' Sutch observes to the cameraman. 'Should be with me around!' quips Cynthia, who has by now sidled up. Bad news, though: a Tory has arrived, and Sutch is stood down. 'We can wait,' he says, plaintively. Sutch got 266 votes.

At the end of the 1980s, Sutch was chosen by Heineken to head up its new TV advertising campaign. In the advert, he is shown clutching a pint of the stuff and entering Number 10 Downing Street to the voice-over punchline, 'Only Heineken can do this.' This single job, he later admitted, made him £5,000. And not all his relentless Loony Party campaigning was as desperate as Glamorgan. In the European Elections of 1989, where he stood in the London Central constituency, he was rewarded with 841 votes – coming sixth out of eight candidates. This time he stood for the Loony Euro Sausage Party, picking up on British distrust of bureaucratic European Commission food regulations that, in the apocalyptic scenarios of the popular press, threatened to do away with the great British banger. Sutch adapted Mungo Jerry's 1970 smash hit 'In the Summertime' as his campaign signature tune, 'In the Sausage Time', which he performed, accompanied by Mungo Jerry's frontman Ray Dorset, while waving around some Euro-shaped sausages. There was one sticky moment in the campaign, during a profile by the London television news programme *Thames Reports*, when he was filmed asking a man whether he would be interested in standing as a parliamentary candidate for the Loonies. 'I will not,' answers the clearly deranged fellow, 'because I'm going away – to Broadmoor or Rampton.' Faced with a genuine lunatic, the professional Loony is tongue-tied. Sutch looks completely nonplussed.

But another programme, *Central Lobby*, inadvertently revealed the essence of Sutch's popular appeal. It shows him doing the rounds with a tray of his Euro Sausages, at one point offering a sample to a bus conductor in a stilted, forced exchange of pleasantries which quite clearly neither of them particularly enjoys. But then Sutch offers his tray to a nearby dog – which promptly turns up its nose and sidles back into the pub from which it has just emerged. Sutch creases up with genuine laughter at the snub, his infectious laugh immediately prompting onlookers to chuckle along.

But loyal Sutch ally Stuart Hughes could no longer see the funny side of his friend and party colleague. Hughes had done well in the European Elections, but felt that Sutch was dismissive and insulting about him. 'Comments such as "We're going to throw him out of the party because he's too serious" and "He's pulling too many votes" – I paid £1,000 to stand for the MRLP and I had a very pro-active campaign.'

Sutch, though, had to be the centre of attention — any suggestion of being over-shadowed by a colleague could not be tolerated.

Hughes quit to start his own Raving Loony Green Giant Party.

The Big Five-Oh

'David was an intriguing and very likeable character and, sometimes, a bloody nuisance ... but by-elections just aren't the same without him'
— NEIL KINNOCK, FORMER LEADER OF THE LABOUR PARTY

The 1990s began well for Sutch and the Monster Raving Loony Party. But it was to be Screaming Lord Sutch's last decade.

If the Loony Party had been started as a joke designed to prick the self-importance of politicians, then Sutch's second campaign of the nineties was the punchline. The Bootle by-election of 24 May 1990 was the high point in Sutch's political career: he effectively put the Social Democratic Party out of business.

The original SDP had by now merged with the Liberal Party to become the Liberal Democrats, but Dr David Owen and his followers had chosen not to be subsumed into the new party and decided to soldier on as the SDP. But in Bootle Sutch and the Official Monster Raving Loony Party finished sixth out of eight with 418 votes, ahead of, and thereby utterly humiliating, the SDP. It was the beginning of the end for Owen. Sutch observed that 'the only reason the SDP has a doctor in charge is because it's a very sick party' and gave Owen the opportunity of merging their two parties. He even spoke of relinquishing the Loony leadership in the doctor's favour but Owen, said Sutch, 'gave a sad little smile and turned it down'. 'Humankind owes him [Sutch] a debt of gratitude,' Ken Livingstone commented, 'for destroying the SDP.'

Earlier in the campaign, Sutch had again called for the Cavern Club to be rebuilt (in years to come it would be), partly because he had teamed up with the former Merseybeat musician, bassist Tony King, of The Undertakers, who now ran a local entertainment agency. King streamlined the Sutch set-up, providing him with the use of a computer, fax and phone-line. 'The notion of any sort of organisation was a dizzying prospect,' marvelled Sutch.

It was also during the Bootle campaign that Sutch introduced the enduringly popular Loony banknotes, which he dispensed with great largesse. The notes, bearing the head of Maggie Thatcher, stated 'I promise the cheque is in the post' and pledged to be worth 'one pound of flesh'. (Various versions would appear in the future and were always well received, particularly in 1994 when their apparent value was pushed up to an inflation-busting £1 million 'of flesh', drawn on the Bank of Loonyland). Boney Moronie (Melodie Staniforth), Sutch's political sidekick, tells how Loony Money came about: 'In 1990 David gave Stan [Boney's drummer husband] a Bank of Greenland pound note that somebody had made for him. The resemblance to the real thing was uncanny. One night Stan passed the pound note over the bar at a local club and the landlord did not notice. David decided to change the 'Greenland' to 'Loonyland' – that's how Loony Money was born.'

After humiliating Dr David Owen, there was only one way the party could go and that was gently downhill. Perhaps Sutch sensed this, but was powerless to call a halt to the political monster he had created. The party had brought together many otherwise unfocused individuals who were dependent on it to offer meaning to their lives, even if it meant basking in the reflected glory of their leader. Previously the party had absolutely nothing to live up to, and no achievements of which to boast; now, beating one of the 'major' parties meant that every succeeding result would be regarded as in some way a disappointment. Some people within the party would start to take it all a little too seriously. Factions and feuds would begin to erupt, just as in a 'real' political party.

But in yet another respect Sutch the joke politician managed to be ahead of his time. During the mid-Staffordshire by-election in March 1990, he had found himself having a conversation with the Labour opposition leader Neil Kinnock, who recalls: 'I knew that we were overhauling the Tories, so I said to David when we bumped into each other, that if his intervention as the Loony Party prevented us from winning, I would skin him alive. His reply was, "Don't worry, if I stop you winning, I'll skin myself!"

'In the course of the conversation, we discussed having a bet on who would be the first rock 'n' roll prime minister but decided that, since I was the nearest thing to a rock 'n' roll opposition leader, I was in with the best chance of getting the next job.

'We agreed to try and think of other names, since it was obvious that a rock 'n' roll prime minister would need his very own rock 'n' roll band for great State occasions, like coronations and the opening of Parliament. David, naturally, was the only member of the future band that we could envisage at that time. He then said that he wanted to discuss appearance and recording fees and, since the title would be no problem, a peerage. I told him to sod off – we parted laughing. Little were we to know, of course, that The Ugly Rumours' rhythm guitarist, young Tony Blair, was to become the first rock PM.'

Sutch toured Finland in May to great acclaim, but acclaim was in short supply in a coruscating and, perhaps, needlessly vindictive putdown in the June edition of the influential rock magazine Q. The writer Tom Hibbert wrote a series of profiles of well-known characters under the heading, 'Who the Hell...?', with those previously selected for such treatment including Jeffrey Archer, Samantha Fox, Steve Davis, Ronnie Biggs, Yoko Ono and Gary Glitter, as well as Sutch's heroes Chuck Berry and Jerry Lee Lewis. Q's editor, Mark Ellen, defined the victims as a 'monstrous regiment of pseuds, dullards and self-loving goons'. These spiteful interviews were certainly not designed to flatter their subjects, but I imagine Sutch was not aware of the intent.

At the start of the interview, according to Hibbert, Sutch handed him two badges, bearing the legends Give Masochists a Fair Crack of the Whip; and Haven't I Fucked You Before Without a Condom? 'Haw!' guffawed Sutch. 'Cor! They're good laughs, them, ain't they?' Hibbert began his savaging of Sutch by calling him 'an exhaustingly tedious, staunchly unribtickling, lecherous old goat'. Here was 'a cruelly wizened figure' who 'hobbles' about the stage, backed by the band Some Like It Hot who 'evidently find supporting duties for the ageing showman something of a chore'. Sutch, wrote Hibbert, is 'radically slurred of speech though he's drinking only lager shandies' and said that 'the befuddled entertainer rattles on less than coherently' with a 'stream of old tosh'.

But his reference to Sutch's father's death elicited an odd reaction: 'It's probably for the best because maybe he wouldn't have allowed me to go into rock 'n' roll.' Did Sutch feel 'at all resentful,' Hibbert inquired, 'still scratching out a living in social clubs when so many of his former sidemen are now so very rich indeed?' 'Oh, well, no, because I've still got a cult following,'" answered Sutch, pointing out that many of his contemporaries were dead.

'Sutch was a duffer when it came to making and selling records,' concluded Hibbert. 'His one talent was, and has been, a bent for self-promotion. Riches never flowed but column inches did.' It is difficult to take issue with that part of his verdict.

With his half-century looming on the horizon, perhaps Sutch decided that he would clear out some of the items connected with his career for which he no longer had any use. Maybe he was short of a few bob. Maybe, as was reported, he was raising funds for his political activities. Whatever the reason, in August, at Phillips' West Two auction house in Bayswater, Sutch contributed a number of lots to their Rock and Pop Memorabilia sale.

Lot 434, coincidentally coming after a collection of Screaming Jay Hawkins memorabilia, was the first of fourteen 'from the collection of Screaming Lord Sutch, either used on-stage or during his election campaigns'. First up, 'a large top hat covered in black velvet with a large butterfly on the front in gold and silver sequins. Do I hear £80?' Er, no.

Next, a more readily recognisable top hat, this one covered with a leopardskin design. This was better received and sold for £80. A pink 'teddy-boy' style jacket trimmed with leopardskin material went for £100. A brass loud-hailer fetched £38. But no one would pay £100 for 'a stage prop coffin made of polished oak with four brass handles'. A leopardskin shirt and pair of red satin trousers, 'both worn on-stage', raised £30.

The most extraordinary item on offer was Lot 446: 'Pink Floyd's touring stage piano with open face with amplification sockets. Measures 102 cm. Together with Pink Floyd sweatshirt, mirror and poster. Used on stage by Pink Floyd and in the recording studio by Julian Lennon.' However Sutch came by this treasure, he wanted £3,000 to £5,000 for it. He didn't get it. Where did it end up?

Finally, Lot 447: 'Packard pump Harmonium organ with carved wooden case, foot pedals and stops. In full working order. Used on-stage by Sutch and by Procol Harum in recording and stage work.' One detects, perhaps, a Matthew Fisher connection here as that early luminary of The Savages went on to join the chart-topping Procol. However, the £200 to £400 price tag deterred would-be buyers.

The sale of Sutch's items raised a total of £323.

In October one Monster came up against another when Sutch travelled to Scotland to take part in the William Hill Monster Hunt Weekend, where he held a packet of British Rail sandwiches above the water in an effort to lure Nessie. Romaine Snijder, my secretary, remembers the Saturday night at the Drumnadrochit Hotel well: 'That night the real David shone through. Throughout the whole meal his tales of the past had us all in stitches. He was not loud or brash, but was very good company, and extremely entertaining.' The weekend set the pattern for her subsequent working relationship with Sutch, as she recalls: 'In one day he managed to make my feelings for him go from extreme exasperation to admiration and fondness. Exasperation – because he was extremely hard to wake up in the morning and get physically to where he was meant to be. But once there he was every inch the professional, happily providing interviews and photo opportunities for hours – no mean feat as the weather was freezing, drizzling and generally very miserable, but David was not bothered. I never heard him complain once.'

For someone so zealously dedicated to self-publicity, however, Sutch was at the same time curiously unambitious as to its possibilities. 'He had a strange attitude,' says Savages drummer Mick Richardson, who knew Sutch for the best part of twenty years. 'He never seemed to take advantage of his coverage to advance his careeer. He was always in the papers, but he didn't seem to pose for recognition as a talented and respected musician. It was enough to be getting the coverage.' It was during the Bradford North by-election campaign in November, where he secured 310 votes, that Sutch met John Tempest, who subsequently became his PR manager and agent. 'He was hopelessly disorganised,' says Tempest, 'and it was perfectly obvious that he needed people. He was great at using people, getting them to do things for him, but he needed more than that, so we came to an agreement. I became his PR adviser and campaign director. It was a commercial deal sealed on a handshake.'

John, who has been 'actively interested in politics for thirty-eight years and worked alongside notables such as William Hague, Tony Benn and Paddy Ashdown', must have put a number of Sutch-related noses out of joint during the time they worked together, for he is not universally liked or praised by the Loony fraternity. As he says himself: 'Let's be quite straight about this, I was never the most popular person in the party.' It should be said, though, that much of the criticism has come from those who seem to consider it unreasonable to provide a service to someone known to you and then charge them. John shrugs off the accusation: 'In fact, I did do a great many things for David that I never charged him for but much of what I did for him put him on a far more professional footing and increased his income. When I teamed up with him he was going out for £600 a gig. I said, "Right, that's too low, we're going to make it £1,200." OK, he may have lost one or two bookings as a result, but the ones that took him on worked harder to get a good turnout and to promote the gig and everyone benefited.'

John's PR nous tempered some of the more enthusiastic but not properly thought-out excesses of the Loony Party. He also found himself having to curb some of David's passion for publicity. 'I stopped him from continuously bombarding people like the BBC and the Press Association with daily phone calls. This could test their patience and undermine the times he had genuinely good stories for them.'

Tempest became a trusted confidant whom Sutch would turn to in times of need: 'He rang me once from Miami, where he was on holiday with Giselle. "John, I've been knocked over the head and mugged – I wanna come home." I rang Richard Branson's people and sold them on the idea of giving David tickets anywhere, anyplace, anytime, in return for a headline that said VIRGIN RESCUES LOONY!'

Another time, Sutch called Tempest from London, complaining

that he couldn't get through to the British Rail call centre to find out the times of trains from London to Manchester: 'When I asked, "Why will I be able to get through any easier than you?" he said, "Well, you're closer to Manchester than me."'

Finally the day itself dawned: on 10 November 1990, David Sutch hit the big five-oh. He celebrated with a party at the Wall Street Club, in London's West End. Amongst the guests were Joe Brown, Jet Harris, Ray Dorset, Chas Hodges and many old mates.

'Dave always told people that I was in his band,' Chas Hodges told me later. 'In fact, I wasn't. I sat in a couple of times. I looked upon it as an honour. I always said, "Yes, I was," and, yes, I suppose I was!'

Everyone's fiftieth birthday is difficult to deal with, so how hard did the inevitable intimations of mortality hit home with David? 'I was amazed to still be here, rocking and rolling,' is his only recorded comment.

Two days later his political credibility received an immeasurable boost when Bernard Levin, the highly respected political commentator, praised him in his *Times* column. Under the headline 'SUCH A SCREAM, WHY CAN'T WE HAVE MORE LIKE HIM?' Levin wrote: 'As far as I know, there is only one politician who admits, indeed, proclaims, his disability, and that is Lord Sutch, who makes much play with his willingness to agree that he is indeed a lunatic.' Levin admired Sutch's proposal 'to stand for all 650 seats at the next general election' and declared, 'His Lordship is a genuine addition to the nation's mirth'. With his participation, Levin said, a 'by-election ceases to be only a mournful parade of po-faced mendacities, and becomes a mournful parade of po-faced mendacities enlivened by a colourful figure who not only *is* mad, but who seizes the nearest loud-hailer to announce the news of his lunacy to the four corners of the earth.' He even dismissed criticism that Sutch's main motive was publicity: 'If you can show me any MP who rejects the very idea of seeking publicity I shall eat my head unbuttered.'

Later that same month, Margaret Thatcher was overthrown by her own party. 'Thatcherism may come and go,' wrote Sutch in a letter to the *Daily Telegraph*, 'but Loonyism, which represents the true spirit of the British people, will go on for ever.' Sutch's plan to succeed her was de-railed when, despite paying £10 to join the Conservative Party, he was ruled ineligible to stand in the leadership contest.

By the time of his death he would be indisputably Britain's longest-serving party leader. Counting back to his first election, the Stratford by-election of 1963, Screaming Lord Sutch clocked up almost thirty-six years at the head of the various parties he fronted, and over sixteen with the Official Monster Raving Loony Party.

In another newspaper interview Sutch gave a hint that he was becoming more aware of his age: 'It's a bit frightening when kids come up to you and say their grannies and granddads used to come and watch you. I have survived for thirty years,' he added, 'just kept soldiering on and seen a lot of big-headed swines with no talent at all come and go.' His latest royalty statement from Dick James Music, however, would have confirmed to him that he couldn't survive on the proceeds from record sales and composing rights. Earnings from 'All Black and Hairy' for the period July–December 1990 were precisely £4.22.

In March 1991, contesting the Lancashire Ribble Valley by-election (278 votes), Sutch claimed to have overtaken the record set by Wing Commander Bill Boaks, who campaigned on a bicycle plastered with slogans, for the number of elections fought. 'There was a slight problem in my claiming the record,' he later admitted in his autobiography, 'as Boaks himself had not been sure of precisely how many times he had stood – thirty had just been his guesstimate.'

Soon after the by-election, interviewed by the well-respected John Dunn for his early evening show on BBC Radio 2, Sutch was congratulated on his record total of by-elections and asked whether he would be considering retirement. 'No,' Sutch told Dunn, estimating he had spent some £60,000 so far funding his political career: 'I'm there for the mass of people who don't bother to vote – I'm their candidate.' He had been approached 'by some of the sensible parties' to stand for them, he claimed, but said he had declined the offers. 'I'd just be a number and lose my whole identity as the official protest party.'

'And what do you protest about?' asked Dunn.

The question prised a rare serious answer from Sutch: 'We protest against the mass of people out of work, the terrible state of the NHS – you either have National Health treatment and die, or if you've got money you can pay for an operation – that's crazy, it should be for everyone.' Another thoughtful comment followed: 'It's more important to have a family than to vote. It's very important to bring someone into this world. It's a great responsibility.'

The following day he was back playing one of the venues he graced in his very early days, the Clay Pigeon in Eastcote.

Here were the two poles of Screaming Lord Sutch's career perfectly juxtaposed: national exposure at the highest level, and the daily grind of club gigs and drumming up a few hundred votes at a by-election. By May 1991, in fact, the Loony Party boasted five elected local councillors – Stuart Hughes and Chris Patch in East Devon; Alan Hope and Charlie Salt in Ashburton and Cheriton Bishop respectively, with Freddie Zapp elected to two councils, Redruth North and Camborne South.

Sutch went to Australia in June to play a music festival – 'It was a lot of my musicians that emigrated over there,' he said of the band he ended up playing with, 'so it was all guys I'd worked with in England' – and he even appeared on television with the Australian prime minister, Paul Keating. In December, to the delight of his mum, he appeared at the Palladium, at a gig to celebrate Chas and Dave's twentieth anniversary in music.

On the other hand, Darren Poyzer, twice a Loony candidate, who was promoting live music at the Wytchwood pub in Ashton-under-Lyne at the time, remembers the night he booked Sutch: 'The night was memorable for two things – a poorly attended but nevertheless very enjoyable gig, and David and his driver staying the night in my flat and kipping on the floor. I'd never thought that a guy of David's age would quite happily doss down rough, but here he was – a portly, middle-aged fella in creased pyjamas, looking tired and in need of a few years' rest and retirement, with toothbrush, intermittently bringing up a few words about how worthwhile it would be for me to stand for the Loony Party at the next election. Despite the splash of toothpaste, it all made the clearest sense.'

In August 1991 one of Sutch's earliest rock 'n' roll friends passed away. Vince Taylor was one of the early successes to emerge from the 2 I's, and for the best part of a year from late 1960 the 2 I's package of Taylor, Lance Fortune, Keith Kelly and newcomer Screaming Lord Sutch had played superb shows across the country. Taylor's song 'Brand New Cadillac' had gained a new life in 1979 in a blistering cover version by The Clash on their classic *London Calling* album. Taylor was fifty-four when he died. Sutch may or may not have been aware that, according to the obituary in the rock 'n' roll magazine *Now Dig This*, he underwent 'long spells in psychiatric clinics' and that 'his career [had] spiralled into self-destruction'.

chapter twelve

Payne's a Pleasure

'I always say to people who are down, nothing ever lasts, not even your troubles'

— CYNTHIA PAYNE

What was perhaps Sutch's most enigmatic relationship began as a complete shock to the other half of it – a woman as notorious in her own right as Sutch, but for less wholesome reasons. He first met Britain's most famous former madam Cynthia Payne in the summer of 1988 when he gatecrashed a television interview she was giving about the Kensington and Chelsea by-election in which she was standing.

Payne's outwardly unremarkable house in Streatham, south London, just off Tooting Common, had become world-famous in the late 1970s as the venue for extraordinary sex parties involving men from the most respectable upper echelons of the English establishment. Payne was ultimately charged with running the biggest disorderly house or brothel in history. She was sentenced to eighteen months, reduced on appeal to six months, plus a hefty fine. Her story was subsequently immortalised in the film *Personal Services*, starring Julie Walters.

'If you really want to do something about changing the sex laws,' her assistant Gloria Walker had remarked, 'why not stand for Parliament? After all, if that Screaming Lord Sutch bloke can do it, anyone can.'

'Who's Screaming Lord Sutch?' Payne had replied. When she went to hand in her nomination papers she soon found out. 'I was about to start talking to an interviewer when all of a sudden this figure jumped out from nowhere and threw both arms around me like a long-lost friend. It was Sutch.'

Adam Boulton, the political correspondent for Sky News and previously ITN, got to know Sutch well over the years of covering his election appearances, and says Kensington is his fondest memory of all: 'Sutch was going green with envy at the prospect of another fringe candidate scoring the elusive "nul points". We had quite a long conversation about how it was difficult not to get votes once you got your name on the ballot.' To achieve no votes at all would have been a Holy Grail for Sutch – to blur the line between success and failure must have seemed irresistible yet unachievable to him. By persuading absolutely no one to (or everyone not to) vote for him, Sutch would have become the most successful political failure of all time – or would he have been recording the ultimate failure to succeed? In the end, though, the result was dire for Sutch: he polled his lowest ever result, at just 61 votes behind Payne's 193. It was perhaps inauspicious that his campaign vehicle was an Austin Princess hearse – 'because we were dead centre of town' – but in the midst of the campaign he had flown to Germany to play in Berlin and Hanover and his vote collapsed in his absence.

The lord and the lady, however, had hit it off, and they began a close and long-term acquaintance. Adam Boulton had mixed feelings about the new alliance: 'Sometimes there was a druggy ambience about his entourage and I felt it was a shame he latched on to the likes of Cynthia Payne and George Weiss, who slightly sullied his image.'

'Rainbow' George Weiss was another maverick politician, who indeed claims to have made the formal introductions between Sutch and Payne: 'I thought they were like brother and sister,' he said (more like Darby and Joan, some might say). But after the *Daily Mirror* dredged up a photograph of himself, Cynthia and David to accompany a report about George being 'busted' for an indiscretion involving a dubious substance – brilliantly headlined 'SEX AND DRUGS AND ROCK 'N' ROLL' – 'Cynthia and David seemed to distance themselves from me somewhat.' Drugs were anathema to Sutch and could have harmed his image. Cynthia's dubious fame, on the other hand, was no problem for him – he wouldn't have been too worried about proximity to sexual notoriety.

On Sunday, 3 February 1991, therefore, an inquisitive audience at the University of Sussex's Gardner Centre in Falmer, Brighton, shelled out up to £7 a ticket to see an unusual combination of a madam and a political rocker in a show called 'Sutch a Payne'. David and Cynthia chatted, told anecdotes about their lives, answered questions and, in Sutch's case, played some music. Subsequently they also entertained the good folk of Harrogate and north London before the short tour came to an end. According to Cynthia, there was something of a disagreement about the fees involved, but in a May 1991 letter to Sutch's friend Pat Hellier, Cynthia confided, 'Harrogate Theatre was a great success. Sutch was a lot better, but he still looks very depressed. I really do think something bad will happen to him in the end if he doesn't change his ways and take life more slowly.'

Cynthia Payne's infamous house in Streatham, when I visited, was packed with pictures of her with celebrities such as George Michael, Sean Connery, Julie Walters and Arnold Schwarzenegger. There was also one of Sutch and Cynthia at a William Hill betting shop during the Kensington campaign, prominently displayed. Cynthia keeps herself well for her advancing years. She talks quickly and often unguardedly, and seems to rely a great deal on her assistant, Gloria, who is treated brusquely if not unkindly, rather as Sutch treated anyone available as a convenient helper.

David was going through a tempestuous stage in his volatile relationship with Giselle when he met her, Cynthia confirmed. He was living with Giselle at her house in Notting Hill, but started to spend more and more time with Cynthia. Ultimately he moved in on a more or less permanent basis: 'I allowed Sutch to live here since Gloria was my part-time assistant, answering telephone calls for him and me – it made things easier and this was particularly good for Sutch as, this way, he never paid rent, nor wages to anyone. He didn't like spending money at all. In all the time we were together I think he only took me out for a meal twice, and I had the devil's own job of getting any contribution towards my phone bill out of him, even though he monopolised it for days on end during his election campaigns.'

Cynthia developed her own suspicions about David's fragile mental state: 'I used to go and visit his mother because I felt sorry for the old girl. She was at her wit's end with him. I saw his mum shortly before she died. I stayed with her for several hours – she was lonely – and I said to her, "Look, I don't want to be rude, but is David all there? He does very weird things, you know." She said to me, "Well, he has been in a couple of depression clinics, he's always saying he is under stress." That night on my way back on the tube I had a horrifying headache which scared me so much I went to see my GP. I was still worrying about Sutch, but never got round to ringing his mum again. If I had I may have found out what was really wrong with him – I'm still annoyed I didn't.'

Sutch's own bouts with depression, Payne suggests, did make him unusually sensitive to other people's depressions: she highlighted an instance when he did something for her that no one would ever manage to do for him. 'When I was ill in 1989 I had to have quite a nasty operation and I was really scared about it. Sutch was wonderful, and came to see me in hospital and cheered me up. He got me out of quite a depressed state, which no man had ever been able to do.'

But even when Sutch moved into Cynthia's house more or less full-time, Giselle was never entirely off the scene. Cynthia thought Sutch was intimidated by his girlfriend. Once, when Cynthia was working at the Edinburgh Festival, she wanted Sutch to join her, but he didn't come, and Cynthia thought she knew why. 'It's such a shame that he can't do anything with her [Giselle] around,' she wrote to a friend at the time. 'I wonder why he is so scared of her. I can only think it's something to do with money, as that's the only thing he worries about losing!'

'Sutch always said Giselle loved and responded to flattery,' Cynthia told me, 'but my dad brought me up to distrust it.' She added that she and David never had an affair but admitted, 'Certainly there was a spark – I was very fond of him.'

Was Sutch and Cynthia's relationship a potentially sexual one? Promoter of their shows Arthur Martin suggested, 'I think Cynthia was secretly in love with him – they had a very deep friendship.' More likely it was perhaps the kind of mother-son relationship he'd have preferred – according to Cynthia, he even called her 'Mumsy'.

One day, however, completely out of the blue, Sutch stunned Cynthia by asking her to marry him. 'He said, "Imagine the publicity we'd get if we announced our engagement." He really meant the publicity he would get. I never had any intention of doing it so I'm not sure how far he would have gone.'

Naturally, a conversation with Madam Cyn is bound to steer one's thought towards matters of a carnal nature. The sexual side of Sutch's life has not often been aired in public, although he confessed in *Life As Sutch* that 'I've known plenty of groupies', describing them as 'a rough and ready lot'. He added: 'The more carefree days before AIDS led to regular visits to the gonorrhoea clinic for some painful treatment.' Somewhat surprisingly, Sutch also declared that 'political groupies are not only cleaner, but more sophisticated. They are also much thinner on the ground – but you can take it from me they're usually a much hotter property between the sheets than the blondes in skintight leather micro-skirts who hang round the pop scene.'

In the video of the Adam Boulton interview at the Vale of Glamorgan by-election, Cynthia and Sutch become wary when the subject of Lindi St Clair, alias Miss Whiplash, comes up. A campaigner for prostitutes' rights, she also claimed relationships with a number of MPs. Sutch's uncharacteristic unease about the association may have had something to do with the fact that he was once allegedly involved with St Clair. According to her, she was yet another of Sutch's 'occasional shags' when he had lots of groupies around in the late 1960s. 'We were a proper couple for about three months,' she told me, adding that he was 'a great lover and always had several girls on standby. I never forgot Dave and was thrilled to meet up with him again on the hustings. I tried to rekindle our sexual liaisons but Cynthia put the kibosh on it.'

Like other partners before her, Cynthia finally found Sutch's obsessive hoarding too much to live with. It caused their biggest row. 'He just brought in more and more stuff, leaving it all over the house. I told him it had to go, I didn't care where. In the end I had it all stacked up outside on the pavement and made him shift it. He was furious. About this time he told me he was going into a London clinic – he claimed it was for an operation on his nose, but now I wonder.' She also said that around the same time Sutch was worried about his health and underwent a brain scan, which revealed nothing untoward.

But Sutch appreciated Cynthia Payne's role in his life. 'I think she's quite fond of me,' he said in an *Independent on Sunday* interview with Isabel Wolff in July 1995:

Cynthia's very kind and listens to my problems. Cynthia and I will always be pals. I've had my ups and downs with her, because she tends to argue a lot and gets set in her ways, but she doesn't do that so much now. What would I miss if I didn't see her? Well, certainly not her cooking, but her happy, smiling face.

He also told a story about Cynthia which revealed something about his own nature, suggesting, somewhat surprisingly, that perhaps he was a little star-struck:

I was at her house once and she got a call from this bloke who said he wanted to invite her to his party. He told her that he'd send a limousine to pick her up. She said, 'Who are you?' He said, 'George Michael.' She said, 'Who? I've never heard of you,' and put the phone down. When she told me who it was, I couldn't believe it. I told her she'd got to go, because there'd be all sorts of celebrities there, like Elton John and Paul McCartney. But she'd never heard of them, because she doesn't know the pop scene at all. She only knows people like Frank Sinatra or Tom Jones. George Michael had the guts to phone her back and ask her again, so she went.

Cynthia and I chatted on about various things and then she said: 'I'll always be a brothel-keeper at heart. I'd like to have been known for something else, but it wasn't to be. I've had a taste of what being famous is like, and a lot of people I have met are very false, continually buttering you up. Sutch always had people around to help him. He did attract lonely people, though,' she concluded, leaving me wondering whether she included herself in that category or whether they had simply recognised in each other a kindred spirit.

She thought back to the last time she saw David, who had invited her to see him play in Hammersmith some six weeks before his death. 'I was curious as to why he was so insistent and made a big effort to go. He was there with Yvonne. I watched him closely on stage but he seemed to be just going through the motions and I thought, "You've really gone down".' Cynthia was tired and left after the show. 'As I went to the door I looked round at him. He was flexing his leg which had been giving him a bit of trouble and he gave me a look as if to say, "You won't be seeing me any more". He never contacted me again.'

The several hours I'd spent with Cynthia and Gloria had positively flown, and I began to make my excuses to leave. As I stood up to go Cynthia said, 'I asked Sutch once whether he ever ejaculated on stage.'

I looked at her. 'And?'

'He gave a sly smile and said, "It has been known to happen."'

As she opened the door to see me out she handed me a card, in the style of the luncheon vouchers that were famously used by her guests to pay for their pleasures. On the back of it she had written: 'To Graham, Thanks for your past custom. Cynthia.'

chapter thirteen

A Year in the Life

'He guards his celebrity with the venom of a six-year-old with a new bike. The winds may blow and the seasons may change, but still David Sutch will rave on, outlasting any transient pop star that comes along'
— ALAN CLAYSON, MUSICIAN AND WRITER

*L*ife *As Sutch*: The Official Autobiography of a Monster Raving Loony was published in October 1991. A month later, on his fifty-first birthday, Sutch was the guest of honour at a gathering in the producer's former home studio, for LWT's documentary 'The Legendary Joe Meek'. He led a communal singing of 'Jack the Ripper', cut his black-coffin birthday cake, acclaimed Meek a 'genius' and flourished his latest album, *The Screaming Lord Sutch Story* and a copy of the new autobiography.

Chippindale had had his work cut out to get the book written, as he recalls: 'At one point Sutch had the proofs to check and the publisher was anxious about the schedule. So I rang him to ask how he was getting on. 'Not very well,' he said. 'How far have you got?' 'Page nine,' he said. 'David, you're never going to read it, are you?' I asked him. He admitted he wouldn't, so we agreed that I should finish it off to get the publisher off his back.'

So Sutch never proofread his own book (his probable dyslexia would have made it tough to do so unless he had found someone to read it through with him), which makes it difficult to know how reliable the content may be as, through no fault of his own, Chippindale's voice often seems to make itself heard over Sutch's.

On page thirteen, however, when Sutch may still have been interested enough, he makes a remark that sounds all his own: 'The historical role which most interested me was that of the court jester ... But if you were a jester and your jests were no good, they had your head. You found yourself literally dead for what you said.'

The book is as disordered as Sutch's own life. Dates are notable by their absence, Sutch's memory is clearly unreliable, and the amount of political fantasy contained in the pages suggests that Chippindale had to pad out the book when Sutch was unable or unwilling to give the project sufficient attention and input.

The book's dedication reads: 'For my mother, Annie Emily Sutch'. For an epigraph he chose two lines of Bob Dylan: 'There's no success like failure, and failure's no success at all.'

'It didn't sell very well,' Chippindale told me, 'but it was enormously popular with library borrowers. We both stood to make a decent sum through the Public Lending Right system. As an established author I was careful to register my half of the rights, but even though I made sure David's form was completed and ready to send he just couldn't be bothered to take it to the pillar box and post it, so the payments he was fully entitled to went begging.'

This was an out-of-character oversight by Sutch, which suggests that his depression was influencing his attitude at the time.

To mark the book's publication, the *Kilburn Times* took Sutch back to his former home in Kilburn:

> On arrival, Lord Sutch recalled, 'We named it the Dead End Street, me and my friends were the Dead End Kids.' At the sight of his old house, its paintwork peeling, the exterior fallen into disrepair, Lord Sutch started checking his finances. 'We are going to need to do it up a bit before we make it a party office.'
>
> Then, from a neighbouring upstairs window, Mrs Esther Callaghan, 79, called, 'Hello, David.' A wide-eyed Lord Sutch was rooted to the spot. 'You still here? I didn't know any of the neighbours were still here.'
>
> 'I have been here since 1941,' she said. 'He is a right nutter, you know – no, not really – he has always been a clever lad.'

A mark of how far society had come during the thirty-year career described in *Life As Sutch* was a Hallowe'en show staged at the London Dungeon that autumn for which Sutch put together an eleven-piece line-up. 'The most famous English pop singer who never had a hit could hardly have been witnessed in surroundings more blood-curdlingly appropriate,' observed Alan Clayson later. The show had been conceived and was broadcast by BBC Radio. 'They insisted I did all the numbers the BBC had once banned,' Sutch reflected afterwards. 'The producer said, "You were too far ahead of your time."'

When the paperback edition of *Life As Sutch* was launched the following August at Peter Stockton's Johnnie O'Boogie rock 'n' roll bar café in Leicester Square, Sutch uncharacteristically put his relationship with his one of his closest and most long-established friends, Pat Hellier, at risk, when a mix-up over who was looking after his cherished loud-hailer led to someone blithely walking out of the club with it. Sutch eventually got it back, but in the meantime had had to apologise to Hellier for swearing at her in front of all the people at the party. 'That was the only time David had a go at me,' she remembers. 'Most telling-offs were with great humour, like the time he gave a stranger his camera – when he went to take it back the guy had gone. I got the blame, because, "If you had been there you would have been in charge of the camera."'

Sutch would often leave his props lying around Pat and her late husband Ken Hellier's house. 'The coffin was here because David had nowhere else for it – and the bat was being repaired so that it could be rigged up to fly across the stage.' It seems that nobody could stay cross with Sutchie for long.

Over the next two years several events give a conflicting picture of how organised and focused he could be on the task in hand. For the general election in April 1992, he carried through an audacious plan to stand against all three major party leaders. He took on John Major and the Tories in Huntingdon, and polled 728 votes; Neil Kinnock and Labour in Islwyn – 547, finishing fifth; and finally Paddy Ashdown and his Lib Dems in Yeovil where he ended up with 338 votes, fifth out of six. His bold move resulted in a (top) hat-trick of lost deposits. The following May, for his first by-election outing of the year, in Newbury, his attempt to make a mark by paying his deposit in German currency (earned while touring Europe earlier in the year) was foiled by Town Hall officials. He appeared as himself in a Carlton Television drama, *A Woman's Guide to Adultery*, starring Sean Bean and Neil Morrissey.

For Christmas 1992, however, Sutch was booked to appear in pantomime in Scotland alongside the singer Andy –'Donald Where's Yer Troosers' – Stewart, in a touring production of *Robinson Crusoe*. Savages' sax player Dave Dix says Sutch was to play the prime minister of the island, although others say he was cast as the Sea Monster Raving Captain. Whatever, on 7 December, the *Today* newspaper reported that 'Lord Sutch missed the first night of his pantomime season after falling through the stage.' Tony Dangerfield and Pat Hellier later told me that Sutch had been looking for an excuse to get out of this commitment, having been unable or unwilling to learn his script. 'He'd been sent the script ages before but never opened it,' confirms Dave Dix, 'and by the time rehearsals came around he had done nothing – he could have breezed it if he'd put himself out a bit. Instead, he went downhill rapidly, worrying about it. Then he had the accident, which got him out of trouble.'

Jack Irving, in The Savages at the time, recalled that the accident occurred in Nottingham: 'We were on a bill with Dr and The Medics. Their manager checked out the stage and warned us that there was a small gap in it which might prove a problem. Sure enough, Sutch put his foot straight in it and fell over – he had me worried for a while before he got up. To be honest, I think it may have been deliberate to give him the excuse to get out of the panto, which had been worrying him. Not all the band members agree with me on this, though. That night he had not looked well when he had turned up – he looked as though someone had just woken him up.'

'He made some insurance money, which was a nice little earner,' says Dix, 'and had a ready-made excuse for getting out of the panto.'

In the August of 1993 Sutch celebrated 'thirty years as a party leader' with a conga over Westminster Bridge. 'I'll probably be elected once I'm a pensioner,' he told reporters. 'That's the right age for an MP.' He unveiled a new policy: 'We should all work a two-day week with a five-day weekend.' In the same month, he was one of the first visitors to take advantage of the opening up of Buckingham Palace, 'where I hope one day to be knighted.' And at the Loony Party conference later that year, he was presented with a large, yellow cake, adorned with a trophy and the words: 'Lord Sutch, Thirty Years of Failure'.

For the following year in Sutch's life, 1994, we have a unique insight into his existence, thanks to an extraordinary piece of luck. Nearly ten years later I came upon, and was fortunate enough to be able to acquire, his personal diary for the year, which came to light on eBay. A well used, small, pocket-sized, AA Motorists' Diary, a week-per-page book, it is stuffed with contact names and numbers, together with detail of gigs, financial transactions, doodlings and ideas for songs and policies. The diary offers a fascinating insight into Sutch's state of mind and thought processes (as well as giving a good idea of his idiosyncratic spelling).

Thanks to the diary, 1994 is perhaps the most accurately recorded year of Sutch's life. It provides an intimate look into Sutch's domestic and private life, cataloguing the minutiae of his daily existence. It obviously continued in use well after the end of 1994, as it includes the phone numbers of friends, musicians, journalists, outfitters; and business cards from cab companies, recording studios and Giselle's Paris shop, L'Heure du Bijou. There is a card from the Charter Nightingale Hospital with a doctor's name written on it, and another from what seems to be an escort agency. Suddenly, my own name and number jump out from the top of a page, immediately above the telephone number for the House of Commons. Further down there is a number for publicist Max Clifford.

Most fascinating of all are the casual thoughts jotted down: 'Advice comes to [sic] late when a thing is done'. Under a small tag from a 36B Wonderbra, stuck onto the top of a page, is an old joke: 'Don't get married. Just meet someone you don't like and buy them a house.' There is a doodle about 'Rock 'n' Roll Madhouse Nutcases, Madmen and Geanius's [sic]'. Sutch lists Arthur Brown at number one, ahead of Viv Stanshall, P.J. Proby and Roy Wood. I can't decipher number five but at number six Sutch has inserted his own name.

Then there is a receipt from 23 February 1995 for something measuring $17\frac{5}{8}'' \times 4\frac{3}{16}''$, and costing 75p. Most poignant of all is a sad (but unintentionally funny) list, headed 'To Do – My Body – 1. Teeth 2. Eys [sic] 3. Bum 4. Face lift 5. Fat off belly 6. Get fat off me.'

The diary (which includes a month either side of the calendar year) reveals that at the beginning of December 1993 Sutch's earning power was in decent nick. However, it also shows just how hard he had to work to get it. On Sunday, 5 December, he records a payment of £200 for performing at Cardiff's Llandaff Rowing Club. A cheque for £250 was added to the kitty for his show at Gassy Jacks in Cathays, also in Cardiff, the next day. Aberystwyth Arts Centre was the venue on Tuesday, bringing him £550. A couple of days off, before Carmarthen's Trinity College on Friday brought in £1,200, while Saturday meant a dash to Worthing FC in Sussex to rake in £600. An appearance on BBC Radio 5 earned him £100 on Tuesday, 14 December, and the next day he collected £550 at Christchurch's Highlander Club in Dorset. On Thursday it was off to Wembley Arena to see Gary Glitter, and the Friday saw him playing at Thames Valley University for £1,000.

That's thirteen days, eight gigs, £4,450. How much had to be shared with musicians is not recorded – nor is the taxman's share!

There is an intriguing entry for Monday, 27 December, which just reads 'Lis Wilmer Voice Coach'. Was David planning a New Year's Resolution to improve his vocal technique? If so, it would suggest a previously unadmitted crisis of confidence in the untutored, shouting style which had served him well enough thus far.

Sutch's diary entry for 1 January suggests he was making other more domestic New Year Resolutions, too:

Sell houses.
Sell junk off.
One house, one car, go farr [sic].

On the same page he has written lyrics to a song called 'I Got A Car, Public Enemy'. It seems unfinished, but you get the drift:

I don't deal in drugs I don't smoke dope
I don't take crack, cause that is a joke.
But I drive a car, so I'm public enemy number one
Caught speeding, caught drunk, no road tax, MoT ...

Sutch had clearly tapped into public opinion again – and these were the days *before* speed cameras.

On 4 January, Sutch makes a note in red ink and underlines it: 'Tristan 19teen'. Three days later he was back to work for £140 in the High Rock pub in Tunbridge Wells. On 2 February he was off to Miami Beach, spending '£219 each' and recording in his diary that the moment had come to spend some 'quality time together' (presumably with Giselle). He had also written a new song – touchingly, he writes, 'Tristan to sing it':

> Papa do you still wanna rock 'n' roll,
> Papa can you still do the stroll,
> Papa can you dance to a rockin' band,
> Papa are you too old to move your feet?

From Miami he sent Melodie Staniforth and her husband Stan a postcard: 'Weather great, having a nice rest – and just one gig.' He forgot to mention that on arrival, with Giselle too tired to drive, he jumped behind the wheel of their hired car and promptly drove them into an alligator-filled swamp. They survived unscathed but minus one of Giselle's – non-alligator-skin – shoes! Two days later, jet-lagged or not, he was appearing with Jess Conrad and Wee Willie Harris in Edmonton, earning £700.

He was still confiding to his diary his concerns over his weight and diet, though. In what may be another song, or simply a message to himself, he writes:

> All I want for Christmas is a lettuce, yes a lettuce. I want to get rid of my pot belly and lose at least 20lbs of fat. I'm gonna give my turkey to the dog and cat, I don't want no Christmas puddin', No jelly and ice cream – I'm gonna get back to a decent weight, it ain't no dream. I'll eat a melon but spit out the pips – there won't be any stodgy food pass my lips; On the 3rd day I'll have boiled fish – but without the chips.

This seems to be some sort of resolution to go on a diet, because a couple of pages later he writes: 'I'll stick to my diet. I'll be a brand new man for a brand new year. I'm gonna eat carrots, celery and peas. I'll stick to the program, just you wait and see, and when I've lost all the weight I'll buy

Screaming Lord Sutch in his prime and in his element: stylishly and raffishly good-looking, playing out a mock-horror role leavened with a tasteless yet self-mocking humour.
Courtesy of Rollercoaster Records

Looking for all the world like the eleven-year-old bundle of mischief immortalised in the Just William books so popular in his childhood.

An early taste of the limelight for David Sutch (middle row, second from right). Despite being one of the smaller members of the boxing squad he had a pugilistic talent that won him school and district honours. He would punch above his weight for the rest of his life. *Courtesy of Rollercoaster Records*

The last person to be acclaimed as one of the world's great drivers, Sutch nevertheless loved cars — owning over the years, among other vehicles, a hearse, vans, a Rolls-Royce and a Cadillac. A casual attitude towards speed limits, car tax and insurance saw him attending court and being fined on a number of occasions. Here he turns up for a hearing. *Courtesy of Rollercoaster Records*

A terrific, idyllic shot of David (hands on hips) and classmates on a school trip.

With the basic rock 'n' roll group format beefed up with brass, this February–May 1965 line-up of the Savages proved uneconomic to keep on the road for long, but was impressive while it lasted, featuring the Four Saxes, Ritchie Blackmore, bassist Avid Andersen and drummer Tornado Evans.

His hair-raising singing style was in stark contrast to the clean-cut crooners of the pre-Beatles days.

The early sixties, and Screaming Lord Sutch introduces his 'Wild Man of Borneo' image, which rapidly attracted attention from rock fans and the media.

His uninhibited, over-the-top stage antics made the band one of the leading attractions of the time, but never made the transition to record success.

This moody, sultry style, somewhat reminiscent of early Human League-era Phil Oakley, had David staring meaningfully into the camera lens and projecting a persona his musical direction could never sustain. *Courtesy of Rollercoaster Records*

Sutch is perfectly relaxed in leopardskin, horns and little else, hamming it up with a plastic crocodile and a huge axe. Band members (left to right) Nicky Hopkins, Ritchie Blackmore, Carlo Little and Ricky Brown wish he'd opted for a more conservative approach. *Courtesy of Rollercoaster Records*

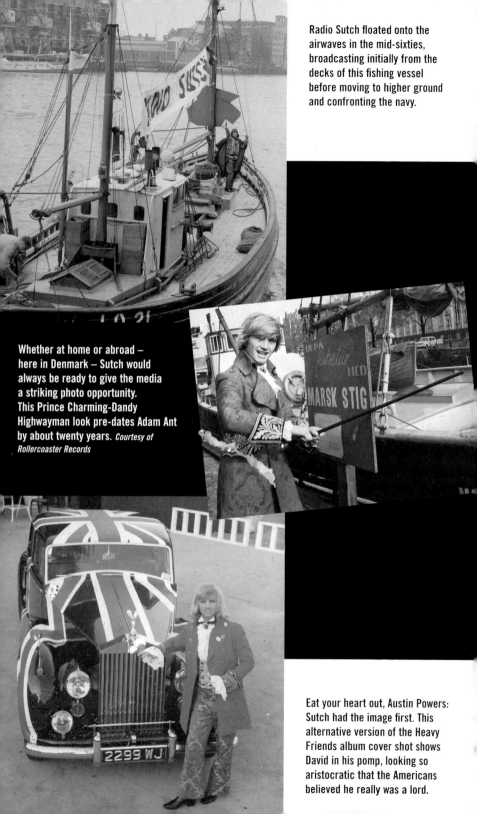

Radio Sutch floated onto the airwaves in the mid-sixties, broadcasting initially from the decks of this fishing vessel before moving to higher ground and confronting the navy.

Whether at home or abroad – here in Denmark – Sutch would always be ready to give the media a striking photo opportunity. This Prince Charming-Dandy Highwayman look pre-dates Adam Ant by about twenty years. *Courtesy of Rollercoaster Records*

Eat your heart out, Austin Powers: Sutch had the image first. This alternative version of the Heavy Friends album cover shot shows David in his pomp, looking so aristocratic that the Americans believed he really was a lord.

Even at just a few hours old, Tristan Sutch is asked to perform for the cameras. Thann looks radiantly happy, but David is as concerned with getting the picture right and branding his baby son as Sutch Minor as he is with his new role as a father.

Perhaps a more realistic expression of the troubled relationship between David and Thann.

As always with Sutch, every picture tells a story. This studio shot of him with legendary axe-man Jimmy Page hides a dispute over the guitarist's role on the *Heavy Friends* album. *Courtesy of Rollercoaster Records*

'A kind of Zelig figure, who might be mistaken for Chauncey Gardner in a bad light' – Alwyn W. Turner. This double-page spread illustrates Sutch's knack of getting in the picture with a very wide selection of celebrities over several decades. First, with Keith Moon, whose unhinged antics finally proved too much even for Screaming Lord Sutch. When Moon persuaded him and Vivian Stanshall to parade around London clubs in Nazi attire, Sutch initially went along with him, but bailed out when Moon wanted them to take to the streets. *Courtesy of Rollercoaster Records*

Having introduced Little Richard to soccer on the pitch at Wembley Stadium when they both played there at a big concert, Sutch stayed pally with the camp rock 'n' roller. *Courtesy of Rollercoaster Records*

Giselle's favourite photograph of David Sutch, snapped with Mick Jagger before she met him

Middlesex schoolboy champ shapes up to 'The Greatest'. Muhammad Ali made a decent fist of singing, even achieving a minor hit with an early single. Sutch is at least managing to stay upright here, which is more than most of Ali's British opponents could do.

Gary Glitter's onstage refusal to compromise the show he presented contrasted with Sutch's scaling-down of his own performances. But off-stage demons would overwhelm the lives of both men, condemning one to suicide and the other to exile. *Courtesy of Rollercoaster Records*

Can you tell who it is yet? Perhaps Rolf Harris inspired Sutch to take to the canvas and create the mysterious paintings that appeared under his name.

Sutch gate-crashes a prime minister for the first – but far from last – time. This shot of him cadging a light from Harold Wilson was sent round the world by the media, and appeared on his personal Christmas card that year.

A Loony Conference team photo. Left to right: Loony Lord Tiverton; the author; Tim Fordham-Moss, PR for William Hill; Sutch; Freddie Zapp; Cynthia Payne; Alan Hope.

The jacket Giselle bought for Sutch shortly after they met in the mid-seventies. After his death it turned up at auction, to be snapped up by the author.

Relaxing with Giselle (far left) and friends at her home in Paris.

The pig's head is quite easy to understand; Sutch would always don it for the song 'I'm a Hog for You'. The symbolism of the toilet seat around the neck remains elusive.

Tony Dangerfield (centre), one of the 'keepers of the flame' for the Savages, and Jack Irving (right) were convinced that towards the end of his life David was keen to rekindle his rock 'n' roll credentials at the expense of his political aspirations.

David loved his trips to Wales each year for the William Hill Man Versus Horse Marathon. Here, he and the author hand over a cheque for £5000 to the first mountain biker ever to complete the 22-mile course faster than the first horse home.

David, his 'Ma' and her dog, Rosie. *Courtesy of Rollercoaster Records*

When several paintings purporting to be by David Sutch turned up on eBay following his death it was news to many of his closest friends, who had never known his artistic talents to extend beyond matchstick-men. Is this intriguing 'Self Portrait Reflected in a Spoon' a crude forgery or evidence of a hidden talent?

David sings live for the very last time, at the Neuadd Arms in Llanwrtyd Wells, mid-Wales, on the night of 12/13 June 1999. Three days later he would commit suicide. *Susannah Green*

An alarming sequence of passport-style photographs taken shortly before his death, which show an unfamiliar, somewhat unhinged look in his eyes ('crazy', Thann called it), emphasised by the facial hair.

Clothes found laid out on David's bed after his death.

When David's house in Watford Road, Sudbury, was emptied out before being sold in August 2003, much of his property, including this stage coffin lid, was just dumped in a skip.

Tristan stands amongst a jumble of 'stuff' as he clears David's mother's house in Parkfield Road, South Harrow.

This hopeless clutter hints at the state of mind of the man who had allowed such a terrible confusion to reign in his home and his head.

The kitchen was as crowded and untidy as the rest of the Parkfield Road property.

Tristan and Thann in May 2003, outside the house where David killed himself. *Graham Sharpe*

Under the permanent memorial to Sutch unveiled in Llanwrytd Wells in June 2004. Left to right: Yvonne; Alan Hope; Yvonne's daughter Alex; and 'Sir Dangerous Dave'. *Graham Sharpe*

Carlo Little, without whom Sutch's career might well have taken a very different direction, stands alongside his mate's grave in June 2003. Little had just been diagnosed with cancer, but pledged to continue celebrating Sutch's life at the annual 'Sutch A Night' tribute gig for as long as possible. *Graham Sharpe*

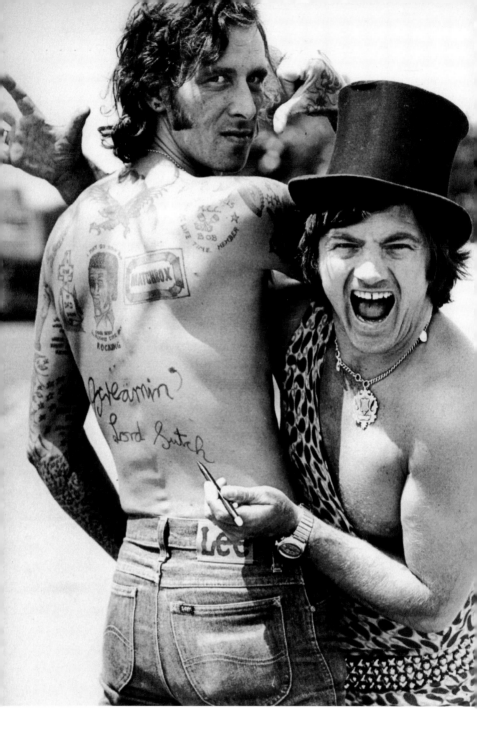

Sutch signs off by adding another illustration to the back of his great friend drummer 'Wild' Bob Burgos, the 'tattooed sledgehammer' of rock.

a brand new suit for the new me.' Around this time Sutch made an appearance with Cynthia Payne at Crufts Dog Show, reportedly causing chaos at the Pedigree Petfoods Luncheon taking place there.

Elsewhere in the diary, Sutch ponders on the nature of time as he doodles with the lyrics to another song:

Time is strong,
Time is never rong [sic],
Time can be good,
Time can be bad,
Time can rush,
Time can drag ...

The song ends poignantly yet inaccurately in the light of what would happen: 'Time you can't control, when your time is up you go.'

He had gigs on and off for the rest of April. A diary entry for 25 April reveals yet another song idea which looks likely to have been autobiographical:

If you're too old to rock n roll you might as well be dead
In your box under the rocks.
If you're too old to rock n roll, the hair gone from your head,
Too old to rock n roll, the bounce have left your legs ...

In May, Sutch was campaigning for the Rotherham by-election. In his manifesto he exhorted voters: 'If you agree with Loony policies, put a big X against my name. If you're not sure, just put a little x.' He polled 1,114 votes, his highest total yet, and, remarkably, no less than 4.16 per cent of the vote. Numerically, this was Sutch's finest hour, as he was just 200 short of saving his deposit. The election was won by Labour's Denis MacShane. Sutch's diary entry for the day simply reads: 'No fee, all exs went to John Tempest.'

Sutch held his Loony victory party at The Zone, on the evening of polling day, 5 May (he would often wittily celebrate anticipated victory before the results came through) and stayed that night, as he had throughout the campaign, at John Tempest's home. 'I noticed he seemed to have trouble sleeping,' recalls Tempest, 'but put it down to the rock 'n' roll lifestyle and timetable he was used to. My fondest memory of David,' he continues, 'was during the by-election when we returned in the early hours. We were greeted by my other half holding our fourteen-month-old-daughter, Jessica, saying, "Well, you take her then." She'd had a bad night. I duly did.

'But both David and I wanted a cup of tea – in David's case rather more than a potful – little Jessica was still at the milk, no tea stage. So, I gave our little bundle of fun to David and they sat on the couch together. After a while I heard these strange noises and went to investigate. Jessica was sitting on David's knee, playing with the badges on his coat and going, "Ooh, ooh." And David was going "Ooh, ooh," and I'm thinking, "Which one of these two is the most childlike?"'

On 12 May, Sutch recorded in his diary: 'John Smith dead, only 55 years old', referring to the deceased Labour leader. Two days later, disaster struck: when Sutch played Barry Island Conservative Club one of his favourite top hats was stolen. He succinctly noted: 'Lost hat.' But the show must go on, hat or not, and the next day he played at the Home Guard Club in Ely, Cardiff. By 17 May, a relieved Sutch had been reunited with the headgear. On 23 May he was broadcasting to 'our boys' on the British Forces network, picking up a fee of £40. On Saturday, May 28, he flew to Berlin but on 6 June was asking his diary about his appearance on Radio Luxembourg: 'To get paid fee?'

By the middle of 1994 the diary shows Sutch's health beginning to give him problems. He was still doing gigs and contesting by-elections, but he had now started recording his ailments: 'I had bad headache for 4 days,' he wrote on Friday, 17 June. An appointment with a Harley Street doctor at 3 p.m. is noted in the diary – along with a figure of £140, presumably the fee. On Saturday, 25 June, he records that he 'woke up with bad headache'.

The next day he was at radio broadcaster James Whale's 'tea party' in London with Giselle – his first direct mention of her for the year. On 27 June, he indicates a fee of £1,000 which he attributes to 'Carton [sic] TV' – probably for his participation in a stunt to stage a show by 'the world's biggest band' on Clapham Common. On 1 July he dined at Giselle's with her friend Vivienne Westwood before heading for Canvey Island for a double-bill with the band Dr Feelgood. He picked up £400. Perhaps he would have been gratified, too, to read in a July edition of

Melody Maker that Sutch's 'horror spectacle' of a show was 'copied almost prop for prop by Alice Cooper'. In view of his altercation with his American equivalent some twenty years earlier, the *Melody Maker* article must have seemed like a belated vindication.

On Sunday, 3 July the diary notes: 'Woke up with bad headache in two eyes, went to Paris with car + Gis 11pm – got stuck in Paris car jam, got to Ablon 10am. No sleep so best time to leave London 7-8pm'. They were in France 'to get house ready' for *OK!* to take photos to accompany the feature for which they had been already been interviewed, and which appeared in January 1995.

Sutch was off to Kensington Roof Garden's Night of 1,000 Stars on 11 July, but then the next day records 'bad headache'. On 15 July he flew out to Munich for a rock 'n' roll festival, featuring Carl Perkins, then flew back on Sunday but 'had bad headache in left eye'. Another bad headache on 21 July was followed by yet another two days later. A week after this he cancelled a gig in Eastleigh.

He jotted down details of a Jet Harris gig in London on 1 August, then notes: 'Sekonda Watch on 8 August'. This is presumably when he began work on the first of the television adverts in which he was taking part. The *Daily Mirror* reported that Sutch earned £20,000 for this campaign.

He recorded three adverts in total. The first, 'Broadcast', was a spoof party political broadcast with Sutch proclaiming: 'We urge you to go out and buy these £5,000 watches, and not a perfectly acceptable Sekonda which looks similar but sells for a fraction of the price. You'd have to be barking mad [cue shot of dog wearing Loony rosette] to part with five grand for this ... I did.' The second ad, 'Field', showed Sutch declaring: 'I didn't get where I am today by wearing a Sekonda', and the third, 'Jeweller', had a voiceover saying, 'And this watch, m'Lord, is very similar to the Sekonda, but is nearly a thousand pounds more.' Sutch cackles with laughter: 'I'll take it.' In all three advertisements Sutch is shown in dimly-lit close-up wearing a black polo neck, leopardskin jacket and top hat, with red hair sticking out at all angles. 'The only trouble with doing these ads,' he told the *Daily Mirror* later, 'is now I've got to be on time everywhere I go.' *Not* a discipline he would adhere to.

On 20 August the date is ringed in his diary and labelled 'Anti-junk day'. The day before, Thann Rendessy, now forty-one, had got married in Texas to David Benavidez (whom she would later be convicted of murdering in self-defence). Four days later Sutch confided to his diary: 'If I get depressed I shop and buy junk that I don't need and I don't want.' Was he finally trying to face up to the problem that had helped to drive Thann away and blighted much of his life?

For the rest of the year, Sutch's diary records more gigs, together with the amounts he had been paid. The day after the August bank holiday he writes, 'bad headache and start of flu', confirmed a day later when he manages to record: 'I was ill with flu'. A bizarre entry for 2 September complains, 'gig not paid, band late on stage, swearing too loud' – it is not clear where this happened. Flu seems to have been a continuing problem because on 5 September he writes, 'Ma's had flu as well – I'm at Parkfield Road for car', and the next day, 'Very bad with full flu.' On Wednesday, despite the flu, he somehow managed to fit in a 'Paul and Linda McCartney party', then on Thursday, 'Dizey [sic] with flu' and 'I was too ill to go to Tooting Benefit gig'.

By mid-September he must have improved because he flew out both to Italy and to Giselle's house in France (and he was still going over to 'Ma's house to eat dinner'). A contemplative mood seems to have come over him as he wrote in his diary: 'Whatever is the past is the past, now I look to the future. Get rid of Hastings and Watford Road. Stop bills, do up houses. Not too many gigs or PAs. Do houses and sell stuff off.' Could he have been contemplating retirement? Or emigration? He also wrote in the space for 17 September, 'In winter go to sun to work'.

In October the death was reported of Nicky Hopkins, the keyboards player who was an early Savage and went on to work with top bands like The Rolling Stones and Quicksilver Messenger Service. He had suffered some years of chronic health problems. Oddly, Sutch's diary fails to mention it. On 4 October Sutch played at Blackwood Snooker Club, but seemed, understandably, disappointed with the reward: 'Paid only £110.' There was better news the following day at TJ Rock Night Club in Newport when he earned £250. On 7 October it was 'photos for Sekonda watch ads'. A day later he recorded: 'Hats Portobello Rd' and a visit to Ealing Hospital Level 5 North, along with the name Mary Rose. Later in the month he flew to Paris to see Vivienne Westwood's new fashion show before flying on to Germany:

'German tour – 2 x £500 a gig + 2 at £300 gig'. The rest of the month was taken up with parties, gigs and various interviews, although on 27 October he noted details of antibiotics and tablets for 'flu'.

On 2 November, however, there is an entry that strikes a chord with many authors: 'My books 4000 at 30p, £1200'. Like so many who have been offered the chance to buy remaindered copies of their own book, Sutch probably couldn't bear to think of all those copies of his book being pulped, so snapped them up at a knock-down rate. This was pre-eBay, so to acquire such a vast number of books with no genuine prospect of shifting them, even at gigs, just demonstrates his continuing inability to free himself of 'stuff', all of which had to be kept some-where. Perhaps the exercise depressed him, for on his birthday on 10 November there is no indication of any kind of celebration, just a stark '54 yrs old'. (Apart from his own, Tristan's and his mother's, no other birthdays are noted in his diary.)

The Dudley West by-election in December went ahead without him. 'The count will not be the same without you,' wrote Richard Heller of the *Independent* in an open letter to Sutch. 'Reports say that you were forced to withdraw because you accidentally threw away your £500 cheque for the returning officer when clearing out rubbish from your home. Even for you this is a novel way of losing your deposit.' Paying tribute to Sutch's persistent attempts to be elected, Heller claimed:

No one has spent so much on getting into Parliament since the days of the 'rotten boroughs' when MPs actually paid for their seats. [In an interview a week before his death Sutch estimated he'd spent £80,000 on his campaigns.]

You have given voters a chance to underline their disenchant-ment with the mainstream political parties. It is healthier for them to express this through you rather than an extremist of Left or Right or a messianic billionaire; better a Monster Raving Loony with capital letters than a real monster raving loony without them.

Then Heller made a startling suggestion:

As Britain's longest serving political leader you are, by long-established convention, entitled to a life peerage on your retirement. I urge you to claim it and become, at last, a real Lord Sutch – you would look great in ermine robes, and nothing you could do or say would seem extraordinary in the House of Lords.

Three days before Christmas Sutch was in Wellingborough for a show at the Thunderbird Club, for a fee of £750. 'Paid OK,' he notes. Then for Boxing Day there is a tantalising entry: 'I could drink her bath water.' Whose, I wonder?

On 28 December he played Eastleigh's Railway Institute for £500 (probably to make up for the cancellation there in July), and that seems to be that for another varied but hardly lucrative year. Perhaps Sutch was even considering a change of direction: amongst the phone numbers at the back of his diary is one for Andy Roberts. Sutch notes: 'Great black singer for recording with me.'

The total fees listed in the diary between 22 November 1993 and 1 January 1995 add up to £23,320. To that you could add a few hundred pounds apparently paid by the 'tenant' of one of his properties, together with whatever he made from the Sekonda ads.

Given, as we shall see, that a new and alarming financial crisis was looming by now, in the shape of the house Sutch had purchased in Hastings, it is not difficult to calculate that he was not earning enough to sustain his lifestyle. Across a map of England towards the back of the diary, he wrote: 'Yogic breathing in, count 8, hold, count 8, out to count 8.' Sutch would need all the yogic calm he could muster to face what lay ahead.

chapter fourteen

Battle of Hastings

'However difficult his own life had been, he had brought gaiety to the nation, as well as political wisdom. He was not only the soul, but the life of the party, was he not?'

— DAVID ROBSON, *DAILY EXPRESS*

Having spent the majority of his life in a cosseted cocoon into which the real world could rarely intrude, David Sutch was forced to confront the big bad wolf in the shape of financial ruin. Reality was about to gatecrash his personal Never-Never Land.

He began the financial transaction which would lead him to the verge of bankruptcy while he was still living at Cynthia Payne's house.

'He was looking for a bolthole well away from Giselle,' Cynthia told me, and his friend, Lord Tiverton [a fellow Loony Party candidate] who lived in Hastings, told him about a property he knew there. I went down there with him – it was up a cliff with concrete steps up to the house, which had five bedrooms and a recording studio.

'I wasn't over enthusiastic, but he said it would be great for storing all his stuff and it would be somewhere for him to retire to when he got old. The owners were dying to get rid of it and kept ringing him for a decision. It would have been easy to tell them no, but he was determined to go ahead even though he had to take out a six-figure mortgage. I told him he must sell the place he had in Wembley before committing to this deal, but he didn't. He had received some money for a Heineken advert he'd done – about five grand, I think – and he used that as the deposit.'

Giselle also thought the purchase a bad idea: 'We fell out over the Hastings house. When I first met him I thought he had only one house. Then I found out he had another one, then another one – suddenly he had four; then he bought another, and that was five. They could and should have been a good investment. Lord Tiverton persuaded him to buy that terrible house, which was far too expensive ... [David] wanted to buy the house, but he hid the papers from me. I did not want to go and live at the English seaside, not at all. I did not think it was a good idea. He thought it was an excellent idea – and he was going to retire there, become an OAP with Lord Tiverton. We broke up first, maybe for a year, and then he bought the house. I had been stopping him because I could not share his enthusiasm. Then I accepted that we were not going to see each other.'

She tried constantly to persuade Sutch to sort out what she called the 'Hastings mess'. 'After we got back together, I said, you're paying so much each month on that bridging loan, you should do something about it.'" Sutch's response, though, was entirely predictable: 'He would not talk about it.'

Sutch referred to the house as 'my Chequers' and did indeed buy it after staying in Hastings with his pal 'Tivers', a millionaire who had bought his title after making his fortune from a chain of health food shops. 'Sutch got up at three or four a.m. and sat in my garden as the sun came up,' Lord Tiverton recalled, 'and fell in love with old Hastings.' It would be only three years after this optimistic dawn that Sutch's rash acquisition would almost bankrupt him – financially and emotionally.

Jack Irving, one of the Savages, remembers that when group members heard about the purchase they thought, 'Great! We can live upstairs and record downstairs.' With the recording studio in the basement (Sutch told everyone that the house had belonged to Mike Oldfield, but in fact it had been owned by Oldfield's sound engineer, Tom Newman), certainly Sutch could have invited other bands in to defray costs. But Irving says Sutch cleared all the recording gear out and sold it, using the space instead for storing the multitude of items he had acquired over the years: 'A very strange thing to do.'

By mid-1992 Sutch was beginning to realise that 'Chequers' was not a wise investment and came up with one of his barmy schemes to get rid of it. On 9 July, the *Sun* reported: 'He wants sixteen punters to gamble £10,000 each for the five-bedroomed property – on the spin of a roulette wheel.' Needless to say, the required number of interested parties failed to materialise.

Undeterred, he tried again in January 1995 (typically also hoping to reap some PR benefit into the bargain). The media revealed that Lord Sutch had 'announced he is selling his seaside home in Hastings, to finance 100 candidates at the general election in his biggest assault on the corridors of power. He said: "There could be a snap election. I have to be on red alert."'

That was the PR – now for the financial desperation. Sutch decided to auction the house at the town's White Rock Theatre on 18 January. 'I hope that the sale will raise £100,000 for the candidates. The house is my country retreat. I am making a £65,000 loss on the house – but it will be worth it,' he said. The auction produced no buyer.

By May 1995, with UK property values generally on a downward spiral, Sutch's finances were in dire straits. That month, *The Times* ran a front-page story revealing that he was 'threatened with bankruptcy over a £194,000 debt to Barclays Bank'. This of course could have far-reaching consequences: ultimately it could lead to his departure from the political scene, since bankrupts cannot stand for election.

Then the worst happened: Barclays issued a civil writ for £193,945.87, claiming Sutch had defaulted on a £120,000 bridging loan, plus interest.

In public, at least, Sutch was still trying to make a joke of the whole thing: 'They knew they were lending the money to a raving loony, I can't see why they're complaining now.' This was not likely to impress the bankers. On behalf of William Hill, I then pledged to fund election expenses for the Loony Party up to and including the next general election; there was nothing I could do for his personal finances, however. Unable to accede to Sutch's request that she buy the place herself, Cynthia Payne wrote to a National Lottery jackpot winner, suggesting that if he wanted to do some good with his windfall, he might consider buying Sutch's house to get him out of trouble? The answer was negative.

It was a media lawyer called Gary Jacobs, now deceased, who, according to Cynthia Payne, finally stepped in to rearrange David's finances, decreeing first that Sutch's property around the corner from Giselle's house in Notting Hill had to go (it sold for about £150,000). Sutch's PR John Tempest also helped out, contacting Barclays' chairman to request that he intervene to avoid bad publicity. By early June Barclays Bank announced, 'we have come to a mutually beneficial agreement concerning the outstanding monies' and Sutch's debts were reduced to a manageable level. He made only one rather downbeat and relieved comment: 'The bank had it in their power to make me bankrupt and they have declined to do that – they have been kind to me, I must admit.'

But the Hastings affair shook Sutch up more than he would confess at the time. 'It took him to the brink,' says Paul Barrett, one of Sutch's regular promoters, 'knocked away his security and was quite a blow to him. I think he realised that now he'd never catch up – he didn't have another thirty years in which to start over – he would now be chasing something he could not catch.' In a later interview for TV, carried out by Dave Painter of Hot under the Collar Productions and never screened, Sutch confessed: 'Between you and me, I had trouble sleeping – it kept whirling round – £196,000 [still exaggerating]! Then I did five gigs in one week and I gave that to the bank manager, and he said, "Thank you very much – but that doesn't even cover the interest." So then I did worry – and worried – and in the end I sorted it all out. I sold a house, sold it for peanuts, lost a lot of money, paid off the bank, and now I don't owe them anything, which is much clearer in the head because, after all, it's only bits of paper – and bits of paper are to wipe your bum on – that's all it is.'

Bob Gilbert, Sutch's long-term driver and right-hand man, believes that having to relinquish the London property caused Sutch to relapse into depression and anxiety. Sutch and Giselle had once planned to live there, renting out her house (a plan which never came to fruition). Sutch had moved a lot of stuff to Giselle's, mainly because whenever Giselle was away, he would pile up his booty there before having hurriedly to spirit it out to the other house on her return. Four storeys high, the Notting Hill house was now, like his other homes, filled to the brim with stuff and yet more stuff. There was a tenant living in the basement (who later lived in Sutch's house in Watford Road, Sudbury, which he still owned when he died) but 'the rest of the house,' says Gilbert, 'was virtually unliveable. He couldn't face up to emptying out the house, which Giselle and a friend of Sutch's had to do – they cleared eight skips full of rubbish. He got really uptight about it all.'

Gilbert was already well aware of Sutch's obsessive collecting: 'Once we were driving down the street and he shouted, "Bob! Bob! Stop!". He jumped out and dived head-first into a skip, emerging with a lump of wood which he insisted on taking home as it might prove useful. I think you can put an obsession of that kind down either to childhood conditions or to an inherited genetic make-up. His mother collected nick-nacks – she wouldn't throw things away – but she was nowhere near as extreme as him. He had to hire or buy garages to put his stuff in.'

While Sutch was trying to extricate himself from the Hastings debacle and throw himself back into the campaign trail (506 votes in the Islwyn by-election in February 1995 after Kinnock had resigned in January), a new scandal broke. Friends and fans were shocked to open the *Daily Mirror* on 3 March to read the headline: 'DARKER SIDE OF THE LOONY LORD: NOT SUTCH A NICE CHAP'.

Under an 'exclusive' tag, journalist Caroline Sutton revealed that Sutch's ex-girlfriend, Thann Quantrill (another new surname), was now claiming that the 'good-natured image he fosters hides a sinister side to his character'. Thann reported that Sutch 'once beat me up so badly I had two black eyes and a busted lip'. She was speaking out in response to the *OK!* feature in which Sutch had claimed that Tristan was studying politics at an American university in Houston and suggested that 'one day I'd like him to succeed me as Screaming Lord Sutch Jr.' She felt Sutch had neglected his financial responsibilities towards their child, and said that her twenty-year-old son was 'working in a grocer's store. He's struggling to make ends meet.' Tristan was quoted as saying: 'He doesn't know me very well. There's no way I would want to follow in his footsteps.' Thann alleged that Sutch had attacked her early in their relationship, after she called his mother 'a fat cow': 'He laid me on the bed and put his knees on my arms and started slapping me. I was terrified.' She did say, though, that the incident had never been repeated and that afterwards he apologised and bought her presents.

Sutch later defended himself: 'I admit I did hit Thann once. It was years ago and she had insulted my mother.' He said that he had been misquoted about Tristan.

Later, when Thann was charged with the murder of her then-husband, Sutch immediately rallied to her defence: 'He came from a Mexican family and was a bit hot-headed. They had an argument.' Thann was found guilty of murder in self-defence and sentenced to five years' probation; she said of Sutch at this time: 'He offered me support and never doubted my innocence. I could have gone to the electric chair.'

Meanwhile there was the Tayside, Perth and Kinross by-election in May. 'We decided the Jocks needed waking up,' John Tempest recalled, 'so we came up with the idea of tartan sheep. Most of the farmers weren't too impressed with the idea – but eventually the owner of the Auchingarrich Wildlife Centre saw the wisdom of supporting us and he and three friends brought four sheep. There was a man at each end – one to hold the book about tartans, and one to spray the sheep. Reuters flew a photographer from London; Channel 4, Sky and the local press arrived. David was persuaded to pose at the top of the hillside. This was to prove his undoing as the sheep decided to get their own back on this intruding Sassenach. They headbutted him, and the last thing the TV viewers saw was David sliding down the hill on his backside, with arms, legs and top hat going in different directions.'

The eventual tally was 586 votes.

Shows in Holland, France, Germany and Austria followed, and then in June a feature on Sutch appeared in the *Daily Express*'s magazine, *This Week*, in which he revealed that his favourite aunt, Enda (her real name was Edna but as a child he called her Enda), had died recently of cancer (this was the mother of his cousin, Linda Oliver). Later in the piece he bemoaned the state of his finances: 'I only play rock 'n' roll gigs in pubs now, so I don't earn much.' Signs of depression were evident as he told the reporter Jackie Holland, with an audible sigh: 'They say things come in threes. My aunt dies, my ex-wife is charged with murder and the bank slaps a writ on me. Life is very complicated. I thought I would be taking it easy by the time I reached my fifties.'

He managed to raise his game, nevertheless, to be the co-presenter of a live Radio Two concert at the end of June to celebrate National

Music Day, in which Showaddywaddy carried his coffin on stage for him to introduce 1970s acts like Les McKeown's Bay City Rollers, The Real Thing and The New Seekers. He contrived to double-book himself in July for gigs in Hammersmith and Milton Keynes, but still turn up at both, and in the same month hammer an upstart icon at the Greater Manchester by-election when the Loonies beat Mr Blobby by 782 votes to 105. Neil Crespin, Mr Blobby's agent, revealed to me that preliminary talks about an amalgamation of their parties stalled over the problem of whether to name themselves Bloonies or Lobbies.

Faced with something of an explosion in the number of frankly joke candidates – all no doubt taking their cue from Screaming Lord Sutch's indefatigable example – the BBC had wanted to restrict their coverage of minor candidates at this election to a two-minute pre-recorded interview. John Tempest was having none of it: 'Why should a well-established candidate like Sutch with a proper party,' he thundered as self-righteously as Alastair Campbell in defence of Labour, 'be treated the same way as some one-man band who came up with the idea for a party in the pub a day earlier? We took the BBC off our media list, and they eventually backed down.'

In August Sutch performed 'London Rocker' and 'Loony Rock' with the band Good Rockin' Tonite for the Platinum Films movie, *Over Exposed*. He mimed much of the first song, swigged at a bottle of bubbly then sang the wrong lyrics to the second.

Sutch absented himself from that year's Loony Party conference. He was believed to have been undergoing treatment for depression. Captain Sensible, formerly of the punk band The Damned, with whom Sutch had done gigs back in the early days of the New Wave, did attend, however, declaring that he joined the party because 'there are real lunatics in government at the moment and the Loonies certainly couldn't do any worse. At least we are honest about ourselves.' Still, Sutch was back early in the New Year to be fifth of ten with 652 votes at the Hemsworth by-election in West Yorkshire, and then to go to Holland for more gigs. At least one admirer over there was impressed by his political celebrity. Paul Barrett, one of Sutch's promoters, recalls a Dutch friend of his telling him, 'One Sunday we had Henry Kissinger on our top current affairs programme, the next week I saw your friend Screaming Lord Sutch as guest on the same show'.

But by now his mother's health was causing him significant concern: his appearance at the South-East Staffordshire by-election in April (506 votes) would be the last he would take part in for some fifteen months.

John Major's Conservative government was now seriously weak, and all parties were gearing up for the inevitable General Election in 1997. In September, therefore, the Loonies launched their election manifesto. *As Sutch: The Political Manifesto of the Official Monster Raving Loony Party*, published by McNaughty Books, was ostensibly written by Sutch himself, but actually ghost-written by Alwyn Turner, though the 'Sutch Fact File' section, listing his favourite things, was, apparently, his own work:

Colour:	Blue
Drink:	Tea and lager
City:	London
Country:	America
Occupation:	Feeding the birds
Band:	Creedence Clearwater Revival
Singer:	Little Richard, Ray Charles, Chuck Berry, Elvis
Film:	*Citizen Kane, The Maltese Falcon, Treasure Island*
Actor:	James Cagney, Humphrey Bogart
Book:	*Animal Farm*
Hobbies:	Collecting junk and records
Sport:	Boxing
Time:	1 p.m.
Animal:	Jack Russell terrier, parrot

The 'lager' reference is interesting, given his teetotal reputation. 'Maybe I saw him drunk once or twice,' Giselle told me, though rock 'n' roll promoter 'Just Janice', who has a reputation as a 'healer', told me Sutch asked her 'if you are able to help with drinking?'. The erudite choice of movies is a little surprising, given that Giselle said he liked *The Texas Chainsaw Massacre*, which suggests he had moved on from Hammer horror melodrama.

The manifesto contained its usual mixture of the almost sensible and the inane. On the one hand, 'All British hospitals will be twinned with hospitals in other countries, so that you can decide where you want to convalesce'; on the other hand, 'We will solve the problem of overcrowding in prisons by releasing all the innocent prisoners.' I like to think that I may have influenced another of the party's ideas for constitutional reform: 'Opinion polls will be banned during elections because they're too boring. Instead, daily odds – compiled by Lord Sutch's favourite bookmaker, Mr William Hill – will be quoted on all TV news broadcasts.' Another radical suggestion recommended that people who died prior to an election 'can leave their vote in their will'.

To launch it, Sutch, clad in gold suit, leopardskin top hat and sandwich board, spoke at an open-air meeting on London's Westminster Bridge, haranguing a John Major look-alike and unveiling the party's new slogan, 'New Loony, No Danger'. He committed the party to 'improve the weather by encasing London within a plastic dome and using heaters to recreate the tropics,' and his latest pledge to abolish January and February even made the headlines in the po-faced *Financial Times*: 'ABOLITION OF WINTER A LOONY PROMISE'. Sutch also supported the cause of British beef, then tainted by Mad Cow Disease or BSE: 'I've been eating it for years,' he declared dead-pan, 'and look at me.' At the party conference that year (where the guest of honour was the 1950s singer Ruby Murray) Sutch came up with one of those occasional and inspired flashes of wit which, in later years, had become rather less frequent. Asked about Loony ideas for reducing the dole queue, he replied: 'We'll make them stand closer together.'

One of the enduring myths about Screaming Lord Sutch is that he changed his name by deed poll to acquire the title 'Lord'. I had never been convinced that he had actually completed the necessary formalities, even though he is registered as Lord David Edward Sutch on Tristan's birth certificate, and my suspicions were somewhat confirmed by never-broadcast footage of an interview with him at this conference when the subject came up. 'I added the Lord on,' Sutch is shown explaining, 'because I wore a top hat and tails many years ago. No one objected to it, so I became ... squatter's rights, shall we say, on the title Lord – and as it went so many years without anyone objecting, I was able to put it on my passport and also my driving licence.' However, whilst rummaging through a pile of Sutch memorabilia towards the end of my research for this book, I came across the proofs of a series of photographs showing him, circa 1970, proudly displaying deed poll documents, although whether he ever got round to completing them may never be confirmed. Contrary to popular belief, there is no central register in the United Kingdom and no requirement to register a name change.

At the start of 1997 the new edition of the *Guinness Book of Records* made Sutch's record as the longest-serving political leader in the UK official. 'He has contested thirty-nine elections or by-elections and lost his deposit every time. Bookmakers William Hill offer shorter odds for Elvis Presley crashing a UFO into the Loch Ness Monster (14 million to one) than for Lord Sutch becoming prime minister (15 million to one).'

He may have lost every deposit, but in February, his name was brought up in Parliament during a debate on betting as an example to the whole House. 'My constituent, Screaming Lord Sutch,' said the MP for Harrow, Robert Hughes, 'has bet on himself and on the number of votes that he might receive in the many by-elections he has stood in and, in most cases, that is how he has paid his election expenses. It is a very good tradition.'

A general election was duly announced for 1 May 1997, but this time Screaming Lord Sutch would not get the chance to bet on himself. Two weeks before election day he announced in the *Daily Telegraph* that he would not be standing, 'because his elderly mother is ill'. Now eighty-one, she had gone into hospital. Julia Rothnie, a social worker at Northwick Park Hospital, to which Annie Sutch was admitted, recalls lengthy discussions about it between herself, Sutch and his mother: 'She wanted him to carry on, but he wanted to stand down for her sake.' Sutch had already cut back on his gigging since the tail end of the previous year, citing his mother's failing heath. But whether his concern was entirely genuine or conveniently excused the relative paucity of bookings is a moot point. 'This is the first time I have missed a general election since 1964,' he declared, 'but when you have family they come first,' which might have caused his son Tristan to raise an eyebrow.

Maybe this was an apposite opportunity to return to his first love – rock 'n' roll. Too many people, he felt, now only knew him for his political spoofery. He wanted to restate his rocking credentials, believed Savage Tony Dangerfield – and Ken Rumens, who promoted him in the West Country, recalled Sutch's reaction when Rumens had referred to him as a 'comedian'. "'I'm not a bloody comedian, I'm a rock 'n' roll singer," he said quite sharply. I think he resented the fact that he was no longer seen as the King of Horror Rock.'

John Major paid tribute to Sutch as a 'national institution – at the last election he was by far my most intelligent opponent'. The Liberal Democrat leader, Paddy Ashdown, said he hoped Sutch's absence would 'not last too long'. Unable to forfeit the limelight completely, Sutch maintained an election presence of a sort by promising one of the thirty-five Loony candidates, Nick Marsh (standing at Westminster), that he would attend as a supporter. He commented wistfully, 'It wouldn't be the same without me, would it?' His spirits might have lifted somewhat at the news that the confectioners, Thorntons, had already unveiled some special 'Sutch lollies' to go on sale during the election. But even at this time of personal turmoil – or perhaps because of it – Sutch was utilising his favourite political device of being economical with the truth. Far from this being his first absence since 1964, I can find no record of him having stood at the general elections of 1974, 1979 or 1987 either.

chapter fifteen

Keeping Mum at Loony Funeral

'Dave was never the same after Annie was gone. He lost everything, really'

— 'WILD' BOB BURGOS, FORMER SAVAGE

Annie Emily Sutch, also known as Nancy, died in Northwick Park Hospital on 30 April 1997, the day before the general election. Many believe that David Sutch's spirit effectively died with her. She passed away just after six o'clock in the evening: Sutch and his driver, Bob Gilbert, had been on their way up to her ward when a nurse intercepted them: the hospital, she told him, had been trying to reach him with the news that his mother had died shortly before. But it wasn't until 6 May that the news was made public, when John Tempest issued a press release on Sutch's behalf. Sutch was quoted as saying that 'my mum was most supportive of the Loony Party and she was popular with the candidates and members of the party. I didn't want to prevent them from having a good election by making the announcement sooner.' Annie Sutch died in the same hospital where Tristan had been born, and where Sutch's body would in due course be taken after his death.

According to Giselle (still Sutch's partner at the time), there had been plans for Mrs Sutch to enter a nursing or residential home when she left hospital, but they quickly went awry. 'The hospital was surprised that she died; they did an autopsy. Before she went into hospital she wasn't really eating properly, she'd lost her appetite. David was at a loss because he didn't know how to cook, and if I wasn't there he'd just go and get some fish and chips, which she did not eat ... I think she was in pain because she was always laying on her belly in bed. Then she fell in hospital and broke her hip.' Giselle understands that she eventually died of peritonitis.

Sutch reacted to his mother's death with a series of bizarre public comments. In an interview with the *Daily Telegraph*, for example, he linked her loss to defeat in politics: 'I've lost more than John Major [the outgoing Conservative prime minister who'd just been defeated in a landslide by Tony Blair's New Labour]. He's only lost a few seats. She meant everything to me. I would give up all I've got – I'd just stand here in my underpants – if I could bring her back.' For a man approaching retirement age, Sutch gave the impression that he was still extremely dependent on his mother.

'His mother was a sweet old lady,' recalls his friend Sid 'Elvisly Yours' Shaw, 'and he was devoted to her, driving her mad many times a day, constantly on the phone. Somehow she never got flustered and was a pillar of strength handling the press, rock promoters, girl-friends, politicians and all his weird and wonderful contacts in her stride.'

Everyone has to come to terms with both the fear and the reality of eventually losing their parents – and few people would regard a life of more than four score years as ending prematurely. Was he really grief-stricken for his mother, dead at eighty-one, or for himself, orphaned at fifty-six?

But he was unwilling to let her go easily. Seemingly unable to resist the chance for yet more self-publicity, he announced the 'First Monster Raving Loony Funeral' for his mother: 'A lot of my party will be there, because that's what she wanted.' But was it? It is hard to see how such an event could maintain or add to his mother's dignity. The public at large neither knew nor, therefore, much cared about Annie Sutch, and would hardly be expecting the opportunity to join a public outpouring of grief: to announce the news in a press release looked far more like a clumsy attempt by David to exploit his mother's death. Everyone who knew him was well aware that this was not the case (not consciously at least) – but it certainly looked that way. Perhaps (as his last girlfriend

Yvonne Elwood believed) Sutch was still beating himself up for not having been with his mother at the actual moment of her death.

Before the funeral Sutch was interviewed by Jane Kelly of the *Daily Mail*. He came slowly to the door, she wrote:

> Soberly dressed, with a pallid face and dark rings under his eyes, he looked utterly defeated. 'I dropped out [of the election] to look after Mum and thank God I did. The whole election passed me by. I was in a daze. I didn't know what I was doing. I was supposed to be with my candidate in Westminster. I went but I wasn't very good. I am supposed to make people laugh, but I couldn't even smile at people.

Kelly was struck by the state of Sutch's living conditions at his mum's house in Parkfield Road, which would shortly begin to deteriorate: 'In a room cluttered like a Victorian parlour with nursery pictures on the discoloured walls, pot plants, ornamental lamps, tea pots, three phones and piles of Loony Party election paraphernalia, he sat at a table clutching Rosie, his mother's Yorkshire terrier.' Sutch also confided to Kelly that 'Rosie wouldn't eat until I took her to the hospital for my mother to feed her.'

Kelly asked Sutch about the early years with his mother: 'I was very spoiled,' he replied. 'I never thought I had to help her at home. She did everything for me. An uncle of mine once told me to wash the bath out after I'd used it, and I was very surprised. When I first went to school I thought all the toys were for me. It took me a while to learn how to share anything.'

Whilst he clearly had no problems with being spoiled and becoming selfish – he continued with these traits for the rest of his life – he obviously felt stifled by his mother's attentions. He began to rebel but tried not to offend his mother in the process. For example, when she wanted him to get a respectable job he did, but at the same time began to grow his hair long, displaying the more ebullient side of his personality outside the house. 'At home he was a dutiful boy,' Kelly noted, 'but on stage he could be a raving monster.'

But try as he might – and he didn't, really – Sutch could not escape from the embrace of his mother's influence:

I've always been involved with women, but there was always Mum as well. Since I was a boy I felt sorry for her being on her own. From 1968 I didn't let her work and I supported her entirely. I was always on call for her – I came back from America if I thought she needed me. Girlfriends found this very annoying. Every woman I've ever been out with said I spent too much time with my mother, and they were bloody right.

Is that 'bloody' an expression of regret, or of defiant self-approbation? One wonders why his mother didn't help him cut the apron strings and move on. Her son, who all his life was surrounded by friends, managers, girlfriends or paid helpers, could not live without attention and assistance from others: perhaps his mother was just as needy of attention and love as him.

Perhaps one clue lies in a remark Annie made in 1991 to the journalist Marina Cantacuzino: 'He's always in so much of a hurry and there's never any time for him to do things for me round the house like clean my windows.' Had I been the interviewer I might have told Mrs Sutch that David was not the only window cleaner in town. She also said that she hated the idea of her son being without a proper family life 'when I'm dead', yet she hardly went about helping him develop one while she was alive. For instance, Sutch also confessed to Jane Kelly that even when Thann had the infant Tristan to care for, he 'often left her, to spend half the day with my mother. I'd do all her repairs and she'd give me chicken dinners, hot pot or lovely oxtail in gravy … I'd forget about time passing. Then it would be midnight. It wasn't fair.'

As Thann herself said: 'He would always look after her – she'd call, and no matter what it was, any little thing, he'd run over there and do it, and leave me, and I didn't know anybody. I hated that. Stuck in the house, knowing nobody, not able to drive over here. I think he was probably running away from his responsibilities.'

Giselle had to endure the same divided loyalty, says Pat Hellier: 'Giselle actually hated Mrs Sutch because of the bond she and David had. David would be round there, at perhaps three in the morning, and Giselle would be sitting outside in the car with her hand on the car horn.'

In another interview in 1995 Annie Sutch said: 'He's never married and, I think, never really left home. He still has his own room in my house and sometimes he'll stay here for up to three days at a time. I've always encouraged David to get married. I don't want him to end up alone and lonely. But these pop musicians, they're not really the marrying kind, are they?'

But Thann is not entirely convinced that Mrs Sutch was being honest: 'She hated me while I was here [in England] – as soon as I left she liked me, but then she didn't like Giselle – because nobody was good enough for her David.'

Some mothers, of course, do find it difficult to accept that any woman can be good enough for their beloved son. According to some sources, it was actually Mrs Sutch who forbade David to marry Thann. She seemed to be more enamoured with other girlfriends – but these were the ones he quite clearly had no intention of living with, let alone marrying, and who therefore presented no threat.

Perhaps that was why he jumped at the chance of teaming up with Cynthia Payne when his relationship with Giselle was under pressure – in the hope that his mother would find it hard to object to·someone almost closer to her own age than his. And although Cynthia is clearly telling the truth when she says that she and David only ever had a platonic relationship, there was that strange habit he had of calling her 'Mumsy'. Sutch may well have resented his mother's disparaging reactions every time he wanted her approval for someone he saw as being special. Did he keep running back to her, hoping that she would finally give him 'permission' to allow another female into their complicated relationship?

Cynthia told the *Sunday Times:*

When he was at his mother's he'd say to her, 'I'm just going out to get some milk' – and he'd be gone two weeks! Instead of saying to her, 'Look, I want to get away from you for a while,' he'd tell a lie. Because he didn't like to hurt people's feelings, he would cause more trouble. And, instead of telling a girlfriend, 'Look, we're finished', he would just disappear and get himself in such a mess.

He was happy – desperate, even – to be treated as a son, but, as we have seen, strangely unwilling to carry out his own paternal duties. Yet in his discussion with Kelly, Sutch was still unwilling to accept any responsibility for Thann walking out on him: 'My mother was partly the reason – but it was also to do with the British climate.'

He ended his interview with Kelly in defiant, yet unconvincing mode. 'The future is bright, really. I do feel that my mother is here with me in spirit. At the next by-election I will be back. That is what she would have wanted. Just wait, I will be back bigger, stronger and even loonier – if that is possible.'

Sutch's first public appearance following his mother's death was a party on 10 May in Kensington for fellow Loony candidates. He announced on stage – and in the media – that the night was dedicated to Ma: 'She started it all.' How, other than by giving birth to him, she did so, was not explained and, in fact, she was not exactly supportive of his original career path in his formative years.

The funeral was delayed for a few days to allow his close friends Pat and Ken Hellier and Kim Roberts to return from holiday. It was eventually held on 14 May at the South Harrow church, where Sutch's own funeral would take place just over two years later. 'Friends and family wore outlandish outfits,' reported the local newspaper, 'to reflect the spirit of Annie Sutch, who died on the eve of polling day.' But she was never outlandish.

A fiddler played outside the church and Sutch handed out badges to mourners that read 'Annie Emily Sutch Lives On'. Many of the mourners, who were mainly made up of Sutch's friends and business associates, and included an Elvis look-alike in the person of his great friend Leyton Summers, another who would die tragically, felt uncomfortable about the badge. John Tempest chose not to wear his. Sutch had arranged for his mother's favourite song – 'Rose Marie' by Slim Whitman (a hit in 1955) – to be played (Legendary Lonnie had sent Sutch a copy of the record when he couldn't find one). The Loony Party's deputy leader Melodie Staniforth was one of those present: 'He asked if we would take a piece of Yorkshire stone down to place in his mother's grave, so that she would have a bit of Yorkshire with her.' Sutch threw a rose into the grave.

According to some reports, Sutch and Giselle argued that day and she later sent him packing. Giselle told me that she regarded the funeral as a pivotal moment in Sutch's life: 'I think he probably decided to die then ... I remember I saw the car going away with his mother's coffin, and I saw in the hearse a huge photograph of him with his mother – as if he was going to be buried with her. I should have understood the meaning of that. He bought a double plot. I think he planned it [his suicide]. When we were standing with him in the church and they were playing the music his mother loved, he was crushing my hand. I think there and then he was going to go with her.'

She feels that the fact he had no headstone put on her grave was significant: 'It was not necessary if he was going to go. Don't forget, he was extremely depressed by that time – extremely. He'd been on Prozac for so long and he was taking so much medicine that his mind was swimming.'

But surely his medication was designed to alleviate his symptoms?

'Prozac will give you the strength to commit suicide,' is Giselle's bitter riposte. 'Everybody will tell you that.'

'Dave was never the same after Annie was gone,' says Savages drummer 'Wild' Bob Burgos. 'He lost everything, really. Shortly after his mum went he split up with Giselle. He tried to carry on, but I could tell his mind was elsewhere. He was in a dream world. He'd lost his fighting spirit.'

After Sutch's death, the psychotherapist Susie Orbach wrote a piece in the *Guardian* about the reaction of men to their mother's death. 'What do Screaming Lord Sutch, Lenny Henry, David Hockney and the new Poet Laureate Andrew Motion have in common?' she asked. The answer was that in every case these well-known men had found the experience of losing their mother indescribably painful. Orbach then suggests that our culture is not very accepting of the 'important relationship' between a man and his mother. 'All the more surprising, then, when a mother dies and the son's distress becomes destabilising. We don't expect it. We're made uncomfortable, as though it's unseemly to recognise the significance of this relationship.' She asks, 'Are we right to believe that Screaming Lord Sutch was continually desperate for his mother's approval, needed her to acknowledge his outrageousness as a way to manage how suffocating she was? Is it right that her death took the stuffing out of him so that there was not reason enough to live?'

Certainly it is the perceived wisdom amongst the majority of those who knew both Sutch and his mother – and very many that didn't – that Annie Sutch doted on her son and that the feeling was mutual. Mrs Sutch's sister-in-law, Mary, told me that Annie was herself a great collector of Sutch memorabilia: 'She told me she went to markets and bought anything she could find in connection with Lord Sutch.' Ray Wade, Mrs Sutch's neighbour, who frequently accepted her invitations 'to pop round for a cup of tea', found that she 'talked about David the whole time'.

'At first mother didn't quite understand,' confesses Sutch in the 1965 *Arena* interview, around the time he first bought a home for his mum, 'but now I've bought a nice house and different odds and ends, we live very comfortably where we used to live in just a couple of rooms.' Television footage of the Watford Road home shows his love of obscure accessories already beginning to flourish – a pet rat sits on top of a speaker while Sutch shaves. Large vases and mantelpiece ornaments are visible. 'I think she's very, very pleased that I've got on the way I have,' he continues. 'Everyone was against me at first, really – including my mother.'

Cynthia Payne, however, believes that the mess he made of his mother's house with his hoarding and collecting was not to Annie Sutch's taste at all: 'She used to cry sometimes because she was so embarrassed when people came into her house.'

But although David Sutch made great play of his close relationship with his mother, even the very matter of his mother's headstone seems to offer some evidence to the contrary. When he committed suicide his mother had already been dead for over two years – yet he had still not organised a headstone on her grave. Some theorised that to do so would have been too final an act for him, forcing him to accept that she had gone for good. Yvonne Elwood believes this was why he never visited his mother's grave.

But Sutch never, I discovered, even made an application to the local council for permission to erect a headstone. One possible reason is his renowned financial tightness: Harrow Council confirmed that it did not make an additional charge if one grave was used as the final resting place of two members of the same family. In this analysis, the cash-canny Sutch went for a bizarre kind of burial buy-off, figuring it made sound financial sense to invest in a two-graves-for-the-price-of-one deal that would save him about a thousand quid and perhaps defer the bill for a headstone for both of them to be footed by someone else.

Iris Little, wife of original Savage Carlo, told me a fascinating story about Yvonne Elwood, Sutch's last partner, attempting to do some clearing up in the kitchen at Parkfield Road after his mother had died, and coming across a misshapen old piece of marble which David's mother would use to make her pastry on. Yvonne wanted to throw it out and told David to get rid of it. 'But that's Ma's marble!' he protested, suddenly downcast at the thought of having to dispense with the redundant object, and instead took it outside to the garden, where he sat considering it for some while. 'When he came back in he had a smile on his face,' Iris recounts. '"I know!" he said. "I'll have Ma's headstone made out of it – she'll like that."'

Sutch grew up almost exclusively under female influence – and only one strong female at that. His father, William, had died before his first birthday and his mother's one long-term dalliance with 'Uncle Benny' does not seem to have yielded much in the way of male input. In the 1965 *Arena* interview, Sutch claimed not to have missed a father figure in his life: 'As a child I never noticed that I didn't have a father because my mother was so good at seeing to all of my needs. Also I used to go and stay with her family in Yorkshire where my uncles always took a great interest in me.' But Thann says that David would never tell her what had happened to his father – 'His mother told me.' When she was sorting through Sutch's personal effects after his suicide, however, she discovered a sympathy card from his father's funeral, perhaps given to him by his mother or found amongst his mother's things when she died.

From adolescence onwards, however, he did lead his social life within a close, almost familial, male-dominated circle, and certainly Sutch once confessed to a journalist that 'I would have liked a father to confide in and advise me on money matters. He might have stopped me going wrong in the sixties when I was making good money.' Perhaps this is one reason why Sutch in adult life was so keen to develop and sustain relationships with older male role models, such as Reg Calvert, Alan Hope, Carlo Little and Lord Tiverton. But given his mother's account of his father ignoring him as a young baby, whether his own

The Man who was Screaming Lord Sutch

father would have fulfilled these desires seems debatable. Like father, like son?

It is an irony that Sutch's own son, Tristan, would also have to come to make do without a permanent father. To an extent Sutch's chaotic lifestyle made this inevitable, although even when Tristan was living thousands of miles away in America he did sporadically endeavour to keep tabs on his son. 'I remember Dave speaking to me once and looking very worried,' says one of Sutch's close friends. 'He told me he had to go to the States because Tristan – who must have been in his early teens at the time – was playing up and getting involved in petty crime. Dave was going to talk some sense into him – and I believe he did just that.'

Peter Stockton, occasional backing musician and friend, who knew Sutch for nearly twenty years, tells of how, during a long telephone conversation, Sutch once confessed to being 'consumed with guilt over his mother's death. He felt that if he had spent money on private treatment, she might still be alive. I tried to reassure him with the story of my own mother's death, but all to no avail.' Which begs the question: if Sutch truly believed he might have prolonged his mother's life via private treatment then why did he not try to get it for her?

Cynthia Payne feels one of David's deepest problems was his complicated relationship with his mother. Even after Payne and Sutch broke up and Sutch was with his last girlfriend Yvonne Elwood, it was still problematic. 'I told Yvonne I felt he had a guilt complex about his mum,' she told me. 'He didn't take her out enough, and I always told him he'd be lost without her and to do what he could for her while she was still around. There was a time when I noticed his mum was wearing stockings with holes in them – no woman likes that – and she told me she'd asked David to get her new ones but he wouldn't so I got some and sent them to her.' (Sutch's loyal friend and helper Pat Hellier also told me that she shopped for Mrs Sutch. 'He'd phone me up and say, "Do you think you could get her a pair of slippers?"').

Yet David would help other people's mothers. Wild Bob Burgos remembers, 'Sutch would always treat my Mum with great respect and would go out shopping for her. I would come round to find him out in the garden trimming and pruning plants for her.'

'He cared about his mum – but he didn't care enough,' confirms

Cynthia's assistant Gloria Walker (who co-wrote *Sexplicitly Yours: The Trial of Cynthia Payne* and acted as election agent for Sutch on a number of occasions). 'I think he was actually ashamed of her and her working-class background. He didn't love her as much as he should – and she didn't approve of his lifestyle. She wanted him to work. He loved the idea of his mother, but was ashamed of the person she was and probably resented her. He would never even spend Christmas with his mother, but would drop everything if Giselle called.'

'When Giselle said "jump" he would jump,' agrees Cynthia, adding that Mrs Sutch 'hated Giselle, because she kept David away from her'.

Ursula Symonds, wife of Savages drummer Martin, and a good friend both of Sutch and Giselle, thought Mrs Sutch had implanted feelings of guilt in her son which he found difficult (if not impossible) to reconcile, a view shared by many of his friends: 'He had come from the background of an over-domineering, over-loving mother. His rebellion against convention was in response to his childhood when he was over-protected by his mother who had just given him too much love. He needed to get away from her but felt guilty. He always felt guilty when he was at Giselle's beautiful, 300-year-old house near the Seine – he had been brought up to feel guilty when he was happy. After his mother died, David suddenly elevated her to sainthood, which was an absurdity. He suddenly made a monster into a saint, and he split with Giselle and took up with Yvonne, who was the same kind of woman his mother had been … His relationship with his mother was so muddled, and it became even more confused when she died – he started to look at Giselle through his mother's eyes. She had once referred to Giselle as "that French tart".'

According to Thann, David's sudden post-death devotion to his mother took on a quasi-religious aspect when he built a bizarre shrine to her in the corner of the living room in Parkfield Road. 'He collected all the flowers from Nancy's casket and took them home,' Thann told the *Mail on Sunday*. 'He built this altar to her with pictures and the flowers, which ended up drying out. It was a little shrine to her. The relationship was always unnaturally close. It was one of the reasons I left him.'

Later she told me that 'he continued to buy gifts for his mother, writing: "To Ma" on them – even though she was dead.'

Could there even have been an altogether darker reason for Sutch's ambivalent relationship with his mother? Is it possible that he was sexually abused as a youngster? A couple of people who knew him well and thought carefully about him suggested this independently of each other. Could he subconsciously have blamed her for letting it happen? I discovered no evidence to support this theory but it could explain some of the more extreme elements of his long-term behaviour and his inability to sustain personal commitment.

Perhaps it was only by elevating his mother to untouchable status that he was able to purge the guilt he felt at treating her in a neglectful manner. It certainly appears that on one level he found it easier to deal with his mother dead rather than alive.

Psychologists would no doubt find it interesting that Sutch took his own life in his mother's house. A tribute to her or the ultimate act of rebellion?

chapter sixteen

Life Must Go On?

'He is a British institution. Some say he should be inside one'
— JAMES CUSICK, THE *Independent*

Sutch was at a very low ebb following his mother's death when fate intervened. His long relationship with Giselle had been in trouble for some time, but now a new woman unexpectedly arrived on the scene. Those who would believe that Sutch's suicide was an inevitable consequence of his mother's death would argue that he took up with Yvonne on the rebound from 'Ma'.

Yvonne Elwood was an attractive divorcee, younger than Giselle, with a couple of grown-up kids who 'hadn't had a boyfriend for years'. They met when Sutch was campaigning in the Uxbridge by-election in July 1997. 'I joined the party to have some fun but ended up falling in love,' Yvonne told me. They canvassed together up the Uxbridge High Street, then retired to a pub (as usual, Sutch ordered a pot of tea). Yvonne vaguely understood him to be in a relationship and was 'confused at the way he was flirting with me'. When they said goodbye he gave her a kiss 'and held my hand. It was love at first sight.' But Yvonne came with some baggage from a previous relationship – a family – which David may have been unwilling, or unable, to take on.

Sutch's fortunes seemed to be looking up: shortly after the by-election he was hired to open the Erotica Exhibition in Stoke-on-Trent, carried into the hall in a sedan chair by half-naked body-builders and girls who wore nothing but latex paint. In the Uxbridge campaign itself, despite suffering from a trapped sciatic nerve throughout, he once again dealt a political death-blow to a party leader. This time it was Alan Sked of the Eurosceptic UK Independence Party, who (long before their subsequent successes in 2004 when joined by the charismatic television personality Robert Kilroy-Silk) trailed behind Sutch's 396 votes. Sked, an academic, learnt his lesson and quit.

At the end of September, Sutch began filming – at Giselle's house – for the television programme *Through the Keyhole*, even though his affair with Yvonne was secretly developing. (The programme is all about guessing the identity of someone from the inside of their house – but they couldn't possibly have done it from the rubbish-filled dump of Parkfield Road, Sutch's real home, which would have been a more appropriate subject for *Life of Grime*.) According to Yvonne, she and Sutch slept together for the first time at the Loony Party conference in September but 'did not have sex'. By October though, Sutch's relationship with Giselle was effectively over: 'I didn't want to end up as his bit on the side,' said Yvonne, and by November Sutch had already moved in to her house in Reading . Yvonne acceded to his wish that she give up her work as a supply teacher to look after him: 'I found the prospect of looking after him attractive because he seemed so neglected. His mother had made him lazy.' Once again he was playing out one of the central conundrums of his life: the inability to fully commit himself combined with his inability to fully live alone. Straight away Yvonne was confronted with the other central issue of Sutch's existence: 'He had an inordinate amount of junk – records, books, bric-à-brac, everything. My house was filled with it.'

Around the same time, Sutch also had a falling-out with Bob Gilbert, his driver for almost eight years. 'I moved David out of Giselle's when he left to live in Reading with Yvonne. After that it seemed that his timekeeping went out of the window. I used to tell him he had to be somewhere earlier than he really did which meant he might just get there on time, but once he was with Yvonne he wasn't getting himself to places on time and he began to acquire a reputation for not being too reliable.'

In *Life As Sutch,* Sutch explained his timekeeping philosophy: 'My own sense of timing has been known to try the patience of even my best friends. I keep what I describe as a flexible attitude to appointments.

That way, by not having set up the expectation of being on time, I do not disappoint when I am late.'

But now Sutch's timekeeping became so erratic, Gilbert told me, as to cause him to miss at least three gigs: 'On one occasion I turned up to take him to a gig up north only to find him in his pyjamas and unshaved. I had to wait for over an hour while he got himself ready.' The crunch came when Gilbert organised a gig at the Railway Hotel in Wealdstone in the November, a couple of days before Sutch's fifty-seventh birthday: 'Everyone else arrived on time at 8 p.m., but David didn't turn up until midnight. That was the final straw.'

Was this his already established tardiness or the escalation of depression? Yvonne recalled the incident well. She told me they had been out during the day at Portobello Market, 'which he loved', where David lost his car- and house-keys. When they eventually found them there was still plenty of time to get to Wealdstone – that is, until Sutch insisted on a full, sit-down tea. 'It was getting later and later but he wasn't at all concerned – he just presumed we'd be there in good time. When we finally arrived, at about eleven, people had already begun leaving – and they were not happy. Because we hadn't been together long I think people thought I was responsible, but I wasn't.'

Guitarist Paul Green was in the band that night: 'Dave walked into the hall as though nothing was wrong. After the gig he told the band they wouldn't be getting paid as the amount due to them would just about cover what they owed him for the extravagant room bills they'd run up in a Hamburg hotel when they'd been there with him recently.'

But Sutch's general profile was still high. At the end of November he appeared on the hugely popular Saturday evening BBC television programme *Noel's House Party*. The following month he was a guest (appropriately enough) on *It's Later Than You Think*. But that November's by-election in Winchester, though he did not know it, was to be his final political hurrah. He would never again contest another election.

Sutch managed a respectable fifth place out of eight. It made a total, during his long political career, of forty-one parliamentary elections, in which he had polled 15,657 votes along the way. He had also had a crack at one Euro-election, with the odd local council campaign thrown in. Only a Canadian, John 'the Engineer' Turmel, according to the *Guinness Book of Records*, could boast a more prolific political CV.

With Giselle and driver Bob Gilbert now out of the picture, Yvonne began her efforts to organise the famously disorganised Loony. At the end of the year they went on holiday to Cyprus, where she says Sutch proposed to her. Instead of a ring he gave her a gold medallion from around his neck: 'I said yes,' says Yvonne, 'but we made no real plans.' Even on holiday, though, Sutch was unable to resist the lure of publicity, telling Radio Napa he wanted to set up a Loony branch on the island. Away from the UK Sutch noticeably relaxed. 'No one knew who he was,' said Yvonne. 'He liked that, he could be anonymous.'

The first time Yvonne ever saw Sutch depressed was the February of the following year, 1998: 'He had been on anti-depressants but suddenly came off them. He did it without guidance and was very low.' He kept up a jokey presence in the political arena, in April talking up the possibility of his running in the contest for London's first elected Mayor – 'I want to introduce heated pavements which will benefit pensioners. I'd also have a pirate ship in the Thames alongside Parliament, and any MP found lying would be forced to walk the plank' – and even offering a job-share deal to his fellow candidate (and the eventual victor) Ken Livingstone: 'I get on very well with him. He could do the mornings and I'd do the afternoons and evenings.' In the summer, with the sensational revelation of the American president Bill Clinton's affair with Monica Lewinsky, Sutch immediately expressed his 'reluctant willingness' to step down as leader of the Monster Raving Loonies in favour of Clinton, in the event of him having to renounce the Presidency. Although clearly a joke, similar to the time he had offered to stand down for David Owen, perhaps this was the first genuine sign that Sutch was tiring of the political merry-go-round and hoping to find a way to get off.

Tragedy intruded into his life again in May when Melodie Staniforth's twenty-one-year-old daughter, Sammy, died. At the 1998 Loony Party conference, which attracted media from Mexico, Thailand and Poland, Sutch did not seem on top form: at one point he appeared for an interview still wearing his pyjamas and dressing gown, with shaving cream on his face. Melodie Staniforth later took a photo of him smiling in the kitchen of the Golden Lion in Ashburton, where they were having a chat and a cup of tea: 'He told me he had made up his mind to leave Yvonne and go to live back at his mum's house and sort things out. Then the strangest thing happened: he gave me his mobile telephone number and told me to ring him. I had never known Dave have a mobile before. I still have the number.'

Ian Scouler, drummer with a band called Thee Waltons who frequently backed Sutch, recalled another poignant incident at the end-of-conference party. The band started playing the old hit, 'Wipeout', and Alan Hope screamed out Sutch's name, with the light shining on the doorway he was supposed to come through. 'And ... nothing,' recalls Scouler. 'Again he shouted, the crowd applauded and ... nothing. Eventually someone went to look for Sutch. He was found, slumped at the bottom of the stairs, having had one too many Babycham shandies. Trouper that he was, he got straight up, top hat on, marched in and gave it large amounts of "All Black and Hairy".' This is a very rare suggestion of Sutch over-indulging in alcohol.

And how would Sutch have felt about the dubious accolade of seeing his *Heavy Friends* album – his best ever seller – picked out that September on the BBC website as Worst Album of All Time? The news item followed the publication of Colin Larkin's encyclopaedic book, *All Time Top 1000 Albums*, but while some 200,000 votes were collected to determine the number one choice, it turns out that Larkin alone was responsible for declaring *Heavy Friends* the pits. How did the pressure of continuous failure weigh on Sutch? Did the realisation that he was celebrated only for his failures contribute to his fate?

He could count one small victory that year, however: the belated introduction, decades after he had first proposed the mad idea, of passports for pets. Now, he told the *Daily Express,* he planned to take his parrot ('called Ziz-ziz because that's all it ever says') to the States.

For the rest of the year his friends and acquaintances saw differing sides of him. A trip to Newcastle to visit a record fair, after Sutch had volunteered his services to help raise cash for the Sunshine Fund charity, turned into a memorable weekend. According to Ray Nicholls, the local record shop owner with whom Sutch, Yvonne and former Savage Alan Clayson stayed, David was a star at the fair, selling souvenirs he'd brought with him, signing autographs and 'chatting with anyone and everyone', but in terms of organisation, he was 'an absolute shambles. Yvonne [with whom he had now reportedly bought a house in Reading] had to arrange everything for him. She totally looked after him and was his "crutch".'

'It took absolutely hours to drive to Ray's,' said Yvonne. 'David insisted on stopping for tea at almost every service station en route. It was past midnight and we still weren't there so we booked into a hotel which didn't accept animals and smuggled Rosie in by cramming her into my case.'

The remainder of the weekend included an unexpected meeting with Jimmy Savile, who happened to be in town for the Great North Run, and with whom Sutch spent some time reminiscing, the escape of Rosie, and the best part of the day at the local A&E for Alan Clayson having a tetanus jab after the ungrateful dog savaged his hands when he finally caught her.

Sutch was still managing to perform occasionally: a tribute concert at Sudbury's Rising Sun pub alongside Joe Brown, P.J. Proby and Clem Cattini in aid of an ailing Wee Willie Harris, and Hallowe'en night in Hamburg for a 'Star Club Remember Concert', where Sutch shared the bill with Gerry and The Pacemakers and Dozy, Beaky, Mick and Tich. The German music writer Thorsten Schmidt, recalls the time Sutch spent after the gig, 'signing photos, selling some of his books and talking with people', as 'the highlight … It was a really funny hour, a great pleasure for all.' Looking portly but happy, he attended Carlo Little's sixtieth birthday party in December. In his leopardskin shirt and black-and-white top hat, he stood out in the 'official' photograph amongst the crowd of conservatively dressed fifty- and sixty-somethings, who had accepted their hell-raising days were past.

In the November, however, he had appointments with doctors working for the Wokingham and District Mental Health Service, including the psychiatrist who would later give evidence at his inquest. In December he was prescribed fifty-six tablets of Lithium, a mood stabiliser for patients already under treatment for depression, and a drug whose potential benefits are very dependent on abiding by the dosage instructions.

Just before Christmas, he turned up for a meal at one of his regular haunts in South Harrow. 'He looked awful,' remembers Jasmine Bearman of The Café. 'I gave him something to eat and he said it was the first meal he'd had in five weeks.'

There can be no argument as to whether David and Yvonne were 'an item' that Christmas: the card he sent to friends Pat and Ken Hellier was signed 'David Sutch and Eve [sic]'.

On New Year's Eve, when the rest of the nation was preparing to celebrate the imminent arrival of 1999, David Sutch went to see his doctor again.

chapter seventeen

Sutch's Last Love

'Here today. God tomorrow'

– DAVID SUTCH

To many of David Sutch's friends and associates, Yvonne Elwood is variously seen as having foisted herself upon an unwilling victim (whom she then tried to inveigle into matrimony), or else as a bad influence, manipulating and dominating a defenceless Sutch against his will. She was known to some as 'Roadrunner'. Even my William Hill colleague, Romaine Snijder, recalled Sutch – the Loony – saying, 'She's barmy.' It seemed that everyone I spoke to for this book had an opinion about Yvonne: that never in a million years would David have willingly chosen to commit the rest of his life to her – and hadn't she proved herself a disruptive presence at his funeral, trying to muscle in on the arrangements, suggesting that she was as entitled to whatever David was leaving behind as anyone else? Most of the stories I heard about Yvonne Elwood, however, also seemed to come from somebody who had heard it from someone else; few were first-hand and hardly anyone was prepared to go on the record. Some were just plain malicious.

Obviously I tried to hear everything direct from the horse's mouth, but for a while all my efforts to contact Yvonne failed. Finally I tracked down a telephone number for her through a model agency where she used to work. The woman who answered was charming and accommodating and chatted away openly, even indiscreetly. She had not returned to her old job of supply teaching after Sutch's death and was now living in a house in Worcester Park, Surrey, which she was renovating: 'I suspect I've picked the wrong time to do that.' It was she, of course, who had found Sutch's body. She still has flashbacks to the terrible sight that confronted her when she opened the front door.

Finally, early in 2004, Yvonne agreed to come and see me. She arrived with a kiss of welcome, but in true Sutch style was so late that I'd virtually given up on her. She was full of apologies: 'David got in quite a bit of trouble over his lateness. I'm quite a punctual person and I used to be worried for him because he'd arrange to do a gig but not get there. I remember driving up to Stone in Staffordshire when there were floods. We left much too late and it took us so long that by the time we got there they were packing up to come out. He just had time to have a cup of tea, turn round and go back again after taking five hours to get there. Agents would be phoning up to say, "Where is he?" and I'd be saying, "We're just leaving now", but we wouldn't be. He'd be saying, just one more cup of tea, and we should have been there an hour ago. He wouldn't care. Time had no meaning at all for him. He'd say, "I'm just going into this shop." And I'd be sitting in the car and he'd come out an hour and a half later.'

I suggested to Yvonne that perhaps this was a consequence of an over-indulgent parent never chiding him: 'No, I don't think it had anything to do with his mum.' Her take on it was both more banal and more illuminating. Sutch had simply begun to 'get lazy – all he ever wanted to do was read the papers, go to the shops, feed the ducks – we'd go out at one or two and still be sitting there at six or seven. I'd take a book. He tended to let down a lot of people at that time – he'd phone them and say, "I'm ill", or that the car had broken down.'

This lassitude may have been due in part to the medication he was taking – anti-depressants are downers, tending to slow one down – but Yvonne believes that he was clearly falling out of love with the hard grind of his dual life: 'I think he was ready for semi-retirement. We liked to wander round the charity shops. He loved to watch telly – why should we drive up to Leeds and do a gig? But there was something in him – he couldn't stop completely but was being more selective. I think that if he were still alive he would have cherry-picked the gigs he wanted to do – he still would have gone to Wales, for example [for the Man Versus Horse Marathon] but I don't think he felt the need to work as much. Likewise, with the politics, I think he would have just done less of everything. I don't think physically he was a well man … He never stopped eating well, though – he had a very good appetite. He liked steak – I'm a vegetarian but I had to cook him steak nearly every night.

'He was, though, almost addicted to painkillers – some days he would take fourteen painkillers. He'd say, "I've got a headache", but the pills were causing the headaches – the more you take, the less effective they are.'

Very soon after they met, Yvonne took over all the driving (Sutch's driver Bob Gilbert had already quit): 'The last time I remember him driving was in 1997 – we had finally moved the last of his gear out of Giselle's in about October. He nearly killed us coming along Goldhawk Road – there was a mini roundabout and he just went straight over it. There was a lorry coming the other way – I don't know how it stopped. He was just unaware; most people look at other cars on the road but he didn't do that. After that he let me take over the driving.'

Yvonne recalled their time together fondly and seemed more at ease with herself (and with David's place in her life) than I'd sensed when we had met before. She spent much of the three hours we had together concentrating on positive memories, emphasising the fun they had together and the way David was forever playing practical jokes.

She told me about the early days of their relationship: 'When I first met him I had a job, but I packed it up because he expected me to be there all the time. A week after the 1997 party conference he moved in properly with me and my daughter. Very soon after he got her the job with Circus of Horrors.'

A few years earlier Sutch had got to know Dr Haze, one of the principal performers with this gruesome but excitingly entertaining touring revue, very much in the spirit of Sutch's ghoulish early live shows. The job for Yvonne's daughter, Alex, involved squeezing herself into a tiny bottle on stage.

But very soon after they moved in together, Yvonne became aware of the anguish his continual collecting caused him: 'When we were in Wales that last weekend [before he died] he was saying he wanted to totally clear out the stuff in Watford Road and Parkfield Road, sell them both and buy one nice new house where the heating worked and the windows opened – those were his words, not mine. We'd made a start by going up to the paper bank with bags of newspapers, some of which were ten or fifteen years old. That sounds normal to me and you, but to him that was a really difficult thing to do. It was almost heartbreaking.

'This was his terrible conflict – logically he did actually know, "I've got to get rid of this stuff, I can't move on with my life, it's dragging me down." We decided to get rid of the old rubbish, take the things that had no real value to charity shops. The valuable stuff he was going to put in an auction. We made a start but it was a drop in the ocean. If I was away, when I came back he'd have brought in more stuff. He didn't want to do it. He wrote down, "I must get rid of this stuff." It worried him.'

Yvonne then offered up a startling theory about the cause of Sutch's obsessive collecting: that he suffered from Asperger's Syndrome. The syndrome, on the mildest end of the autism spectrum, is, according to a website dedicated to the condition, 'characterised by severe and sustained impairment in social interaction, development of restricted and repetitive patterns of behaviour, interests and activities. Adults with Asperger's have trouble with empathy and modulation of social interaction – the disorder is usually lifelong. Idiosyncratic behaviours are reported. Depression and bipolar disorder are often reported in those with Asperger's.' Certainly Sutch displayed some of these characteristics.

While I can't be sure this was ever professionally diagnosed, Yvonne is adamant that they both thought it to be the case. She certainly believes David knew he had it: 'He hoarded everything – I believe that was part of his illness. Many of the things he did were not eccentric, they were symptoms of what was wrong with him. I just wish I'd understood more about it at the time.'

It is only since Sutch's death that Yvonne has achieved a certain perspective on their time together. 'I mean, probably, OK, yes, he was mad. Probably I had to be mad myself – we were two nutters. I've been told his mum used to tell people he was mad – she knew he wasn't like a normal bloke. Until the time he died I was mentally an adolescent. His death made me grow up.

'It was a very fun time – the time of my life. The rest of my life I'd give up for those two years. It was a very short, but strange, period. I'm confident we would still have been together now. If we rowed they were rows like fifteen-year-olds would have – "Oh yes you did, Oh no you didn't." I realised I was never going to be number one, I couldn't replace his mum, but I think he also realised he wouldn't find anyone to look after him so well.'

She went on to make a strange revelation: 'He did do a lot of very naughty things, and he'd make me do naughty things. It was very good that we never got caught because, looking back, it would have been awful to be in the papers – Lord Sutch and his girlfriend arrested for …' She suddenly became more circumspect. 'Well, some of the things that we did were bad enough to get arrested – yes, definitely. But again, they were mischievous. He'd only tell the papers what he wanted them to know – the things the papers didn't get to hear they'd have liked more.'

What could she be hinting at? I wondered. Nicking towels from hotels? Or something more serious? Yvonne and Sutch as South Harrow's own Bonnie and Clyde? Whatever it was that they got up to, Yvonne wouldn't be drawn further.

Like all Sutch's relationships that had gone before, theirs was an on-off one. In early 1999 they split up temporarily when first Yvonne and then David developed flu. She had been unhappy that he failed to look after her when she had been laid up with the illness, and on New Year's Day 1999 they rowed. She gave him back the engagement ring he had now given her, 'wrapped in Christmas paper'. 'We had a break. I didn't understand the full extent of his illness. Perhaps I was expecting something I would have expected from a normal man. He wasn't a normal man. We were both pretty grotty with flu. He kept phoning me all the time. Perhaps I wanted to punish him a little bit. '"When are you coming home?" he'd ask. Well, I don't know. "I'm going to see so-and-so, can you come and drive me?" Oh, what the hell, I knew I'd go back. I wanted to give him a short, sharp shock. Then we went off to Italy.'

By this time, of course, Yvonne had a fair inkling about the state of Sutch's psyche. 'Once we went to the Isle of Man for a gig and he was very depressed there – he'd stopped taking the Prozac. "I don't need them," he said. "I want to be myself."' She is also convinced that she foiled an earlier suicide bid: 'I was driving home and had got as far as a roundabout leading off to the M4 when a voice in my head said, "Go back, go back." I turned round and drove like a maniac to Parkfield

Road and banged on the door. He came down – he looked at me and I was crying, I said, "You were going to do something silly, weren't you?" He cried, too, and said, "I'm coming back with you now." I think it would have happened then, a year earlier than it did.'

Like many others, Yvonne believes he never got over the death of Annie Sutch: 'I thought he was getting over his mum but he wasn't. He wasn't thinking as a rational person – to everybody that would listen, he'd talk about his mum. I really don't think it was an act. The death of his mother was totally devastating for him. He [still] hadn't accepted it two years later. He wanted to be with his mum. He even realised that if he hadn't accepted it now he never would.'

Sutch was also, said Yvonne, somehow incapable of analysing his own character. It was a trait particularly evident whenever he occasionally upset his friends: 'When David did get nasty with anybody you had to look at it in terms of his illness. Things would happen and I'd say, "Why did you do that?" He'd say, "Oh, they didn't realise," but I'd point out that he may have really upset them ... [But] he'd never accepted there was anything for him to be concerned about in his behaviour.'

For example, he was unpleasantly rude to old friends, singer Danny Rivers and partner Emily, who they were giving a lift home from a party. 'David was annoyed that as she had on a lovely evening dress she sat in the front alongside me. He kept on and on about it, and eventually, we dropped them off to catch a cab the rest of the way home.'

Nor, in private, did Sutch always live up to his practical joker image: 'He could be very serious. Sometimes we'd talk all night about really serious things.' He did, however, remain silent on the question of what should happen to his possessions when he died. Yvonne cannot shed any light whatsoever on why Sutch did not leave a proper will (other than that he simply never got around to it). I believe he was aware that if he didn't, Tristan would get the lot.

But although Sutch was never the most organised of people, according to Yvonne, he did have his own quaint method of keeping tabs on his life: 'Every day he'd write down the names and phone numbers of everyone he met, and all of his thoughts, on his calendar. If anything happened when we went out, if he saw someone who was a bit nutty, for example, we had to follow them, then he'd come back and write on his calendar, "Man in green hat," or whatever, to remember it.' She showed me one such calendar she'd brought with her. Against one date David had written, 'Here Today – God Tomorrow'. 'He'd just sit and write – it was his filing system. He never used a computer. His system was different coloured pens. It worked quite well for us. "Put it on the calendar so I'll know," he'd say, and we both used it in the end.'

Yvonne still feels the need, however, to justify her claims on Sutch: 'Our friends know how close Dave and I were. I looked after his every need for the past two years and he was determined to marry me.' She has a plausible explanation for why the marriage claim came as such a bombshell to so many of his oldest friends: 'He kept telling me not to mention it to anyone because he wanted to do an exclusive deal with *OK!* magazine.' Sutch was booked to top the bill at a Hallowe'en gig in the States in October and, according to Yvonne and others, he was so excited he was showing off advance posters to anyone and everyone: 'We were going to get married ... Carlo Little was to be best man ... [but] nothing definite had been arranged as he had only just got the booking and things had still to be sorted out by the promoter.'

Perhaps the one rumour that irks Yvonne above all others is the widespread belief that the death of his mother's dog, Rosie, somehow sparked his suicide. According to Thann, just as David had continued to buy gifts for his mother after her death, so after the dog's death 'he kept every medical record from the vet and every bit of dog stuff he had bought. He wouldn't have kept it if he hadn't cared.' We have, though, already heard that he could bear to part with almost nothing. 'I want to put paid to all these myths about the dog,' said Yvonne. 'I was very cross when I heard about them – that people would think his life was so trivial. He bought the dog for his mother. Rosie was already six or seven, not a puppy, and his mum had her for only two or three years. The dog was diabetic. David went to the vet, got medication for her. She had to be injected at the same time every day, but David just wasn't up to keeping to that regime and in the end I think she became a bit of a nuisance almost, and he wasn't giving her her medication, so she was getting quite poorly.

'I'd give it to her, but it would be at the wrong time, or he'd say he'd given it to her, then say, "Oh dear, I've forgotten to give it to her." We took her to the vet who said, really it would be a kindness at her age to put her to sleep ...

'[So] the vet put her to sleep and said, did we want him to cremate her, but David said he wanted to take her home, so he put her in this black bag. This was Friday night. He put her in the room downstairs. I said, "I don't think she should be in the house because she'll start to smell." He said he was going to bury her, so I told him to leave her outside where it was cooler.'

Unfortunately though, Sutch had a gig on in Kent the following day (for which, as usual, he was running late), so they didn't have time to bury the dog.

'We got back very late and went to bed,' Yvonne continues. 'On Sunday morning I got out of bed, put my foot down and screamed, because there under my foot was the black sack … He was laughing – he thought it was hilarious. He got up, picked the black bag up and tipped it upside down – it was full of books and boxes that he'd made to look like the dog.'

They finally buried the dog later that afternoon. 'If he was that devastated about the dog would he have done something like that?' Yvonne asks me. 'You wouldn't be so disrespectful to her, would you?' Yvonne also told another story about Sutch once shutting Rosie in the back of his car with a much bigger gentleman dog who'd been hassling her for certain favours. 'I had to make him let her out,' she said.

Afterwards, said Yvonne, Sutch had remarked that life was actually a lot easier without Rosie. She had seen Sutch depressed before, but he certainly did not appear to be overly distressed about Rosie. 'You could always see it in his face when he was depressed,' Yvonne had told Maggie O'Riordan of the *Daily Mail* in an earlier interview. 'From being such a smiley person he would suddenly be terribly morose. He would be unable to face people and cancel all his gigs. If he was really bad he would just go to bed.' He had never seemed as bad again as when he'd come off his anti-depressants early in 1998, she said, 'not even before he died'.

The most important reminder of Sutch, said Yvonne, were her memories: 'They mean more than anything else.' She confirmed, though, that Sutch never visited his mother's grave. 'People have said to me, isn't it strange? And yet it's one thing I actually understand, because I can't bring myself to go back to his grave. I don't want to go and see that grave. I thought, why doesn't he want to go to his mum's? Now I know why – it's not really them there, is it?'

chapter eighteen

Beginning of the End

'I'm on my own. I'm my own best friend'
— DAVID SUTCH, 1999

In public at heart, Sutch tried to keep up appearances: in January 1999 he made half-hearted noises about standing in the Scottish Parliamentary elections, on a Loony ticket that proposed a Parliament on wheels to travel the country, turning the Isle of Skye into a tax haven and building a tunnel to it, and decreeing that members of the Scottish parliament wore a kilt at all times – tired gags, many of them recycled.

His enthusiasm for gigs appeared to be waning, too, says Jess Conrad, the suave, good-looking middle-of-the-road singer who became firm friends with Sutch when they met up on the early-sixties revival shows. 'Towards the end he didn't much care about his act any more – he had no stage props left, he'd even go on stage in street clothes – although they were pretty bizarre anyway. There wasn't much reality in his life – a man of that age, turning up late for everything, always talking about showbiz, not real life – for example, he never mentioned his son at all.' David Parker, editor of *Beat* magazine, later recalled how Conrad had told him of a lengthy motorway trip together when Sutch had turned to him and said, 'Jess, we can't carry on doing this, can we?'

Sutch's friend, Trevor Fontane, is an entertainer who kept a collection of scrapbooks about Sutch's career, prompting Sutch to tell him once: 'You know more about my life than I do.' He had been organising his own fiftieth birthday party for the end of January in Cornwall – even arranging gigs for Sutch on either side of the big day in order to make it worth his while coming such a long way – and Sutch had agreed to be there. But he let Fontane down. 'It wasn't like him,' the friendly former postman told me. 'He'd rung up to say he would be there but next day he said he had flu and couldn't make it. I later found out that he'd been letting people down left, right and centre around this time.' A note later found in Sutch's house, dated 21 January, read: 'Feeling the hole [sic] world is against me, I'm on my own. I'm my own best friend.' He had also written down the telephone number of a help-line.

On 3 February, he did appear at a gig at the Lord Nelson in London's Holloway Road organised by the Joe Meek Appreciation Society to commemorate the anniversary of Meek's death, and earlier that day joined a large delegation to gather outside Cliff Cooper's World of Music store in Denmark Street to try and persuade Cooper to hand over more than 3,000 tapes of unissued Meek recordings which he had pledged to give to the National Sound Archive two years previously. 'Let's have them now,' demanded Sutch, whose own material is believed to be on the tapes: 'I don't want a pile of dust.'

Colin Pryce-Jones, guitarist with The Rapiers, was part of the gig that evening. He'd been with Sutch for a previous Hallowe'en gig at a Manchester club called Quaffers, which could accommodate thousands of revellers, and cherishes the Spinal Tap-like memory of Sutch coming on to explosions, smoke, lights, on a stage that slowly rose to eye level, and 'as we reached the level of the club and the smoke faded, we were horrified to see only six people – sitting at one table. This was our audience. Sutch gave a show that was second to none.' That night, in the seedy dressing room before they went on, he had looked across at Sutch, who was resplendent in his usual leopardskin, and 'asked him to remind me of the count into "Jack the Ripper". "Three screams and in," he replied, in all seriousness. We all erupted into fits of laughter and David, not realising what he had said, joined in; his high-pitched giggling nearly drowning us out.' Pryce-Jones also recalls being with Sutch when he was stopped at customs on his way to a rock 'n' roll festival in Munich. Asked by the customs officer what was in his big red bag, Sutch replied: 'Severed head, swords, axes, knives, toilet seat, surgical implements.' 'Very funny, sir,' said the officer. 'Would you open the suitcase?' Sutch obliged, pulling out a severed head, swords, axes...

During that Lord Nelson gig, a photograph was taken which sparked a bizarre theory that Sutch's death was part of a 'Joe Meek Curse'. Snapped by amateur photographer Bill Musyk, the picture showed seven people, including the former frontman of The Tornados, Heinz Burt, who died from a stroke in April 2000, the singer Kim Roberts, who had once been Sutch's girlfriend and who died in June 2000, and Sutch himself. The photo spooked long-serving Savage Tony Dangerfield, who was also in it. He burnt his copy. 'It's like I'm travelling under an endless black cloud being pushed towards some horrible destiny,' he said. Two other individuals associated with Meek – Geoff Goddard, a songwriter, and Tornados guitarist Alan Caddy – were also to die in 2000. The date of 3 February was also portentous: it was the day Buddy Holly died in 1959, as predicted by Joe Meek following a séance he had attended. And it was on 3 February 1967 that Meek shot himself dead.

By mid-February, Sutch and Yvonne were reconciled, and she accompanied him on tour to Italy. 'On Valentine's Day he gave me back the engagement ring,' she later told the *Mail*. 'From that moment we barely had a cross word. He had come off the tablets briefly before he died ... but went back on them and seemed OK.' This was Sutch's last significant tour, Yvonne told me: four gigs, using a band called The Goodfellas. 'We had a fabulous time. If anything, our time together from February onwards was almost stronger than even the very early days.'

In March Sutch officially opened the world's first millennium party, staged in the 'alternative millennium dome', the Roundhouse in London, by his much-loved Circus of Horrors and featuring all manner of strange and wonderful acts. He seemed to revel in his role as 'alternative prime minister'. Later in the month he recorded a lucrative television advertisement for the breakfast cereal, Coco Pops, and asked the agent, Patsy Martin, who negotiated the deal for him for more of the same kind of work. 'He used to ring me for long chats after his mum died,' she said. 'He'd showed no signs of depression. He never gave me a problem as long as I worked with him.'

But on April Fool's Day, at a gig at the Prince of Wales pub in Hammersmith – 'official London HQ: Raving Loony Party' – he was not his usual self. 'He seemed strange, weird,' recalls Terry Clemson, the lead guitarist, 'but I didn't know why. It was just a strange gig. He used none of his usual props and changed his act round. In the middle of "Jack the Ripper" he went off at a tangent – it seemed as though his heart wasn't really in it and he had something on his mind. I was thinking, "Is he bored with it all?" Over the years his act had become less and less interesting, with fewer things going on compared with the earlier days.'

Peter Stockton, the other guitarist, agrees: 'He hadn't gone to the usual trouble to prepare himself for his appearance. He just had a cape and a top hat and hadn't got dressed up as normal. He wasn't on top form.'

Sutch and Stockton (who had organised the launch party for Sutch's autobiography a few years earlier) kept in regular contact by phone. 'He was complaining of headaches, for which he told me he was taking medication,' Stockton remembers. 'He was also unhappy that Yvonne's daughter, Alex, who should have been keeping a note of calls for him, wasn't bothering to do it properly.' This was a little harsh, coming from someone who was hardly well organised himself – but typical of the way he always expected people to put themselves out for him regardless of the inconvenience to themselves. 'There were times when David could get obnoxious when he was on pills,' Melodie Staniforth had told me. 'He once had a go at one of my children for not taking a phone message for him.'

Stockton was one friend who was certainly unaware of any marriage plans: 'As far as I am concerned, that is so much piffle. The impression David gave me was that he was looking for a way out of their relationship.' Sutch was also reportedly worrying that someone was helping themselves to items of memorabilia from the huge stash he kept at his mother's home and other locations – though how he would have been able to tell is a puzzle.

Val Bird, Sutch's old friend (and ex-girlfriend), did think there was 'something weird' going on when David contacted her twice within a week shortly before he died: 'He was usually so selfish, yet he rang me to have a conversation about my dog which I'd had to have put down, and then a couple of days later to ask whether I was all right. I thought, "Hang on, this isn't the normal David."'

Val had long resigned herself to being 'good old Val,' someone Sutch knew he could always come back to. But she is convinced that in the time leading up to his death 'he was not a happy man'.

'I have never met Yvonne Elwood,' she says, 'and when I heard that he had moved in with her within weeks of meeting her, I spoke to him to ask him what he was doing.' In committing himself to a long-term relationship with someone he hardly knew, she felt Sutch was being uncharacteristically impulsive.

What matters were pre-occupying David in his final days? Did he feel trapped in a relationship that had taken on a momentum of its own and which he now felt powerless to halt, or even slow down? Or perhaps all this is just erroneous conjecture on the part of long-time friends uneasy about Sutch taking up with a 'stranger'? When we get to know someone over many years we can often feel we know what is good, or even best, for them, even if they appear to disagree.

In May, Loony Party member Chris 'Screwy' Driver became an elected councillor on the Isle of Sheppey and later became Mayor of Queenborough-in-Sheppey. The Loonies weren't meant to get elected! Were they losing sight of their raison d'être? By June, however, the party announced it would be unable to contest the European Elections owing to lack of funds. Phew.

Though a gig at the beginning of the month, at a packed London pub, the Blue Angel, in City Road, had gone well – 'the girls went wild,' remembered guitarist Andrew McCafferty – in Gillingham on 15 May, at a birthday party for his old friend Rockin' Dave Robbo, Dave Savage, who was on first with The (Northern) Savages, remembers that Sutch had been 'sat outside waiting for us to finish', perhaps 'because he didn't want to upstage us by walking in halfway through our show – but it was strange and so unlike him not to want to sing.' Savage now believes the signs were there that night 'that something was weighing on his mind', that Sutch was 'wearing a very thick mask'. Robbo himself remembers David and Yvonne arriving with bags of presents for everyone, all of which came from his beloved secondhand shops, including a rocking horse for Screwy and Alma Driver to take to Lingfield Races for the

Lord Sutch day (which he would not live to see). 'Perhaps, knowing what was going to happen, he was saying goodbye in a way,' Alma says. She thought Sutch looked ill. Robbo had employed a professional photographer to take pictures at the party, and most of them show David 'with a very sad face'.

It was soon afterwards (around the time of Rosie's demise), that Sutch rang Darren Poyzer of the Loony Party, who had suffered his own stint, as he puts it, 'at the beck and call of the mental health system'.

'We talked long distance,' Poyzer recalled, 'or rather he talked about his sadness, his loss, his mother … Here was a man who was utterly distraught and yet I had no words that seemed to comfort him. It was quite surreal because I thought, as happens with most people, that he would have some positive points to discuss, and yet his despair was seemingly without limit. It was a level of sadness that I couldn't get my head around.'

Later that same month, long-time fan Keith Knight bumped into Sutch at a charity appearance in a local Red Cross shop in Ruislip. 'He talked enthusiastically about Radio Sutch. He told me he had been back in the forts recently and that they were very rusty.' Was he re-visiting old haunts for the last time?

In private, it was a different matter. At home, alone, he wrote a short but harrowing note: '18 May 99,' he scrawled: 'Not Good Day. Depression Back Today In Evening About 8pm. My Depression.' Another note, undated, seemed to list the times the depression was kicking in: 'Back About 1.45'; 'Back About 4.30 p.m.'; 'Today Came On 10pm Rest Of Day'.

On 24 May, Sutch registered with a Harrow doctors' practice and underwent a full health check from the practice nurse. His weight was recorded at 87kg, his height 167cm, blood pressure 130/80. His Body Mass Index was recorded as 31.2, sufficient for him to be officially classified as obese. Sutch spoke to one of the doctors 'about his low mood'. He was given a variety of medications – Lithium Carbonate, Fluoxetine (also known as Prozac) and Zopiclone (for insomnia) – and referred to the practice's psychologist. The use of Lithium would suggest he was suffering from a relatively serious depressive mental illness. The practice was aware that he had been treated for depression, which had been diagnosed as early as 1992 at Wokingham Hospital.

Subsequently, Sutch shelled out £84.60 to prepay for twelve months of prescription charges – hardly the actions of a financially 'careful' man who wasn't intending to stay around to use those them. On the form he filled in, he gave his name as simply 'Sutch – David Edward'.

Later that same day Sutch went along to the South Harrow Baptist Church for a concert given by another luminary with links to Harrow, Rick Wakeman. Rob McNeill, the *Harrow Observer* reporter who attended, noted that Sutch was 'on his own, looking unkempt and a bit battered, wearing ordinary clothes'. Wakeman had been in the Boys Brigade in Harrow in 1962: this concert was part of his Half a Century Church Tour to celebrate his fiftieth birthday. Perhaps Wakeman's music was not really up Sutch's street: according to McNeill, Sutch merely said hello and 'sat through the keyboard doodlings', but he and Wakeman spoke at length after the show.

'I remember seeing Sutch for the first time way back in the sixties,' says Wakeman, 'and being totally amazed by the sheer showmanship of the stage act. It was wonderfully over the top. I became an instant fan.' They'd actually met years later helping Children in Need at a radio station in Southend and stayed friends thereafter. 'That night without my knowing, David showed up,' Wakeman recalls. 'I introduced [him] to Ramon Remedios, the opera singer with whom I had been working that night. I was completely stunned when Ramon started reeling off tracks that David had done way back – it seemed that David's prowess had even spread to the operatic world!' Wakeman remembers that Sutch asked him if he would be interested in taking part in a charity event for a fellow musician in about a month's time. Wakeman said he'd be delighted, and the two of them agreed to be in touch. Then: 'Within three weeks David was gone. I remember picking up the newspaper, reading the headlines of his apparent suicide and saying out loud to myself, "I don't believe this." And I still don't. The publicity died away as fast as it came, and the verdict on his death went by unchallenged.'

Either later that night (or one day either side of it – both events are recorded as taking place on 25 May) Sutch attended the sixtieth-birthday celebrations of sax player Pete Newman, at a pub near Aylesbury. Pete had played sax on Sutch's first single after his sister Pat became friendly with Sutch – 'She brought him home from

Cricklewood Roller Skating Rink in, oh, it must have been around 1957. He was wearing pink trousers and purple shoes, really outlandish clothes. This was before hippies, before any of that. My dad wanted to throw him out of the house.' That night Sutch brought Pete 'a present and card – he was smiling, being really nice to everybody – he was the old Dave. I'd known him for over forty years and he spoke to me nearly every week. It could be any time of day or night, and we'd discuss every subject under the sun – but he never mentioned his personal situation – I had absolutely no idea there was anything amiss.'

Pat Hellier confirms this: 'He seemed to be going round talking to quite a few people, catching up with them. Strangely enough, he didn't mix with people socially very often other than at gigs and shows.'

That night he sought out another long-standing friend, musician Jet Harris. A massive star in the 1960s when he was part of The Shadows, Harris had also known Sutch for some forty years, and when he was a recovering alcoholic and suffering dreadfully from nerves, Sutch had supported him: 'Anybody going through problems in those days didn't admit how serious it was. He'd say to me, "Come on, you're great, what are you worried about? They love you!" I couldn't see it, I'd pace up and down ... He'd give me a cuddle and great support.' Harris's experience brings home just how many of those with whom Sutch had lived, worked and partied had suffered debilitating ailments and dysfunctional lifestyles.

Harris had undergone a bizarre but virtual miracle cure for his problems in Italy a couple of years before. Sutch had somehow heard about his treatment and, says Harris, 'he got me by the shoulders, looked me in the eye and said, "Jet, you've got to help me. Can I have his address? I'm getting these terrible headaches. They're so intense. I can't take any more." Three weeks later he was dead. I didn't know just how serious he was. He had seemed to be enjoying Pete's party.'

Around this time Sutch took old sparring partner, backing musician and writer Alan Clayson for lunch in a local café. 'The residual depression exacerbated by his mother's death was still evident but he was trying to be optimistic,' says Clayson. Twelve days before he died, he called into the offices of the *Harrow Observer*. 'He'd come to collect ten copies of a recent photograph in our sister paper *The Informer*, showing him working voluntarily at the Red Cross charity shop,' recalls

the paper's reporter Christian Duffin, who also remembers that Sutch 'looked ill. He wanted to give copies to friends in what was to turn out to be a last memento of the man who loved to help others … For a man who seemed obsessed with death, it was as though this was a kind of swansong.'

On 7 June he was back at his GP's, telling a nurse there how keen he was to lose weight. He was advised to join Weight Watchers. 'A week or so' before his death, Sutch rang Tony Ellis, a former Savage and a fellow depressive, 'out of the blue to tell me there was a programme on depression on BBC2. Around midnight the same night he rang again, wanting to talk about it.'

The man who claimed to have invented horror rock was now set to confront his own demons head on and set in motion the only means he could devise to escape from what had become a living nightmare. But he was still trying to keep up appearances and, during what was probably his last radio interview, on Southend-based Breeze AM, the week before he died, he declared: 'The [Loony] Party lives on and on. We're going for 2000 and 2010.'

But he didn't mention that the party would be continuing without him.

chapter nineteen

Dying for Publicity

'People saw him as a performer. He wore a mask of happiness. The real friends saw the other side of the mask'
— TONY KING, MUSICIAN AND CAMPAIGN MANAGER

Is it too much to suppose that a man who lived for publicity might finally have been prepared to die for it?

When Yvonne Elwood opened the door of David Sutch's late mother's house at 10 Parkfield Road, South Harrow, on the afternoon of 16 June 1999, and found his body hanging from the banisters, she had thought it another of his black jokes. So the first thing she did was to take a photograph of him. 'He'd ask me all the time to take photos – I've got over two thousand,' she said, and claims that Sutch had done similar things before, although she didn't elaborate. 'I really did think this was another…'

But this was not a joke, and the memory has never left her. 'It comes back to me suddenly from time to time – when I'm in the supermarket, for example, for no apparent reason … I don't think I'll ever really be able to forget it.'

I asked whether she could bring herself to look at the picture: 'No, I've got it stuck behind another one … You probably know, he always wanted people to take photographs. He couldn't be photographed enough. He was desperate for publicity.'

For many of those Sutch left behind that day, the news seemed literally unimaginable. Rumours began almost at once that foul play had been involved: for those who knew him best, believing that Sutch could not have killed himself seemed to be the only way they could imagine his passing. Rick Wakeman, for example, had talked of Sutch's 'apparent suicide', as had Alan Clayson.

In other words, the vast majority of people found it beyond belief that David Edward Sutch did what he actually did. They could not understand what could have triggered such an act.

The news had an instant impact. Savage Jack Irving recalled: 'On the night Sutch died I'd tried to ring him. As soon as I heard I rang Tony Dangerfield. I heard him shout and his line went dead and he wouldn't answer again.'

Suddenly, the whole world seemed to be coming up with theories: he did it because his beloved mother's dog died, severing his last link with his mother; he did it because he was being blackmailed (according to this theory, hand-written notes containing allegations about Sutch's sexuality were found in the house when he died); he did it to avoid getting married.

Then the gossip escalated once again when it became clear Sutch had died without leaving a will, and that certain parties in his life were fighting over his estate. On one occasion the police were called to the Parkfield Road house. Then a newspaper got hold of a story that Tristan was not Sutch's biological son; there was talk of DNA testing. Then Thann told a journalist that at the time of his death Sutch had been trying to reconcile with Giselle. 'He spent so long trying to get away from her,' Yvonne responded, 'I hardly think he'd want her back.'

All in all, Sutch's death provided the media with a field day. At last, again, everyone was talking about him.

I have spent my entire working life either giving publicity or seeking it. I am a journalist, a profession that would cease to exist if publicity were outlawed. For more than twenty years I have worked in the press office of William Hill, endeavouring to keep the company's name before the public eye in any way I can. I suspect such a profession makes one somewhat obsessive, always looking for stories to publicise, forever creating stories to maximise the publicity that effectively pays my wages. But David Sutch was one of the few people I have met whose desire for publicity exceeded my own.

Certainly Sutch's keenness on publicity was partly professional – obviously the better known his name was, the easier it became to make records, win votes or charge higher performance fees. But anyone who knew the man even briefly soon realized that Sutch's need for publicity was all-encompassing. More than anyone, he understood completely the desire for fame for its own sake which fuels such current cultural phenomena as *Big Brother*. He would have been a natural contestant for *I'm A Celebrity, Get Me Out of Here*. Having lived for fame, perhaps he sensed that his extended fifteen minutes in the limelight were almost up. This might not have bothered David Sutch – but it was unthinkable for Screaming Lord Sutch.

A week after Sutch's suicide, the *South London Press* carried an article in which his old friend Cynthia Payne might, it seemed to me, have put her finger on the real reason for Sutch's desperate act. 'Streatham's Madame Cyn has claimed Screaming Lord Sutch killed himself,' ran the story, 'because he wanted to end his life in a blaze of publicity.' The article went on:

> Cynthia Payne believed her 'close friend' was devastated that he wasn't making headlines any more. 'Whenever he got publicity it lifted his depression. I've heard that two weeks ago one of the tabloids was approached by an ex-girlfriend who wanted to sell her story. They said he wasn't newsworthy any more, and he found out.
>
> 'I reckon he thought, "Right, I know how to get on the front page," and that's exactly what he did. He wanted a dramatic exit.'

Cynthia clearly believes this interpretation of his death. The wreath she sent to Sutch's funeral read: 'You were still newsworthy after all.'

Fellow musician Jess Conrad agrees: 'I think he was depressed and demoralised. His brain was not like ours – it was in turmoil. A couple of days before he died he hadn't been able to play at the charity concert. His work was tailing off and much of what he was getting was absolute crap. He couldn't even get on the sixties revival weekends. They're great earners – I do four or five a year for big money – but Sutch couldn't even get himself on to the bills. I think he went home that

Sunday night thinking, "I can get more publicity than those boys. I'll show them that I can still get noticed." What a publicity stunt, and what courage to take that ultimate action just to get his name in the paper.'

'The gruesome manner in which he chose to leave us,' reflected Joe Meek's biographer, John Repsch, 'was all the more bizarre, considering his relish for parodying such macabre events onstage.'

Perhaps, too, as some have suggested, Sutch held romantic views about the early deaths of rock stars. Had he registered the fact that Joe Meek, for example, might otherwise have slipped into obscurity if his suicide had not resulted in him being revered and feted? Certainly he would have recognised that early or violent death had been a shrewd career move for many rock stars: Jim Morrison, Elvis Presley and Jimi Hendrix among them. And neither is there any shortage of rock suicides.

Besides which, Sutch had spent a good few nights of his last years playing at functions for expired pals, each one no doubt reminding him of his own mortality. Did these events cause him to think morbid thoughts, to wonder if he kept going on and on whether there would be anyone left to mark his own passing? Perhaps he figured that, rather than become a sad and forgotten figure himself, suicide was his best way of achieving immortality. 'I was listening to a radio programme,' he told the *People* in 1991, 'and they featured people like Elvis Presley, Buddy Holly, Eddie Cochran, Jimi Hendrix and Janis Joplin – names that I grew up with. And I suddenly realised that all these bloody people were dead. Makes you think, doesn't it?'

It was certainly clear that Sutch did not know how to survive without the oxygen of publicity. Long before his death, he appeared to have confused his private life with his public one to the extent that the 'media' was an almost constant presence in his life. When he called off his marriage to Thann in the 1970s, he apparently had no qualms about letting a tabloid paper write a story revealing that the reason was that he could not give her the children she wanted. When his mother's dog Rosie died, he did his grieving through the media, complaining that he had lost his last link to his Mum. When his long relationship with Giselle went wrong, he came up with a media stunt which suggested he was planning to marry Cynthia Payne. Was the media the only way he had of confirming his existence, of judging his worth? Did he think that if everyone stopped writing about him he would effectively cease to exist? Did he hit on a drastic way of permitting David to return to the comfort of his mother's protection, whilst allowing Lord Sutch to hit the headlines in a more sensational way than ever before?

When I started writing this book I didn't know whether it would turn out to be about Screaming Lord Sutch or David Edward Sutch. There was a big difference.

Many people felt they knew one or the other side of the Sutch personality. Very few knew both. There were major contradictions within that one, multi-faceted brain. He loved his mother, but his actions did not always demonstrate as much. He wanted to share his life with another human being, yet could never commit himself whole-heartedly to a relationship. He wanted a son who would follow in his footsteps, yet he almost forced the son he had to reject his father. He celebrated, was almost a walking advertisement for, failure, but craved success and never stopped striving for it.

By changing his name to Lord David Edward Sutch, he may have hoped that he was bringing his two separate selves together. But he wasn't. He died without ever having succeeded in combining them. Recognition for the sake of it can be a two-edged axe, rather like the one Sutch used to take on stage with him in the early days: if you're not careful the sharp side can bounce back and cut you. 'My act has always been about going wild and mad,' he once declared, 'but it's a controlled sort of showbiz madness and I knew how to switch it off once it was over.' To some, like the private, shy David Sutch, who, one person told me, met and chatted to him several times without ever revealing his identity, recognition is a curse; to others, like the extrovert Screaming Lord Sutch, who told a 1965 TV audience that 'I've found that personally I've got no self-embarrassment. I feel that I could walk into a restaurant completely naked and I just wouldn't bat an eyelid', it's a blessing. Screaming Lord Sutch always wore an outgoing, flamboyant, wilfully eccentric public face. Depression was not a concept he recognised, or acknowledged. David Edward Sutch was a much more self-effacing, modest, vulnerable and insecure person.

Thann recalled that after donning the make-up in which he performed, Sutch was always extremely keen to wipe it off afterwards to 'try and look as normal as possible'. Did he have in mind a 1982 television documentary he had watched, in which Sir Laurence Olivier warned, 'If you're wise, you take the part off with your make-up. People who can't do that suffer very much.' David never quite learned how to 'take the part off'.

'Nobody knew the real David,' says Yvonne Elwood. 'Some saw him as a rock star and others saw him as a Loony politician, but he would spend most of his time by the Maiden Erlegh lake, reading the paper and feeding the fish.'

It was this private self who was terrified of admitting that he suffered from a debilitating mental illness so crippling that it would ultimately kill him. On the other hand, nothing could kill Screaming Lord Sutch. David's headstone bears the name David Edward Sutch, not that of his alter ego. It was this other self who revelled in the label 'professional lunatic', who presented to the world a face untroubled by pain. Don't forget what Alice Cooper said in 2003: 'People who have tried to live their character have died trying to do it.'

Less than a week before his death, Sutch revealed just how much of a strain living with two selves might be. It was one of his last gigs, The Rolling Stones Convention show at the Brixton Academy. Two of Sutch's friends told me stories from that night that might well be about two different people. Guitarist Terry Clemson obviously ran into the private self, David Edward Sutch: 'Somebody told me Dave had been looking for me. I found him and we had a word. He was obviously very depressed, particularly about his weight. He said to me, "I'm so big, overweight – it's a pity someone can't invent a pill to stop you eating. I'm pissed off about it – you're looking so good" (I'd just lost a couple of stone) "but I just look so old and fat."'

But another friend, musician Rick Brown, obviously met the manic, flamboyant Screaming Lord Sutch that night: 'I was really pleased to bump into David – he seemed the same as ever, better than ever, in fact. I gave him and Yvonne a lift home to his South Harrow house and he did something completely out of character when we got there – he gave me a fiver for the petrol!'

Another person who witnessed the two faces of Sutch in the days immediately prior to his death was Sky TV's political correspondent, Adam Boulton. The journalist had got to know Sutch reasonably well over the years, meeting up with him at by-elections, and in the process becoming genuinely fond of him. In the week before he died Sutch visited the Sky studios to record an interview to be screened in America. 'He came in,' says Boulton, 'and I noticed he had very big bags under his eyes. He seemed shabby, wearing chain-store jeans and sports coat, looking down-at-heel and middle-aged. He was carrying his gear in a plastic bag. He put on the top hat and leopardskin, did the interview, then took it all off and left, on his own, carrying the plastic bag, looking like a man who was fed up with it all, a depressed figure.'

How could one man reconcile these contrasting, opposing elements in one personality? One of Sutch's closest friends, 'Rockin' Dave Robinson, reckons he never did: 'I believe he had to live this other person Screaming Lord Sutch for all those years, and his own person, David Sutch, dried up.'

Sadly, Sutch was all too aware which of the two characters held the upper hand in terms of commercial appeal. This is poignantly demonstrated by a contract for a show he signed in August 1974, which stated simply: 'David Sutch to present Screaming Lord Sutch.'

The punters, of course, did not seem to be interested in the 'real' Sutch. In the same way that everyone knows Darth Vader but few care about the actor inside the costume, it was Screaming Lord Sutch the public wanted. During the 1992 general election this was starkly revealed when a friend of Sutch's, his agent Mal 'Catman' Clint, stood in for him at the count at Islwyn. Clint was surprised at the number of people who mistook him for the genuine Sutch: 'I had the same clothes on as he would have worn, everybody seemed to think I was Lord Sutch. A BBC reporter rushed up to me, holding a microphone, to interview me: "Tell me, Mr Sutch, how did you get started in showbiz and politics?"' Clint began to explain in some detail before honesty got the better of him and he confessed. But how did Sutch, who had worked so hard to ensure that everyone in the world knew who he was, react when he heard this story? Did it give him pause for thought that it was the character, 'the image', that people recognised and not the man?

The drummer Mac Poole tells another story, about driving Sutch on a tour of Scotland. Stuck in a traffic jam, he watched Sutch walk ahead to see what the hold-up was, only to be approached by an old woman and asked, 'Are ye no that Lord Sutch off the telly?' 'Yes,' he agreed, his hand entering his pocket for a pen to sign an autograph. The old woman whacked him on the side of the head: 'Ye ought to be ashamed of yesself – grow up and get a proper job!'

To a lucky few who met him, though, Sutch allowed the man inside Screaming Lord Sutch to shine through. One of his greatest fans, musician Trevor Fontane, once took him to meet his father, who already had serious misgivings about meeting his son's hero: 'Father, who was eighty-nine, came in and shook hands with Dave. "How old are you, boy?" he asked. "Forty-eight," said Sutch. "How can a man your age act so bloody stupid?" "Well, it's taken me thirty years of practice, Dad," said Sutch, disarming my father, who then admitted, "He's a nice chap – he's nothing like his character."'

Another rare public glimpse of David Edward was captured on film when he was campaigning for a Devon council election in May 1989. After mugging it up for the cameras for hours, Sutch is filmed in the porch of a polling station chatting to a couple of elderly female volunteer helpers. They look to be about the same age as his mother; he looks completely at ease. For once he appears to have forgotten the camera and another, gentler personality is on display. He tells them that he put this obscure council election ahead of the imminent European election.

'Can't be everywhere,' he says. 'This is more important to me.'

'Why is Budleigh Salterton important?' enquires one of the ladies politely.

'Well, 'cos the area's nice and we're down here campaigning. It's nice. Nice sunshine.'

There is no doubt that, just for this moment, Screaming Lord Sutch was lying dormant and David Edward was putting in a rare public appearance.

Guitarist Paul Green played with Sutch in Germany a year or so before he died and was another who saw both faces: 'I collect posters from all the big gigs I play, but later I caught Dave scraping some confetti off a table and putting it into a plastic bag – it seemed very sad. I couldn't help thinking that there were two sides to him and I'd had a glimpse of both of them – the up-front nutter leaping about on stage and being the life and soul of the party, and the sad little man without much going for him.'

The seeds of Sutch's dilemma might well have been sown right back at the beginning of his career. As early as 1965, in the *Arena* television documentary, he revealed his unquenchable desire for fame: 'I've always dreamed to become a national figure, and I think it took me three and a half to four years, and more or less everybody in one way or another has heard of me – or, I hope they've heard of me – or, if they haven't, I must keep trying and maybe think up some new ideas.' Screaming Lord Sutch had no option: he *had* to ensure everyone heard of him and would pursue his goal for the next thirty-four years.

But what was the motive behind his desire for fame? Why did he need so constantly to prove his worth, as if to himself? One theory is that he felt abandoned by the father who died before his son could ever know him, and that he was abandoned once again by the man who he believed would become his surrogate father, Uncle Benny. His mother had been left, but the boy who was David Edward Sutch had been left, too. I think David had always wanted to feel himself part of an extended, loving family, which is why he was never happier than when mixing with familiar friends from the music circuit like Wee Willie Harris, Jess Conrad and The Savages. But it wasn't the real thing: there was only his mother, and although she and his father had both had plenty of brothers and sisters he'd never got close to any of them. The rock 'n' rollers were his surrogate family.

Whatever the reasons, Sutch died without ever losing his desire for publicity. He still wanted *everyone* to know him. Why else would he ring me, and many others, almost constantly with suggestions for stories which he thought would persuade someone, anyone, to write a paragraph or two about him? Was this curious lack of awareness (or any sense of perspective) part of the same insensitivity which cost him so many relationships? Did he ever wonder why his girlfriends became exasperated by his self-obsession and lack of interest in anything they were doing, unless it directly involved him? Nor, clearly, did it ever occur to him that going home to a mother who never failed to show an interest in his latest antics might alienate the women in his life. Perhaps he tried so hard to present himself as the most loving son of all time in order to cover the fact that while his mother was alive he had used her to shield himself from the harsh realities of life. Might this be the real reason he was devastated by her death – that she had dared to leave him on his own? He certainly acted as if he resented it.

Every single one of Sutch's mature relationships with women depended on his partner telling him how wonderful he was or how important to her he was, and treating him as the centre of her universe (as his mother did). If anyone was talking about him or to him, or doing something for him, he was content. But if anybody (and particularly his partners) expected him to consider their feelings or even to talk about them, he was reluctant. He was certainly unwilling to sacrifice something he wanted for anyone else's benefit.

Sutch did indeed seem to know that he was selfish, yet such knowledge hardly appeared to make him want to do anything about it. He once made reference to his selfish attitude in an *Independent on Sunday* feature, in which he recalled Cynthia Payne telling him 'how wonderful her election agent Gloria had been. So, at the next election, what did I do? I nicked Gloria.' However, he failed Gloria, too, as she recalls: 'He'd rung up in a panic to say he had forgotten to bring his props to a pub in Ilford, and pleaded with me to bring them over, promising to drive me back if I did. I managed to get there, only to see Giselle walk in during the gig, which resulted in them having a furious row. At the end of the night he just said to me, "Oh, you can get home OK, can't you? I'm going with Giselle." There were no more trains or public transport and I ended up having to beg a lift off someone and getting in at 2 a.m.'

Perhaps Sutch blamed such incidents on his alter ego, Screaming Lord Sutch. By so doing, he could distance himself from feelings of empathy for other people and, at the same time, from his own vulnerabilities.

He died as David Edward Sutch. He did not choose to wear the clothes of his alter ego, but – as Yvonne confirms – ordinary day clothes. Here is the clearest sign possible that it was David Sutch finally succumbing to the despair of depression. The only way to reclaim the real, private Sutch would have been to kill off the public Sutch – but that would never have worked. The shadow would have remained looming over him. It was a conundrum with no resolution short of self-extinction, the ultimate proof that he no longer wanted anything to do with Screaming Lord Sutch. Around his neck, as he died, was a small piece of jewellery which Thann now has. On one side is a happy-looking moon face. On the other is another face, dark and desolate.

Screaming Lord Sutch would inevitably live on in true dead celebrity style. But David Sutch was already being forgotten, even as Yvonne Elwood opened the door to discover his hanging body. It was Screaming Lord Sutch who survived, whose name and image endure in the public imagination. Many today have to be reminded that he is dead, when they hear the name Screaming Lord Sutch. Of David Edward Sutch today, though, there is almost no trace, except in the hearts and minds of those who loved him.

Sutch's old friend Melodie Staniforth is one of those, and recalls that 'he used to love a mirror I own, with a picture of a sad-faced clown on it. I would often find him sitting and staring into that mirror. He would ask me if he could have it – I would always tell him no, but he'd keep on asking, and keep on looking into it … The clown was what he was looking at – the sadness of the clown's face. David played the clown … [and] when he wore clown's clothing he was happy and he entertained people, he made them laugh. In the sad clown's face he saw himself.'

Had others seen what Sutch saw when he gazed into the looking-glass, his story might have had a different ending.

chapter twenty

The Last Show on Earth

'Living with depression is the nearest thing to death'
— DAVID SUTCH, 1999

Much of David Sutch's life was a pantomime, some of it was a farce, but its conclusion was a tragedy. Photographs of his mother's old house 10, Parkfield Road, taken in the days following his death, reveal rooms absolutely crammed and piled high with junk, barely leaving enough space to walk through, cluttered and as precariously balanced as his mind, like the box perched at the front of the living room labelled 'Fragile'. There are papers and boxes and bags and scrapbooks, files, ornaments, bar towels, hats, a discarded dressing gown, a clothes drying-rack with the £4.99 price tag still on it. Scattered everywhere are packets of pills and tablets. In the fridge, a pot of yoghurt and one or two jars of jam are the only edible items. A note dated 21 January 1999 that was found – addressed to whom is not clear – reads: 'You like all things to be put away. I like things out so I can see them.'

It seems that by the end Sutch was living on a diet of Prozac and Lithium and cups of tea. The day after she found him dead, Yvonne told an interviewer: 'He'd been on medication for years. Sometimes that seemed to be a bit of a vicious circle because he'd try and cut down and then he'd feel much worse. And then he'd have to go back on it and then he'd feel worse because he felt he couldn't cope with it.'

Did I ever suspect what he was going through? There were certainly times when I'd speak to him and he'd seem to be a little out of it – a beat behind what was being said. The nearest comparison I can think of is Ozzy Osbourne, wandering through his TV show in virtual slow motion, trying to catch up while the world moves around him at a much faster pace. Ozzy gives the impression that he is still considering the last question he was asked when a new one has already been put to him. But then David Sutch was not one of the world's great brains. He was a two-trick pony – which is still at least one more ride than most of us can manage. He spent almost forty years performing the same music and running the same election campaign, over and over. Perhaps a more fertile mind would have needed to develop and refine his acts. But David was content to be incarcerated within his own Groundhog Day, unwilling (or more likely, unable) to break the cycle. The plus side, of course, was that the great British public (who at first despised, feared and pilloried him) finally took him to their hearts once they realised he represented no threat to the status quo. He became another of the harmless, almost exclusively male eccentrics who populate British public life.

'The value of Screaming Lord Sutch,' the renowned columnist Bernard Levin once wrote of him, 'is the same as that of Arnold Bennett's Card – he is devoted to the cause of cheering us all up.' Which invites the question: who cheers up the man whose job is cheering everyone up? As Mike Neal, of magazine *The Beat Goes On*, observed:

> It is sometimes the case that the most outlandish, eccentric and seemingly extroverted people harbour a dark side to their nature, and this was the case with David Sutch.
>
> What appears to outsiders as brash confidence can in reality often turn out to be a mask concealing any number of insecurities. With the passing of David Sutch the demons have also, thankfully, been laid to rest, allowing David to find true peace of mind at last.

Tony Barrell, a journalist who wrote a lengthy feature in the *Sunday Times* about Sutch a year after his death, believes Sutch suffered from bipolar disorder. Popularly known as 'manic depression', it is a condition 'characterised by alternate highs and lows,' Barrell wrote. Andrew Loog Oldham, The Rolling Stones' first manager and publicist in the early days, suffered from and would 'deal with unsuccessfully' severe manic depression for some thirty years. 'Something in your brain is broken,' he writes in his autobiography, *Stoned*. 'Depression is a sly mistress, she offers numbness in exchange for feeling and scolds you for staying away so long.' Joe Meek, who eventually shot himself, had said, according to an article on the meeksville.com website, 'that he felt like two people, as if someone else was in him'. It has been suggested that as many as one in five people with bipolar illness die by their own hand: a percentage approximately thirty times greater than for the general population.

'Impulsive, irrational spending,' adds Tony Barrell, 'is one of the classic symptoms.' Unquestionably Sutch was forever making impulsive purchases, from charity-shop knick-knacks to cars he could barely drive. His purchase of his personal 'Chequers', the house in Hastings, must surely rank as one of his most impulsive (and foolish) purchases.

On its website the NHS defines the manic phase of bipolar disorder as follows:

> You may have excessive amounts of energy and feel little need for sleep. Your thinking and speech tend to be faster than usual, and your thoughts can jump rapidly from one subject to another, making conversation difficult. Inflated self-esteem, loss of inhibitions and grandiose ideas or delusions are typical features.
>
> During a severe depressive episode you may have feelings of hopelessness and despair, of lethargy, broken sleep, over-whelming negativity and difficulty in carrying on with the activities of day-to-day life.

If insomnia is a symptom of bipolar disorder, then there are certainly a million stories about Sutch staying up all night. He kept rock 'n' roll hours anyway, and it was always pointless contacting him before lunchtime. Even if you got hold of him at that time of the day, any conversation proved useless.

Gloria Walker remembers Sutch sitting up making endless cups of tea until three in the morning. He would watch any number of his seemingly inexhaustible supply of videos – 'really nasty horror ones. If you're going to sit up into the night watching things like that, those things lurk in the corners of your mind. It's all right if you're feeling well, but when you're depressed they're likely to come up to the surface.' (And while we are on the subject of tea – and Sutch's tea obsession has already been well documented – Sutch's consumption of at least forty cups of day would certainly have contributed to his insomnia. According to the media GP Dr John Briffa, a high intake of tea can cause 'anxiety, heart palpitations and insomnia'; it would be an irony if Sutch's determination to avoid alcohol by consuming tea contributed to a state of mind already made vulnerable by depression.)

Sutch's cavalier attitude to his prescribed medications didn't help either, says Sutch's former driver, Bob Gilbert: 'He took it when he felt he needed it. He used to take handfuls sometimes, which could be dangerous, or decide that he didn't want to take any at all.' Thann recalls how Sutch would 'take, like, fifteen tablets of Panadol for the migraine headaches'. For someone who thought illegal drugs were anathema, Sutch certainly had no fear of prescription drugs. Tony Dangerfield (a sufferer from depression himself) told me that when Sutch and the band were on the road we 'used to rattle when we were driving over hills en route to gigs – we were nearly all on Prozac and other pills.'

'We'd all go to gigs,' adds fellow Savage Tony Ellis, 'be the life and soul, then go home, shut the door and wait for the depression to creep in'.

Sutch, however, appeared to have convinced himself that the medications he was taking were not associated with the substances that had ruined the lives of other rock stars. 'Mother was concerned about rock's association with drink and drugs,' he told the *Daily Mail* in 1995. 'But she needn't have worried because alcohol gives me a splitting headache. And when people such as Keith Moon and my hero Elvis died as a result of drugs, I knew I was right in never touching the stuff.' The side effects of Prozac are of course well known: they can include decreased sexual interest and/or problems achieving orgasm, nausea, headache, nervousness, insomnia and diarrhoea. The side effects of Lithium include fluid retention and consequent weight gain, nausea, thirst and excessive urination. One wonders if Sutch ever considered what all those pills were doing to him.

My own opinion is that David suffered from clinical depression. This is the most common form of depression and symptoms include feelings of sadness or emptiness, suicidal thoughts, feelings of hopelessness or worthlessness and difficulties in thinking. To me, this sounds very much like David.

But Bob Gilbert believes 'it was more of a neurosis than a psychosis – he would say, "It just comes on." When I first started with him he could hide his depressions quite well, but in the end he didn't bother. He would get anxiety attacks, dependent on what was going on around him. He would lock up, his fingers and hands would be like claws, he was so uptight. He'd be in severe pain with his headaches. The most he could do was go to bed. He even tried to go to gigs like that a couple of times. He'd get in the back of my car, try to relax, go to sleep, then he'd get out and do the gig for forty-five minutes. That was it – he was shot then.'

Sutch rarely acknowledged his problem in public, of course, and only infrequently in private. Writer Tony Barrell pointed out 'a tragic irony staring us in the face here: when you're top Raving Loony – party slogan: 'Vote for insanity, you know it makes sense' – how can you ever talk to people about a worsening mental illness?' Screaming Lord Sutch revelled in the label of professional lunatic; David Sutch was terrified of admitting that he had a debilitating mental illness. In a 1995 interview Sutch hinted that he had suffered problems in the past, but declined to mention his occasional visits to clinics such as the Charter Nightingale. He even boasted: 'I had to do it the long, lonely hard way, by my own self-discipline.' Yet, Gilbert even remembered Sutch checking himself into the clinic, coming out to do a gig, and being driven back afterwards, and says Sutch would make him drive up to Harley Street to see a specialist in the middle of the night: 'He didn't want the papers to know because of the stigma of mental health problems.' I wonder whether David ever heard the family yarn told to me by a distant relative, journalist Kerry Sutch, who recalled her father's story of how 'a complete stranger turned up on his doorstep, telling my mother that he had been researching the history of the Sutch name, and that he had come to warn her that madness ran through the family.'

But, adds Bob Gilbert, not all Sutch's problems were mental: 'I don't think he had much counselling when he went into the clinic. He would get run down through not eating properly, but in the clinic he would eat regularly. Many mental health problems can be triggered by a lack of minerals in the diet, and left to his own devices Sutch would often eat just three bowls of cereal a day. No vegetables or healthy food.' The death of Sutch's mother, he believes, had real, practical implications: 'When he went round to his mum's he would eat well because she would cook for him, right up until the time she had to go into hospital, by which time I think she knew he was in a bad way.'

One of the few times he opened up about his problems in public was in an interview he gave shortly before his death to his old friend and band-mate, Alan Clayson, eventually to be published in *Record Collector* magazine after Sutch's suicide. Sutch admitted he had been ill: 'It took me a lot longer than I thought to get over my mother's death. During that time I felt so terrible that I was just going through the motions. I didn't want to do gigs.'

I probably still hadn't accepted just how bleak David could feel until Cynthia Payne revealed the contents of a note he had written that had been found in the Parkfield Road house following the funeral by his son Tristan. Cynthia Payne made Tristan read the words out to her so she could write them down. Whether it was David's own work or whether he had read it somewhere else and copied the words down, either way, none of Sutch's previous songwriting efforts ever approached the sheer power and desperation of this short note. It was headed 'Depression':

Living with depression is the nearest thing to death. Even more than sleep. In sleep you are out cold. In depression you feel yourself dying and you can't do anything about it. The deep panic and torture you go through is hell. You are awake but you feel the pain of it all.

Yet another note, also found at the house, read:

1. Stress + Dep, bad bad bad
2. So bad can not pick up vac
3. Dep so low walk will not get rid of it or t.v.comady [sic] shows
4. Can not drive bit of daze
5. Can only think dep dep dep

6. Why dos [sic] it just lift?
7. Back to tabs
8. In morning very bad
   I wish I did not wake up
9. Only good thing is to go to bed and sleep at night and day

'It is tragic,' commented Dave Savage, 'that a man like Dave, who had friends in just about every town, couldn't tell anyone how he really felt. A man who was surrounded by people with genuine love for him had to die alone.' Giselle has upsetting recollections of the depths to which Sutch's spirits could sink. 'At one point he could not talk. He was only making noises. That was really terrifying. He was suffering so intensely. I think he pushed himself too hard to keep his name alive – and he died of it.'

Just when the seeds of Sutch's mental torture were first planted it is impossible to say, but I was struck by the lyrics of what seemed to be a self-composition in a notebook of his from as far back as 1961 or 1962. It was untitled and unfinished:

Well, I stopped by the kemest [sic] just the other day:
(Well, he's getting all drugged up)
Just to chase my blues and sorrows away
(Well, he's getting all drugged up)
I've got a splitting headache and my knees are getting weak
(Well, he's getting all drugged up)
How long can I keep standing on my own two feet
(Well, he's getting all drugged up)
How can I get rid of the buzz in my head
(Well, he's getting all drugged up)

He could easily have written those lyrics in 1999. By comparison, here are the lyrics to another (probably unrecorded) song called 'My Brains On Fire' given to me by Thann and Tristan, and almost certainly written shortly before his death:

I get a bit depressed, and I get a little blue
I totally confused [sic], what do I do?

Am I lazy, or am I going crazy,
But my brains, my brains, my brains on fire

Am I going out of my mind? Tell me the truth, try and be kind
Am I mad or just insane, whatever it is I feel real strange
Yes, am I lazy or just going crazy
But my brains, my brain, my brain on fire.

Solo

I need help and I need it bad
I'm upset and I'm feeling sad
Is this, is this all there is to life
I feel burnt out. Am ill, tell the wife.

In a small notebook (whose contents suggest it was in use between late 1998 and early 1999) Sutch also wrote a series of telling notes: 'Its better to burn out than fade away'; 'I'm growing in confidence'; 'I'm nobody and I'm everybody; 'Never give up. All ways tri harder.' But there are the occasional flashes of wit amongst the despair, including: 'Cliff Richard owes it to his fans to be cloned'.

Alan Clayson had been one of David Sutch's closest and most perceptive friends. In his opinion, 'for keeping the faith for so long, the title of king of British rock might belong not to someone like Cliff Richard, Billy Fury or even Johnny Kidd, but to the realm's hitless godfather of horror-rock.' He and I finally met up ('You'll recognise me by the shock of white hair and black winkle-pickers') and toasted Sutch with a glass of champagne. In 1998, he told me, he had, somewhat audaciously, attempted to get David involved in an album of Jacques Brel songs to which he had contributed – and how oddly Sutch had reacted when Alan told him the track he wanted him to record was the sombre 'My Death': 'I just had this theory that it was still not too late for Sutch to get a freak chart breakthrough if he cut a song completely removed from what people would expect him to do. He knew the track – he had quite a good knowledge of Gallic pop music, perhaps because of his relationship with Giselle – but reacted as though it was something forbidden.'

Clayson admitted that it was probably only his affection for Sutch that persuaded him to 'drive to Peterborough to do a gig for thirty-five quid' – a gig that turned out to be one of the last ones Alan did with him. 'It was a wedding, but we must have been too loud, because by the time we were finishing there was almost no one still watching – and I heard David's footsteps as he walked off the stage.'

This show was the inspiration for Alan's tribute song to David, a raw cry of grief, love and despair called 'The Last Show On Earth':

David, oh David, hang on to that daydream,
Hang on to that daydream, if it meant so much
That centuries fade and some smile and remember
The man who was Screaming Lord Sutch.
It was your day that day,
The last show on earth.
But a black carnival shall continue
For those who weren't there for that final performance,
The only one left in you.
You'd identify awe in the constituency,
When counter assistants went coy.
But they'll speak of you less
In the junk shops and cafés
Where you were still a boy.

No one else listened to that dark escort's whisper
Your mind slipped away from the outrage.
When fortune failed slowly
You heard your own footsteps
Walk off the stage.

Cameo therapy, some kind of Hell,
The dressing room was one more cold dungeon cell.
The spotlight it felt bloody warm on your face
In 'Jack the Ripper' during the chase
And a solitary mister, paid off and gone,
You wondered if you had already passed on.
The newsreader's footnote, the punchline unspoken

Transmitting your funeral knell
Still keeping the faith,
You'd packed up and checked out of Heartbreak Hotel.

David, oh David, hang on that daydream
Hang on to that daydream if it meant so much
When centuries fade there'll be some who'll remember
That tears fell for Screaming Lord Sutch,
Tears fell for Screaming Lord Sutch,
The man who was Screaming Lord Sutch.

The CD recording of this song Alan had sent me was in my car's CD player when I pulled up alongside David's grave one Saturday morning. As the track came on, I opened the car doors to allow the sound to ring around the deserted cemetery. During its final minute I noticed a single, large bird on the highest branch of the tallest tree overlooking David's grave – a magpie, or perhaps a rook or a crow. It was chattering away animatedly, but certainly not singing.

The track died away – and immediately started up again. No CD had ever done that before in my player. It kept repeating as I drove home. Eventually I had to turn it off manually.

chapter twenty-one

Posthumousutch

'Rock's most monstrous raving loony may be gone, but his great, batlike wings still cast a horrifying and humorous shadow over us all – and that's probably just the way he'd want it'

— MATT MARCHESE, WRITER

To the people bereaved by suicide,' writes Virginia Ironside, herself a sufferer from depression, in her striking contribution to the book *Threads of Hope: Learning to Live with Depression*, 'your loved ones never wanted to kill themselves. They only wanted to kill the pain they were feeling. Unfortunately, there was no other way to achieve this than to throw the baby out with the bath water.'

Besides its impact on his family and friends, Sutch's death was felt most keenly by the political party he had co-founded. Its website carried tributes from all over the world. 'I hereby would like to give my most sincerely regards to that Monster of Rock and Roll who wrote some of its most bloody and exciting pages,' wrote Alfonso Cameno from Bilbao. 'In Hudson Bay, Canada to see wild polar bears,' wrote Bob Merkin from Massachusetts, 'I found myself with a Southampton, UK, couple and asked them about the OMRLP. I remember the broad loving smile on their faces that talking about Screaming Lord Sutch generated.'

In the month following his suicide, the first Official Monster Raving Loony Party by-election took place without him. Sutch's old friend (and party co-founder) Alan Hope stood at the Eddisbury, Cheshire by-election and won 238 votes. During its 1999 party conference, there was a two-minute scream in honour of Sutch. Perhaps they should have pulled the plug on the party then, leaving only good memories behind. Instead, it slowly began to unravel.

Certainly Alan Hope was not interested in letting the party die. In November he once again contested a by-election, this time in Kensington and Chelsea. But little of the Sutch factor now remained: Hope no longer sprang eternal. He slumped to twenty votes, finishing a humiliating second last out of eighteen. 'For more than thirty years the Loony Party were the self-appointed pranksters of the political fringe,' wrote Jon Ronson in the *Guardian* in an article about the campaign which the party believed damaged its reputation. 'But now, with the death of their long-time leader, Lord Sutch, the party's japes are no longer a laughing matter.'

Sutch's PR John Tempest certainly believes that the party effectively was over once Sutch died: 'It was generally recognised that without David the party would be a shadow of its former self. I stopped having anything to do with the party pretty soon after David's death.'

Soon, the disquiet festering behind the scenes flared up in public. Unbeknown to many, the Loony Party had effectively split into two factions, with one claiming to be the 'real' party. A significant number of loyal Loonies, though, felt that that the show was already over.

Certainly Helen Cronin (who had been Loony minister for pets) felt strongly that the party needed a new direction if it was going to survive. She knew that it had been 'a benevolent dictatorship' while Sutch was alive but now that he was gone some sort of radical change was needed. 'Once he had gone,' she told me, 'it needed to turn into a democracy with a new figurehead leader, but there were people in the party who would not tolerate any sort of democracy.'

Instead, she ended up joining the breakaway Rock 'n' Roll Loony Party, which registered itself with the Electoral Commission and acknowledged its debt to Sutch in its official crest, which read: 'Vote Sensible, Vote Loony – By Appointment to His Spiritualness, Screaming Lord Sutch.' Amongst the leading lights of the new faction were its chief Rock 'n' Roller, Chris Driver, alias Screwy, who had been voted onto Queenborough council on the Isle of Sheppey in 1999, and was subsequently elected Mayor.

'With Sutchie dead,' his wife Alma told me, 'hundreds of us decided it would be appropriate to let the party die with him, so we formed the new party to mark the fact that Sutchie's era had come to an end. We are going on in Dave's traditional way – having fun. We also have our own party conference, but out of respect to Alan Hope, hold it at a different time from the OMRLP's.'

There is one fight, though, that, in all seriousness, the new party set out to win: seeking to ban the use of the widely-prescribed anti-depressant drug Prozac until more is known about the effects of coming off it. David Sutch would call Alma and Screwy at all hours, complaining about 'black depressions'. Alma's nephew, who was also on Prozac, took his own life, too. She is concerned that when people try to stop using it, the side-effects may be potentially lethal.

Chris Driver explained that the new party was not trying to cash in on Sutch: 'We're in no way trying to harp on David's name or score points over other people – but to us, Sutch was the man, and that's the end of it.' Plenty of others agreed, including one of Sutch's old friends and former Loony, Stuart Hughes (now a Conservative): 'The Loony Party doesn't seem to be or mean anything now. David Sutch *was* the Monster Raving Loony Party. Some of those who continued with the party say it is an epitaph to him but they should really be taking it one stage farther – it really doesn't work without him.' It had to work without Lord Tiverton, too – on the eve of being voted chairman of the party in October 1999 he died, followed two months later by Sutch's Elvis-lookalike pal Leyton Summers, from unexplained injuries sustained shortly before David's funeral.

For a while, Alan Hope, the co-founder of the Official Monster Raving Loony Party, kept a bright orange urn in the pub he ran in Devon with a sign reading 'Ashes of Screaming Lord Sutch'. Inside (reportedly) were the contents of an ashtray found in the non-smoking Sutch's home after his death. Not that funny, really. In 2001, in the wake of all the feuding and defections, Hope made a brave, if perhaps foolhardy, attempt to re-launch the party. In true Sutch style, he immediately made his feline, Cat Mandu, joint leader. Based at the Dog and Partridge pub in Yateley, Hampshire, he kept the party going, along with long-time member and treasurer Melodie Staniforth. At the 2001 general election, they fielded fifteen candidates. Their website does sterling work in keeping the name of David Sutch alive, but somehow the effect feels rather like going to a Herman's Hermits concert, as I did once, and watching the band run through all their familiar hits without drawing attention to the absence of Herman.

The day I walked into the Dog and Partridge for the 2003 Loony conference – passing an open coffin, an abandoned cabinet and a mobile bed on the green outside – multi-coloured clothes and hats seemed to be the order of the day, with normal customers going about their business at the other end of the long bar. The overwhelming impression was of people desperately trying to appear abnormal – 'Look at me, I'm a nutter, aren't I?' – rather than Sutch's brand of genuine eccentricity. As a man and a woman both dressed as vicars exited the pub someone said, 'They're not vicars, you know.'

Sutch had been surrounded in the Loony Party by wannabes, never-would-bes and some bloody-well-shouldn't-bes. No one else was remotely recognisable to the rest of the world. He was the only one who really mattered. Lost without Sutch and his reflected glory, many of these undistinguished hangers-on – with a few honourable exceptions – rapidly faded back into obscurity. Many could not bear to admit that it was finished. Former member Bob Winter, alias The Late Henry Henderson, described his erstwhile colleagues as 'basically a set of old fogies having a laugh dressed up as twats'.

Even the illustrious Van Morrison pointed out the obvious in his song 'Whatever Happened to P.J. Proby?':

> Don't have no frame of reference no more
> Not even Screaming Lord Sutch
> Without him now there's no Raving Loony Party.

Mick Green, the guitarist and mainstay of the Pirates, who collaborated with him on the track, told me that Morrison had cried on hearing the news of Sutch's death. Green also praised Sutch's longevity in a music business where 'you're treated like fucking tubes of toothpaste. The longer you're in the game it doesn't necessarily mean you're any better thought of – there are no retirement gold watches'.

In 2005 both of the parties faced major problems as Alan anticipated moving from the Dog and Partridge, costing the OMRLP its headquarters and conference venue. And the driving force of the Rock 'n' Roll Loony Party, Chris 'Screwy' Driver, decided to stand down as leader. ' It's time for us two oldies to pack up work and party,' Alma explained. Meanwhile, the OMRLP's website boasts the slogan, 'Living the Loony Lifestyle in memory of Screaming Lord Sutch'.

In October 1999, four months after his death, the Gold Coast casino hotel in Las Vegas went ahead with the Hallowe'en gig which Sutch had been so thrilled to be invited to headline, although Thann is adamant he never signed his contract. He would have loved it. The Las Vegas Grind featured Jack and The Rippers, and the spirit of Sutch was reincarnated by vocalist Mike Stax, who once said of Sutch: 'For someone who supposedly had no discernible musical talent he sure made some great records.' Stax jumped up on stage to sing, dressed as the Screaming Lord himself.

The following summer, on Friday, 16 June 2000, there was a gathering at his graveside (which at that time did not yet boast a headstone), to mark the first anniversary of Sutch's death. Floral tributes were laid and colourfully garbed mourners discussed the past twelve months. 'His image is still as clear as if I had only seen him yesterday,' said Sutch's old friend, Dave Savage. Carlo Little called everyone to order for the singing of a skiffle song. Later, a jam session was held at the Sudbury Court Sports and Social Club, compered by Doc Cox and featuring Kim Roberts and Carlo's All Stars.

Kim Roberts, who was due to wed Jack Irving of The Savages, died nine days later. Her real name was Rosemary Cottnam, and she had been one of Sutch's first girlfriends, who had been in and out of his life for years. After David's death Kim had written: 'Sleep well, Dave, your demons are gone.' Some believed she was the girl Sutch's mother would have liked him to marry. In an obituary in the *Guardian*, Alan Clayson wrote that her passing was 'the latest among a number of comparatively early deaths among entertainers whose recording careers began at Joe Meek's RGM studio.'

Sutch's penchant for publicity once again echoed from beyond the grave in March 2001, when a headlined article in *The Times* diary declared that 'an auction of clothes and personal effects has prompted outrage among his family and former concubines.'

According to the newspaper the items were being offered by a private collector, but Thann was suspicious, speculating that 'they came from a person who had access to his house', and eventually she succeeded in halting the sale. Bonhams, the London auctioneers, provided me with a list of the goods which would have been offered: 'an incendiary stage top-hat'; a 'faux leopardskin jacket with velvet collar, labelled "Caroline Walker London"'; casual clothes and hats; toy skeletons; a bust of Winston Churchill; five John Major masks; Sutch's answer-phone cassette; publicity photographs; a cassette of Lord Sutch and The Rapiers; and an album of Sutch photographs.

Shortly afterwards, however, my eye was caught by a report in my local paper that some of Sutch's effects were to be part of an auction at Middle Claydon in Bucks – a somewhat incongruous place to find his possessions for sale, and especially alongside such other unrelated items as a 1950s Webbs child's lawnmower and 'a taxidermied Pike'. Once again the provenance seemed dubious – many of the items seemed identical to those from the halted Bonhams sale – but eventually the police confirmed that the sale could go ahead.

The back page of the catalogue was devoted to a colour photograph of a '1960s imitation leopardskin jacket as worn by Lord Sutch whilst performing on stage and also whilst campaigning', which took my eye. I entered a written bid of £400, and got up to read in the *Sunday Times* the next morning that I was now the proud owner of Sutch's jacket. In *Life As Sutch* he writes, 'As a special present for my birthday soon after we met Giselle bought me the mock leopardskin jacket from Caroline Walker in Kensington Market, which became my political uniform.' Sure enough, the original label was still in the jacket. I have since assured Giselle that the jacket is in appreciative hands.

An odd affair was the advertisement for sale on eBay in August 2003 of two 'original paintings by Screaming Lord Sutch'. Brighton-based La Artier Fine Art set a starting bid of £200 for 'a very rare opportunity to acquire an original oil pastel by Sutch. The subject is a reflection of a person in a spoon, signed and dated 1972.' It does bear a resemblance to a young Sutch, and the subject matter would certainly fit. The second painting is a watercolour of a soldier. The signatures on the two items have similarities with, but are distinctly different from, the one he usually used.

Vendor Timothy Williams claimed the pictures had 'come from the house of David Sutch's mother. I could think of no reason for someone to counterfeit them – it would be more worth their while to copy an established artist'. Two more 'Sutches' – one a Second World War scene, another of a horse – are owned by David Sheppard, who bought them for £40 and £30 respectively from Hove Auction Rooms in October 2001 'because my partner thought they had some artistic merit'.

These pictures, I was later told by Stephen Perry of Scarborough Perry Fine Arts, were believed to have come from Sutch's ill-fated home in Hastings – 'no proof, but we accepted them as genuine, if only because they were not worth forging. They might have been a prank but if so, probably close to Sutch.' He wasn't above a practical joke, of course. They could have been pictures he or someone else owned, to which his signature was appended. Sid 'Elvisly Yours' Shaw's partner, Maureen, believes Sutch did paint, showing the results to very few people; Tristan, although he is a decent drawer, says he is unaware that his father may have been, while Yvonne says David could only manage matchstick-men drawings. Pat Hellier is adamant – 'I never knew David to draw anything except the ones that were found after his death in the pockets of one of his stage jackets – drawings of a hangman.'

But, if the 'pictures' are disputed, there is no controversy over the unreleased treasure trove of Sutch tracks I discovered, discarded in a skip, which I hope will eventually be released, perhaps by John Beecher at Rollercoaster Records. Amongst the ten or so useable songs are two terrific sides from 1982 – a kind of adult 'Dracula's Daughter' called 'Vampire For You', which Sutch once said he hoped to use as a 'pension' but which never saw the light of day, and 'Undertaker', a catchy number – 'I am your local coffin maker, with a saw, a hammer and a bunch of nails.'

An eerie revelation, whose relevance to the life of David Sutch one cannot help but speculate on, came in an extraordinary story in *The Times* in May 2003: that 'the brains of thousands of depressed people were illegally removed after their deaths and kept for medical research over a period of nearly thirty years'. The practice continued from 1970 right up until 1999 – the year Sutch died: 'The pathologist would extract the brain, the coroner's office would alert the researchers that they had a good specimen and the mortician would be paid £10 to leave it on a slab of ice to be collected by researchers within hours, all without the knowledge of the dead person's families'. A Manchester woman whose husband committed suicide after suffering depression in 1987 and a doctor from Cambridge whose husband committed suicide while depressed were both said to have discovered that their partner's brains had been removed and used for research purposes. and estimates suggested as many as 10,000 brains may have been removed. We may never know if Sutch's was among them – but even he would never have dared write lyrics as horrific as this scenario, bearing echoes of Burke and Hare, with whose nineteenth-century body-snatching exploits his watching of horror movies had made him so familiar.

In January 2002, Harrow Council's Cemetery Department granted permission to Thann Rendessy for a headstone to be erected on grave number 27 in section J2 of Pinner New Cemetery, where David Edward Sutch lies buried with his mum.

In the meantime, various proposals began to emerge for some sort of memorial to him. Some traders in Harrow, the town he had called home for so much of his life, suggested replacing the long-serving statue in the town centre, of a little girl called Katie and her skipping rope, with one of Sutch. (The irony of substituting an icon with a rather more macabre association with a child's skipping-rope appeared to escape most of those involved.)

Alan Hope had an altogether grander proposal: 'As Screaming Lord Sutch was the longest serving party leader in British political history, we propose that he take pride of place atop a new Sutch's Column in the centre of Trafalgar Square.' On the Isle of Sheppey, Chris 'Screwy' Driver floated the idea of a memorial roundabout to Sutch on a main road, dedicated to him with four plaques.

There were many possible Sutch memorial locations: the site of the now-demolished Railway Hotel in Wealdstone, where Sutch had given many performances. (Indeed, when it had hit hard times, he had suggested that he buy it and turn it into a rock 'n' roll museum, featuring, of course, himself.) Or there was the British Legion in South

Harrow, where, according to Carlo Little, Screaming Lord Sutch and The Savages had played their debut gig; or – Jess Conrad's suggestion – Stringfellow's: 'Sutch loved Stringfellows. Every celebrity night we'd be there, we were great party-goers. We used to go to the opening of an envelope.' The first house he bought his mum, White Lodge? Perhaps even the house in Parkfield Road? (In fact, the latter has since been sold and redecorated.)

Finally I mentioned the problem to Gordon Green, the organiser of the Man Versus Horse Marathon in mid-Wales, which Sutch had attended every year for eleven years, always staying at the Neuadd Arms Hotel, whose bar still boasts pictures of him, together with a poster declaring it to be a Monster Raving Loony HQ. This poster actually fell down at precisely the moment musician 'Dangerous Dave', a former backing musician and political campaigner with Sutch, entered the bar on New Year's Eve 2002. Sutch had loved the surrounding countryside around Llanwrtyd Wells, and had played his very last gig there just three days before he died. Since his death, the race had always featured a Lord Sutch Memorial Trophy, with the winner receiving a model top hat.

Green was soon on the case: 'You know the large metal sculpture of the endangered Red Kite we have on the green outside the Neuadd Arms? Well, I've had a word with the chap who sculpted it and he would be happy to do one dedicated to Sutch.' After discussions with the sculptor, Sandy O'Connor, we decided against a full-size statue and opted instead for a top hat and a rosette, two images strongly associated with Sutch, the top hat (in Loony Party colours of yellow and black) to be affixed to the wall outside the Neuadd Arms, and a plaque under-neath in the shape of a party rosette.

The memorial was unveiled in the presence of Yvonne Elwood, Cynthia Payne, Alan Hope, Melodie Staniforth, Pat Hellier and many other friends of David, on 12 June 2004, to coincide with the twenty-fifth running of the William Hill Man Versus Horse Marathon, incorporating the world's first Loony Marathon, won by Lord Toby Jug. The day also goes down in history as the first time that the man – in the person of Huw Lobb – beat the horse, winning for himself a prize of £25,000. Typical of Sutch to engineer such a unique flourish on, nearly to the day, the fifth anniversary of the death of David Edward Sutch.

Epilogue

'He never wanted anybody to know everything about him'

— PAT HELLIER

Dogs, cats and ferrets 'meeting the necessary requirements' may move freely these days between EU member states if they have a valid EU pet passport. It seems the rest of the world is finally catching up with Screaming Lord Sutch's Loony foresight. Meanwhile, *Telstar*, a play centred on the life of Joe Meek, began a tour of provincial theatres in early 2005; it included a portrayal of Screaming Lord Sutch. A CD of unreleased musical material is imminent from Rollercoaster Records, and there are even plans for a revival of Radio Sutch.

Musically, too, more people are getting the point: one of the world's coolest bands, The White Stripes, perform 'Jack the Ripper' at their gigs, and recorded it on their acclaimed recent DVD, *Under Blackpool Lights*. Jack White, it turns out, is a Sutch fan, and without being aware of this, Tristan was a great White Stripes admirer. I brought them together, and Tristan and Thann attended a gig, which the band dedicated to Sutch, on 16 June 2003 – the fourth anniversary of Sutch's death. Tristan and Thann handed over to Jack one of Sutch's stage-prop coffins for his new house in Detroit, as well as a Lord Sutch stage jacket and top hat. The band played 'Jack the Ripper' as an encore. In an email Jack explained to me that he had a copy of *Heavy Friends*:

I got it as a teenager, because it had members of Led Zeppelin on it. I liked the way his vocals were very intense, but at the same time sort of 'blown off' as not that important. His ideas seemed very interesting to me because he obviously wanted to break some new ground with lyrical and song content. Joe Meek's work with him is pretty amazing. I'm very fond of 'Till the Following Night', which has a great vocal track.

We started to cover his song 'Jack the Ripper' early on in the White Stripes. It actually became a crowd favourite and was often requested. We never recorded it, but we did perform it on different live radio sessions, including John Peel's. It was cool to see new kids getting turned on to the song.

White also remembered borrowing a video tape from a friend which contained footage of Sutch playing the Wembley Stadium gig: 'What was cool was that Sutch came out of his coffin in a gigantic hat and was "shot" several times without falling on stage, whilst saying on the mic, "I'm coming to get you, Alice!"' And White's own thoughts on immortality would have struck a chord with Sutch: 'A hundred years from now, I'd like my skull to be in a junk shop and for someone to pick it up and buy it…'

Towards the end of my research for this book, a chance remark from Cynthia Payne led me to David Sutch's clergyman uncle, Leonard Sutch. A younger surviving brother of Will Sutch, the father Sutch never knew, Len has been a Methodist minister in the Peak District, Liverpool and Birmingham, and is now based in Southport. 'David's mother, Nancy, and David, who was still a baby,' he wrote in a letter to me, 'left my parents' home soon after the tragic death of my eldest brother, Will. They found accommodation elsewhere and thereafter Nancy had very little contact with the family. It was wartime and war work soon took me and my brothers away from London.'

Len Sutch was only a young man himself when his twenty-five-year-old brother was killed in an accident on his way to work during a wartime blackout. But Len remembers him well: 'He was keenly interested in wildlife, and had in the back garden of our house an aviary. He was a member of a "Bird Club", which encouraged members to collect and breed rare and special birds.'

Len had long ago lost contact with his famous nephew: 'The business of our lives got in the way, as it usually does.' However, he sent me a photograph of himself and David, when they had met up for the last time towards the end of David's life, and I noticed that David wore a brooch featuring a bird in his lapel. As I looked at it I recalled Yvonne telling me how in the last weeks of his life, David – truly the son of his father – loved nothing more than sitting in the park feeding the ducks and the pigeons.

The grave that David Edward Sutch shares with his mother is made of black marble with a headstone at one end, topped by the figure of a rather ugly angel, its hands clasped together in an attitude of prayer.

On either side of the headstone are two inscriptions. On the right-hand side are the words 'Annie Emily Sutch "Nancy"' and the dates 1915–1997, 'Dearly beloved mother of David'. ('She's got him back now', observed Julia Rothnie, Mrs Sutch's social worker.) On the left is the outline of a top hat, along with the name 'David Edward Sutch' in white capital letters and the dates 1940–1999. Underneath is a six-line verse:

A lord without peer.
Sutch is the way
It was with him.
And Sutch is why
He'll always
Be with us.

The epigraph echoes a phrase featured twice, with slight variations, in Sutch's autobiography. In the book, these words come to Sutch during a flight of fantasy in which he imagines his hero Winston Churchill telling him: 'For Sutch is the way it is; and Sutch is therefore the way it will be when I am gone.' Then the Greatest Living Englishman pushes him away saying, 'Now, Sutch, get out of my way, you little squirt!'

At the far end of the grave of the little squirt who grew up to become Screaming Lord Sutch is a container in which flowers can be placed. There is rarely anything fresh to be found there.

I started work on this book on 10 November, 2002. The date rang a bell. I checked – it would have been David's sixty-second birthday: a positive sign. So I went to visit his grave – just a mile from my home. I had attended the funeral but not stayed for the burial, and now I searched the cemetery in darkening gloom and persistent drizzle for over an hour in vain. Walking to the exit, defeated, and cursing Sutch out loud, I saw a little yellow Fiat approaching, driven by an elderly lady I'd spoken to earlier who'd been tending her mother's grave.

She pulled alongside: 'Have you found him?'

'No.'

'Jump in.'

She dropped me next to the grave:' Wish him Happy Birthday for me.'

Acknowledgements

At first I kidded myself that I'd be able to write this book just by utilising personal memories and chatting to a few people I already knew who had come into contact with David Sutch. I soon realised how wrong I was when I contacted Alan Hope and began to quiz him about elements of David's life. Alan knew him from both the rock 'n' roll and political angles and he soon began to mention names I was only vaguely aware of and had no means of contacting. He handed over a string of contact names and numbers, which in turn generated more and more of the same. He also gave me access to his own memorabilia.

Without the assistance and freely given access to personal address books of Pat Hellier I would have remained unaware of many vital facts about David and his relationships. Pat pointed me in the right direction so many times and I was devastated to learn that her husband Ken, also hugely helpful, had died in early 2004.

Melodie Staniforth, universally known as Boney Moronie, was another invaluable source of contact details, but also of insights into David's life. Her husband Stan, who played with Sutch, was equally forthcoming.

A book of this nature requires input from those who were closest to the subject. Thann and Tristan, Giselle, Cynthia and Yvonne all shared a home with him at different times – and almost certainly would never share a home with each other – but all were unfailingly helpful and talked freely about their lives with David.

David's surviving blood relatives have varying degrees of knowledge of his life. His Uncle Len and Aunty Mary supplied intriguing insights while his cousin Linda Oliver was circumspect and protective of her relationship with, and opinions of, him. Another cousin, Andrew Sutch, did not know him well but obliged with memories.

Close rock 'n' roll mates via The Savages, Carlo Little (not forgetting his charming wife, Iris, and daughter Giselle) and Tony Dangerfield are widely regarded as the creator and guardian of his musical legacy, respectively. Many others who played with him, whether once, several or many times, contributed gladly. Thanks to: Anji Antanori; Johnny Bedder; Chris Black; Tony Bloom; Rick Brown; Wild Bob Burgos; Jim Byers; Johnny Casanova; Jerry Chapman; Terry Clemson; Mal Clint; Mike Crawford; Sir Dangerous Dave; Dave Dix; Trevor Fontane; Paul Green; Tim Green; Ron Harwood; Derek Holt; Jack Irving; Freddie Fingers Lee; Legendary Lonnie; Pete Newman; Mac Poole; Colin Pryce-Jones; Peter Parks; Mick Richardson; Dave Savage; Johnny Schollar; Ian Scouler; Derek Sirmon; Colin Standring; Martin (and Ursula) Symonds; Dave Taylor; Stuart Taylor; Ian Terry; Pete Thomas; Lord Toby; Dave and Wyatt Wendels; Peter Lee Wenger; Andy Wren.

Then there were those who also trod the boards alongside him, in their own bands, as solo artistes or fellow showbiz personalities. They were all prepared to reflect on the unique character of David Sutch, and for that I am grateful to: Frank Allen; Cliff Bennett; Dave Berry; Mike Berry; Clem Cattini; Alan Clayson; Stuart Colman; Jess Conrad; Billie Davis; Ray Dorset; Rhino Edwards; Matthew Fisher; Ian Gillan; Mick Green; Jet Harris; Wee Willie Harris; Dr Haze; Chas Hodges; Mike Maxfield; Martin Newell; Peter Noone; John Otway; Nick Owen; Mike Read; Bill Roughley; Sir Jimmy Savile; Nick Simper; Peter Stringfellow; Freddie Valentine; Rick Wakeman; Johnny Walker; James Whale; Jack White.

So many people came into contact with David whilst he was out campaigning for the Loony Party whether as helper, candidate, potential voter, or political opponent – again they all had opinions and shared them. Step forward: Captain Beany; Tony Benn; Mark Boyle; Helen Cronin; Alma and Chris Driver; Jersey Flyer; Dave Goddard; Stan Herley; Stuart Hughes; Neil Kinnock; John Lewis; Ken Livingstone; Dennis MacShane; T.C. Owen; Darren Poyzer; Rockin' Robbo; Keith Rothesay; Charlie Salt; R.U. Seerius; Sid Shaw (and partner, Maureen); John Tempest; Baron Von Thunderclap; Gloria Walker; George Weiss; Bob Winter; Freddie Zapp.

A man so frequently in the headlines could not help but become a valuable contact to many journalists, writers and members of the media, some of whom have returned the favour by imparting their impressions of him to me and/or supplying details of stories involving him. I'm also grateful to those who gave publicity to my quest for information about David. Cheers to: Mike Adams; Roger Arthur; Tony Barrell; Jerry Bloom; Adam Boulton; Trevor Cajaio; Chris Charlesworth; Peter Chippindale; John Comfort; Alistair Dabbs; Martin Dawes; Chris Edwards; the late Simon

Ferrari; Sandy Guthrie; Charlie Harris; George Holland; John Kay; Willie Lefebve; Sean Magee; Colleen Maloney; Matt Marchese; Rob McNeil; Tim Moynihan; Mike Neal; Russell Newmark; Dave Painter; David Parker; Roger Plummer; John Repsch; Thorsten Schmidt; Roger St Pierre; Mitchell Symons; Stephen Theobald; Alwyn W. Turner; Richard Williams.

Schoolfriends, early workmates, pals or, in one case, a teacher, from up to half a century or so ago never forgot him – Bob Bassil; Don Bromage; Pat Greenberg; Eddie Jaggers; Rodney Johnson; Arthur 'Nobby' Randall; Keith Rentall; Doug Rosewarne.

Girlfriends, real or imagined, and/or friends who were girls, who retained affectionate thoughts of him even after the relationship had moved on include: Val Bird; Candy Calvert; Jann Clayton-Fuller; Geneveve; Lindi St Clair; Mary Murray; Samantha Kirli; Carole Watt; Angela Wayne.

Those who worked with or for him or for whom he worked over the years: George Apter; Phil Bailey; Paul Barrett; John Brennan; Barry Collins; Lionel Digby; Ritchie Gee; Bob Gilbert; Arthur Martin; Patsy Martin; Nigel Molden; Bob Potter; Phil Reid; Ken Rumens; Mark and Linda Wilsmore.

Those who don't quite belong in any of the above categories, yet contributed importantly to the telling of the story of David's life: John Beecher of Rollercoaster Records; John Briggs; Stephen Burns; Herve Colombet; Roger Cooper; Ken Fagan; Bernard Futter; Bob Gilbert; Gordon, Di and Susannah Green; Brian Gregg; Nigel Griffiths; Roy Hankin; Ian Hawkins; Jean Heath; Vince Hogan; Zak Hussein; Denise Kellerman; Steve Kramer; Moyna Lydon; Tony Marsh; Bill Musyk; Stephen Perry; Sam Rapallo; Julia Rothnie; Jacqueline Ryan; Tom Sheehan; David Sheppard; Roger Slater; Romaine Snijder; Peter Stockton; Mary Timberlake; Desmond Tyler; Timothy Williams; Gunter Zint.

My thanks must also go to Graham Coster at Aurum Press, who commissioned this book, and Susan Johnson, who edited it, particularly for Graham's willingness to act as a sounding board for so much of the material. Without them this book would be a whole lot longer, but a whole lot less accessible.

Many thanks to everyone who took time to speak to me, and apologies to anyone inadvertently omitted. I appreciate your input. Even if it didn't make it into the book it helped complete my overall understanding and interpretation of David's life.

Bibliography

Clayson, Alan, *Beat Merchants* (Blandford, 1995)

Clayson, Alan, *Brian Jones* (Sanctuary, 2003)

Collis, John, *Van Morrison: Inarticulate Speech of the Heart* (Warner Books, 1996)

Cross, Colin, *Encyclopedia of British Beat Groups* (Omnibus Press, 1980)

Ehrenstein, David, and Bill Reed, *Rock On Film* (Virgin, 1982)

Fletcher, Mark, Nic Kynaston, Rhonda Carrier, and Gill Moodie, *The Guinness Book of Records 1998* (Guinness Publishing, 1998)

Fletcher, Tony, *Dear Boy: The Life of Keith Moon* (Omnibus, 1999)

Frame, Pete, *Rock Family Trees* (Omnibus Press, 1980)

Hamlyn, Nick, *Penguin Price Guide For Record and CD Collectors* (Penguin, 2000)

Hibbert, Tom, *Best of Q: Who The Hell ...?* (Virgin, 1994)

Holder, Noddy, *Who's Crazee Now?* (Ebury Press, 1999)

Hounsome, Terry, *New Rock Record* (Blandford Press, 1983)

Humphries, John, *Music Master Tracks Catalogue* (Harrap 1989)

Joynson, Vernon, *The Tapestry of Delights* (Borderline Productions, 1995)

Larkin, Colin, *All Time Top 1000 Albums* (Virgin, 1998)

Marsh, Dave, *Before I Get Old* (Plexus, 1983)

May, Chris and Tim Phillips, *British Beat* (Socion Books, 1974)

Neill, Andy and Matt Hunt, *Complete Chronicle of The Who 1958–78* (Virgin, 2002)

Platt, John, *London's Rock Routes* (Fourth Estate, 1985)

Record Collector, *Rare Record Price Guide 2000* (Parker Mead Limited, 2000)

Rees, Daffyd and Luke Crampton, *Q Encyclopaedia of Rock Stars* (Dorling Kindersley, 1996)

Repsch, John, *The Legendary Joe Meek* (Cherry Red, 1989)

Rogan, Johnny, *Starmakers and Svengalis* (Macdonald Queen Anne Press, 1988)

Sutch, Lord David (with Peter Chippindale), *Life As Sutch* (HarperCollins, 1991)

Sutch, Lord David (with Alwyn W.Turner) *As Sutch: Manifesto of the Official Monster Raving Loony Party* (McNaughty, 1996)

Tobler, John, ed., *NME Rock 'n' Roll Years* (BCA, 1992)

Tosches, Nick, *Unsung Heroes of Rock 'n' Roll* (Secker& Warburg, 1991)

Wyman, Bill, *Rolling with The Stones* (Dorling Kindersley, 2002)

Savageography

'When people tell me they were in the Savages, I look at them and
think, no, mate, I was in the Savages – you just backed Dave Sutch'

— TONY DANGERFIELD

MICK ABRAHAMS (guitar)
Of Jethro Tull and Blodwyn Pig. A Savage but 'only for two gigs when
I was part of Neil Christian's Crusaders. Sutch did exactly the same set
as Christian so it wasn't too hard. He still owes me £15 for the last gig!'

FRANK ALLEN (guitar)
Of The Searchers fame. 'Dave was fairly philosophical about losing his
musicians. It happened a lot. He had a reputation, though, as a training
camp for some of the best and most enduring musicians in British rock.'

ANJI ANTANORI (guitar)
Quietly spoken Scot who played on the 1991 track, 'Loony Rock', but
was – and is – also part of the Dangerfield-vintage Savages.

JOHNNY BEDDER (guitar)
Savages guitarist from October to December 1966. Was there when
they became The Roman Empire until April 1967. Toured with the
Savages to Sweden, where they were locked up when Sutch failed to
turn up with work permits. 'Because he wasn't musical he could be a
nightmare to work with – he'd launch into "Good Golly Miss Molly" but
when we came out of the instrumental break he'd carry on into "Great
Balls of Fire".' Lost contact with Sutch for twenty-five years, then
spotted a Sutch gig near where he was living. 'When I walked in he was

halfway through an interview which he stopped immediately and threw his arms round me.'

NEIL BESMOORI (guitar)
Lead guitarist in January 1976, witnessed Sutch 'set fire to a bass player's trousers'.

CHRIS BLACK (guitar)
Veteran lead guitarist, played with Sutch in the 1980s. Recalled gigs at which Sutch cut chair-legs off with a chain saw. Created a legendary rock yarn by handcuffing Giselle when she came to a show and refusing to set her free even as she became more and more agitated. 'When David died I threw those handcuffs into the grave with him.'

RITCHIE BLACKMORE (guitar)
Arrived at his first Savages' audition accompanied by girlfriend and dad. Joined in May 1962. Nicknamed Bluebell by Sutch: 'He used to just stand in the corner when we first got him. We had to drag him round the stage and put a bit of life into him.' Subsequently found mega-fame with first Deep Purple and then Ritchie Blackmore's Rainbow.

TONY BLOOM (bass)
His Beachcombers supported Sutch in the 1960s. Recalled seeing Sutch perform at his peak in an Earls Court venue: 'He did the full repertoire in front of an audience of about four hundred people. At one point Sutch stopped, came to the front of the stage and said, "Put your hands up anyone who *hasn't* played with me before." Almost all the hands stayed down.'

RICK(Y) BROWN (bass)
An original member of the band.

'WILD' BOB BURGOS (drums)
Met Sutch in 1976, when on tour with Matchbox. Paid tribute to Sutch as 'decent, kind and always thinking of other people'. Recorded an album dedicated to Sutch.

JIM BYERS (guitar)
'Dave was one of the meanest bastards I ever met – but what a nice guy!'

JOHNNY CASANOVA (keyboards)
With Sutch for seven years, and recently called back into band by Dangerfield.

JERRY CHAPMAN (bass)
Believes he could have written Sutch that elusive hit, but doubts whether he would have received his due deserts without a struggle: 'It could be a bugger getting money out of him,' he said, laughing.

TERRY CLEMSON (guitar)
Started with Downliners Sect in the 1960s; has played guitar with Chuck Berry and Bo Diddley. Recalled a series of gigs with Sutch in Swansea's Townsman Club in the early 1970s: 'Sutch was so outrageous that every night there were different complaints – about setting fire to things, spraying water over people, waving dangerous props about. The management gave him such a hard time that by the end of the week he had virtually no act left!'

CLIVE SYDNEY COOK, AKA DJ LEGENDARY LONNIE (guitar)
Met Sutch in 1966. Once visited Sutch at the house he shared with Giselle: 'There was a massive ginger cat in the house. Giselle had been cooking a turkey for guests. She put it on the table and turned her back for a second. The ginger cat pounced, jumped on the table and dragged the turkey down on to the floor. They rescued it, cleaned it up and served it. Later I asked Dave what had become of the cat: "The same as the turkey," he said.'

MIKE CRAWFORD (drums)
Turned bassist with Rock Island Line. Twice accompanied Sutch on German tours in the late 1970s where Sutch was frequently the butt of jokes by the band. The band made a point of travelling separately from Sutch, making sure they got to the hotel first and booked the best rooms: 'Dave took this well until one evening when he and I fancied a pair of sisters – one blonde, one dark. He liked the blonde. That was no

problem, but he said he'd have to pull rank over the rooms: 'I'm the star, I've got to have your room as it's bigger.' I told him that he might be the star on stage but he wasn't in this hotel. He demanded that we should toss a coin. He lost and said 'best of three', lost again and said 'best of five'. He ended up with the girl in the smallest room ... in a single bed.'

TONY DANGERFIELD (bass)

Played with the Savages from January to May 1964. Went off to lead his own band, The Thrills. Returned to the Savages in mid-1966 just before they became The Roman Empire, until April 1967. 'David only lost his edge when Carlo and I weren't there to pull it all together.' Nicknamed Tulip by Sutch. Played bass on 1991's 'Loony Rock', at which stage he helped Sutch put together a regular line-up, including Jack Irving and Anji Antanori, with Dave Dix on sax. Responsible for a legendary prank which Slade's Noddy Holder later confirmed was adapted by them in their movie, *Slade in Flame*, when Tony paid the roadies who carried Sutch on stage in his coffin to stand it on its head up against the wall so he couldn't escape. Fellow depression-sufferer who believes 'what he did was meant – it wasn't a cry for help'. Still very proud of his association with Sutch: 'The Savages are my rock 'n' roll spiritual home.'

ROD DE'ATH (drums)

Appropriately named drummer on *Rock and Horror* album.

DAVE DIX (saxophone)

Highly regarded saxophonist who allows his fondness for the man to overcome his slight irritation at Sutch's reluctance to pay a respectable rate. First met Sutch as the end of the 1970s and tells an amusing story about Sutch's early days on the road: 'He was driving the van with Blackmore and Dangerfield as passengers. They were hungry and wanted to stop for something to eat. David refused to stop. They were sure his mum had made him sandwiches and asked if they could share them. He denied he had any. They found them in his jacket pocket and nicked them. As he drove he tried to slip his hand into the jacket to find his sandwiches, but they were gone – he couldn't complain as he'd told them he had none.' Once misjudged the amount of fuel to put into

Sutch's 'fire-hat' at a gig in France – leaving Sutch singed when the flames leapt up – 'David didn't notice he had a bright red forehead and ears until the next day, when he blamed it on suburn!'

JOHN VICTOR 'RHINO' EDWARDS (bass)
Bassist /songwriter with Status Quo. Made his Sutch debut in the late 1970s: 'I asked about rehearsing and he said, "There's a weird bit in 'Jack the Ripper', be careful", and that was it! I had no idea of the songs he was going to do. I think he came on in some kind of caveman outfit. I don't know about Sutch and The Savages, we were more like the Three Twats Falling About Laughing – it's still the funniest gig I've ever done, and I've been in comedy bands!'

TONY ELLIS (bass)
With Sutch since the late 1970s: 'I was with Café Racers and left just before they changed their name to Dire Straits, but I wasn't envious or resentful. And I never saw Dave show any signs of jealousy that so many of his Savages had gone on to make their fame and fortune.'

MATTHEW FISHER (organ)
Played in The Roman Empire from Dec 1966 to April 1967. Recorded 'Whiter Shade of Pale' with Procol Harum (that's Fisher playing the evocative opening bars – *not* Gary Brooker) but stayed in the Empire (for financial security!) until that single took off: 'We parted on amicable terms. I'd always planned to move on to get a Hammond organ and some well paid work.' Nicknamed 'Ethel' by Carlo, who used to have a go at Fisher for playing classical music when warming up for gigs. Says Sutch 'caused an awful lot of things to happen and gave an awful lot of people a start.'

JOHN GILBEY (guitar)
Formerly with John Mayall. The only direct link between the two great career-makers of rock 'n' roll and the blues. Joined The Savages in early 1964.

DAVE GODDARD (bass)
Played with Shakin' Stevens. 'My main band was The Sunsets, and we

played with Sutch under that name, as both Savages and Savage Sunsets.'
Goddard was with Sutch when, on a German tour, they crossed the
West–East border. There were six in the van, but a flu-suffering Sutch
opted to fly back, so when they returned to the checkpoint their papers
showed six having gone in but only five returning. 'In broken German
and sign language we had explained to the guard that Lord Sutch had
fallen ill and flown home. "Ach, so – ve underschtand – ze aristocracy
fly, ze vorkers zey haff to drive, nicht wahr?"'

PAUL GREEN (guitar)

Calls himself a 'musical prostitute' and joined the Savages in 1997 or
1998, just as Sutch and the Savages were scheduled to fly to Hamburg
for a big 1960s show: 'We were a little late, but Dave turned up even
later – we missed the plane, even though he pulled the "I'm Screaming
Lord Sutch, you've got to let us on the plane" routine, but it had gone.
He was a big man for a little bloke.'

TIM GREEN (guitar)

Met Sutch in the early 1970s when he was with Rock Island Line. They
backed Sutch frequently in the UK and abroad. Green joined Mungo
Jerry before moving permanently to Germany where he produced an
album for Sutch. 'When he came over I invited him to stay in the flat I
shared with my girlfriend. We had a lot of pets, including hamsters.
After we had gone to bed we heard a squeaking noise, so I got up to find
David in the kitchen with a foot on one of the hamsters, pushing it up
and down, apparently under the impression that it was a toy for the
cats.'

RONNIE HARWOOD (bass)

With Sutch from May 1964 to February 1965, when 'the band was
going out for five or six hundred pounds a night'. Sang at the graveside
following Sutch's funeral, which was especially poignant as he had
suffered a breakdown himself many years before.

NICKY HOPKINS (keyboards)

Classically trained and played with many bands including The Who,
The Beatles and The Rolling Stones, but first (and some say foremost)

he was in the inaugural Savages. Sometimes delegated to play the prostitute during 'Jack the Ripper' when he would find himself being stabbed by Sutch, who would disembowel him and hurl previously purchased heart and liver into the audience.

JACK IRVING (drums)
Played on 'Loony Rock'. Came down to London from Glasgow in the late 1970s, at the behest of his pal, Anji Antanori, to join The Shakers. They backed Sutch, and Irving soon became a regular Savage and very fond of Sutch: 'The guy was a gentleman'. Engaged to the late singer (and former Sutch girlfriend) Kim Roberts. Recalled persuading Sutch to drink two pints of lager at one gig – 'he was all over the place'.

HERMIEN JERIAN-DU'FORT (drums)
'I received a phone call from an agency asking if I was free to go to Europe and play drums with Sutch for a couple of weeks. What followed was two years of extensive touring and recording. Along the way came many laughs, drunken nights and the usual array of rock 'n' roll craziness.'

DARNELL KELLERMAN (saxophone)
Sometime James Brown Band member, who played on 'Loonabilly Rock 'n' Roll' EP and *Rock and Horror* album.

FREDDIE 'FINGERS' LEE (guitar and piano)
Handed over guitar duties to Ritchie Blackmore as he turned to piano playing for Sutch, a 'long-time partner in crime' from October 1962 to June 1963. Played with Sutch in Hamburg and also gigged with Jerry Lee Lewis, Chuck Berry and Little Richard. Sutch claimed he made all his keyboards players use the name Freddie Fingers when they were in The Savages: 'The last one, Freddie Fingers Lee from Newcastle, ran off with the name.' Called Sutch a 'greedy bastard' but a 'lovely bloke'. Recalled that Sutch was not only parsimonious with his own band: 'I met up with him one night and we went off for a drink to Scotch of St James where we ended up with Paul McCartney and P.J. Proby. He never put his hand in his pocket, yet he rolled out of there half cut. In the forty years I knew him he only once bought me a drink, and that was a scotch

when I was in pain and needed something to keep me going during a gig.'

CARLO LITTLE (drums)

One of the original Savages, who played with Sutch on and off for most of the 1960s. Still gets phone calls from musicians asking whether he remembers them: 'They say, "I played with you in the Savages once, I stood in for so and so" or they tell me they were on the bill with us at such and such a venue and joined in a jam session. It's impossible to tell how many Savages there have been.' (Tony Dangerfield says that 'nobody is a real Savage unless they played in the band when Carlo or I were running it'.)

ROGER MINGAY (guitar)

Known as 'Scratch and Scrape Bailey' by Sutch when in May 1961 version of band. Left for Outlaws, then moved to Australia.

(ROCKIN') RAY NEALE (guitar)

Had a stint in the 1980s as lead guitarist for Sutch and The Savages, penning 'Loonabilly Rock 'n' Roll' for the Loony Party.

PETE NEWMAN (saxophone)

Played on first single. Pals with Sutch for forty-four years. Remembers a gig in Peterborough when the band finished playing only to find their van had been stolen. Sutch called the police, who drove him around until they found the van – he had forgotten where he had parked it. 'Dave never had tax or insurance in those days, he said he "didn't believe in it" and his vehicles frequently lacked essentials like wing mirrors, windscreen wipers and brakes. This van was no exception, so when we arrived in front of it the copper was looking at it suspiciously as Dave went to get in and drive away. He thought quickly, and said, "Oh, no – not only did they nick the van, they've taken my windscreen wipers and wing mirrors …"'

PAUL NICHOLAS (keyboards)

Versatile TV comic actor. Grabbed job of piano player in Sutch's band from June 1963 to January 1964, and again from May 1964 to Feb

1965, when he was known as Paul Dean: 'Appearing naked in *Hair* was nothing compared to playing keyboards for Screaming Lord Sutch wearing only a leotard.' Sutch was a prominent guest when Nicholas featured on television's *This Is Your Life*.

BILL PARKINSON (guitar)
In 'The Circles' who, from July to September 1966, doubled as The Savages with Carlo and Tony in the line-up. Parkinson wrote Neil Reid's hit, 'Mother of Mine'.

PETER PARKS (guitar)
Played with Nick Simper in Fandango and then Flying Fox, which featured Carlo Little. When the band had a residency at the Brewster Arms in White City, Sutch turned up: 'The impact when he came on was incredible, he created mayhem. You couldn't follow him – it was sheer energy.' Recalled a post-gig chat with Sutch: 'We were still buzzing from the gig, when suddenly Sutch was hit by a wave of depression. He was in tears, asking, "What's it all about?"'

KEN PAYNE (bass)
Played in the second Savages' line-up, in which Sutch nicknamed him 'Hopping Ken Rupert'. Emigrated to Australia.

PETE PHILLIPS (drums)
Drummer from June to August 1963, and May 1964 to Feb 1965. Played on 'I'm a Hog For You, Baby'.

SID PHILLIPS (saxophone)
Played on *Hands of the Ripper* album and *Rock and Horror* set.

MAC POOLE (drums)
Had his own band, Warhorse. First drummed with Sutch in the early days when Carlo was elsewhere, and toured with him in Germany. 'Dave was a lovely guy – but too mean ever to make it big. He was pissed off that he never made his fortune but he was so stupid that rather than pay the great musicians he could call on for his band he

would too often settle for cheaper substitutes – often affecting his own good name and reputation.'

COLIN PRYCE-JONES (guitar)
Played in The Rapiers. Recalled Sutch throwing 'what I thought to be a large plastic knife' at him. 'To my horror a genuine steel knife whizzed past my face and embedded itself into a wooden partition six inches from my head. I was petrified.' Colin's favourite Sutch on-stage announcement was when he apologised to the audience for being unable to sing "All Black and Hairy" because he'd left his shovel in the boot.'

MIKE READ
Most surprising claimant to the title of 'Savage'. The DJ, author, songwriter, singer, actor and *I'm A Celebrity* star called me as he prepared to go on stage in his Cliff Richard musical, which was then playing at the Palladium. Backed Sutch on three occasions, most memorably in Byfleet, where Read 'sweated so much during the show' that he ended up with flu. Said Sutch's 'recognition factor' was phenomenal. 'Any lesser mortal would have capitulated years before but he was still there, making a living, long after others – some much more commercially successful – had come and gone.' Once discussed with Sutch getting together everyone who had ever played in the band for a giant reunion 'Savages party'. Thought Sutch 'always seemed to have an infinite amount of optimism'.

MIKE (MICK) RICHARDSON (drums)
On and off with The Savages for a couple of decades. 'We did the same act for over twenty years, yet every time I turned up for a gig there would be Dave saying, "Right, in this number, we slow it down just here." "Yes, Dave, I know", and, "When I do this, I want you to do that." "Yes, Dave, as usual."'

ROCKIN' DAVE ROBINSON (guitar)
Close to David, especially towards the end of his life. Also the first Rock 'n' Roll Loony Party chairman. An honorary Savage.

DAVE SAVAGE (vocals, guitar)

Perhaps the nearest thing extant to the younger Sutch himself. 'When I first came across Sutch, I was amazed at finding someone who'd managed to put my two favourite things together – horror and rock 'n' roll. I soon bought my first black top hat and long black coat. I joined my first regularly working band and fitted in some of Sutchie's songs. The Sutch-inspired part of my show was always popular, and around 1990 I was asked by Sledgehammer Stan of The 'Northern' Savages if I wanted to come along to a Sutch gig with the band. I travelled to Doncaster and helped carry Sutch on in the coffin. Halfway through the set he shouted to me to come on stage – and for the first time I found myself sharing the stage with one of my greatest inspirations. Back at Stan's, we talked about music and the Loony Party, and Stan said I should join the group and be the singer when Sutch was down south.' Currently stages tribute shows to Screaming Lord Sutch, to crowds of up to 2,000: 'People enjoy it, because I am not doing an impersonation, but manage to capture the Sutchyness and energy that Dave could always find to entertain crowds. We will carry on because we love what we do.'

JOHN SCHOLLAR (guitar)

Backed Sutch on guitar with The Beachcombers: 'I played with another eccentric, Keith Moon. He and I would often drive into Harrow. We bumped into Dave in Sopers department store – he was dressed up in stage gear carrying a pole with a shrunken head on a string on one end of it. He chased the girls on the cosmetics counter, who ran off screaming. Keith thought a great deal of Dave and used to laugh uncontrollably from the wings when he was on stage. I met up with him again some twenty-five years later at a benefit gig for Wee Willie Harris. I saw Dave at the bar and wandered up, wondering whether he would recognise me. He turned to me and said, "Cor, I was thinking about poor old Moonie the other day."'

NICK SIMPER (bass)

Subsequently with Deep Purple. Toured with Sutch and Billie Davis during 1967. Guested on Sutch's *Heavy Friends*. Sutch sometimes misnamed him as 'Simpler': 'Sutch and Johnny Kidd inspired people.

They were so good in their field but never had the hard sell to push them to the very top.' Laments the fact that an attempt to set up a concert in Sutch's honour shortly after his death foundered when every big name appeared to be unavailable or too busy: 'It was bloody sad – too many people get too big and blasé and forget their roots.'

DEREK (LITTLE DEGS) SIRMON (drums)
Brought to Sutch's attention by Ritchie Blackmore: 'I stepped into Carlo's shoes when he left Sutch [in October 1962].They were big shoes to fill, but I had a great couple of years with Dave Sutch. Often, after a gig, we would find a Chinese restaurant and go for a meal. Dave's favourite trick would be to sit with his hat on, his hair bunched up under the hat. If any of the staff asked him to remove his hat he would make excuses as to why he couldn't, but then, when the first course was served, he would take his hat off and let his hair dangle in the meal – the shock reaction was tremendous as, in those days, long hair had not become fashionable.'

MARTIN SYMONDS (drums)
Played with Sutch in the 1970s and 1980s. When he married Ursula, the couple became good friends with David and Giselle and are convinced that 'had David and his beautiful Frenchwoman stayed together he would have been alive today'.

ROCKIN' DAVE TAYLOR (keyboards)
Taylor and Sutch met up in the mid-1970s. Sutch wrote in April 1999: 'Dave caught my attention as a talented young pianist/singer. He hammered the keys to death, played the piano with his feet, chopped it to pieces and even set fire to it on stage!' Taylor claims that he was 'sworn in as one of Sutch's Savages in the mid-1980s'.

STUART TAYLOR (guitar)
Left in January 1964 to join The Tornados.

IAIN 'HOUNDOG' TERRY (vocals/guitar)
Founder member of Matchbox. 'I knew Sutch since 1968. I can honestly say he was the funniest man I ever knew. Sutch was headlining

at an up-market hall in Hamburg, with Rock Island Line providing the backing. There were two gangs of bikers at the show but the band thought nothing of that as they launched into "Great Balls of Fire" with Sutch lighting up his cauldron. Suddenly a Marilyn Monroe lookalike got up on the stage – she had a hairstyle like Kathy Kirby and was wearing a fur coat and red heels. She came up to each band member and rubbed herself against us – then took off her fur coat – and stood there naked.' A riot ensued with a machete and a gun being waved about, but Sutch kept trying to persuade the band to keep playing. 'It turned that "Marilyn" was a local call girl hired to go on stage and provoke the fight by a local gangster, who ran protection rackets, and was a rival to the German promoter who staged the show ... we found ourselves in this farmhouse in Ruschendorf where there was nothing to do for three days until it all blew over.'

LORD TOBY (JUG) (guitar)

Played with the Savages in 1990s. 'He opened up to me about his depression. He would call me at 2, 3 or even 4 a.m. and sometimes end up crying down the phone.' Also a Loony candidate.

BERNIE WATSON (guitar)

A match for Sutch in the oddity stakes. In at the start in 1961 but 'was a bit weird', remembered Matthew Fisher: 'He hated the audience looking at him and once went on stage with something covering his head, and would play out of sight of them.' Sutch called him 'Strawberry'.

DAVE WENDELS (guitar)

A Savage from May to October 1962: 'Every gig, and getting to every gig was an adventure.' Wendels lives in the States, the only Savage whose son, Wyatt, has played in the band, too. He was once married to Kim Roberts: 'Wyatt and I never played together in The Savages. The last time I saw Dave was at a benefit gig. He got to jam with some of his original guys – Carlo, Rick, myself – but looked far from well; grey pallor, and perspiring. It was the same old exuberant Dave, though. If he was depressed, it certainly wasn't apparent on this occasion.'

WYATT WENDELS (drums)

Son of Dave. 'I played with the Savages from 1995 to 1998 as did my dad years ago, and my mum, Kim Roberts, too.' Wyatt recalled a trip to Germany in 1997: 'We were flying out for a Star Club reunion concert with all the usual suspects – (Swinging) Blue Jeans, Merseybeats, etc. After announcements to buckle up and prepare for take off, Dave decided this didn't apply to him, and started to walk down the aisle, saying, "Tony [Dangerfield], I'm having a bit of trouble with ten across – any ideas?", just as the plane was taxi-ing for take off. On the way back he caused chaos by trying to get a newspaper out of an overhead locker as we were about to soar into the sky – he tried to appease the stewardesses with Loony notes.'

PETER LEE WENGER (drums)

Now with The Sunsets. Backed Sutch in the 1970s and 1980s. 'As he got older and fatter his voice was getting worse every year and he would have less and less in the way of props. Towards the end I would never look forward to backing him and would often feel that the audience was being short-changed. He would even sometimes do encores when the audience didn't want one.'

ANDY WREN (keyboards)

Played on first single. Integral part of the stage act between May 1961 and 1962. Became a primary school teacher. Stayed until Nicky Hopkins arrived with Bernie Watson, whereupon he was sacked, returning shortly after for a second stint – this time on a six-month contract worth £17 per week: 'Very few can make a lengthy career of pop – I didn't have the talent to do it – nor did Dave, really. He wanted the glamorous life and his whole heart was in his music – even though he didn't really have a lot of music in him.' Andy recalls an early gig where it was his job to ring a school bell lustily to draw attention to the flames during 'Great Balls of Fire': 'As I swung the bell, Sutch came towards me and I struck him with it, cutting his eye so that blood squirted out as dramatically as in a Henry Cooper fight – the audience thought it was all part of the act, but later we had to take Sutch to the hospital for stitches – he thought it was great.'

UK Discography

Singles

1961   'Till The Following Night'/'Good Golly Miss Molly' (HMV POP953)

1963   'Jack The Ripper'/'Don't You Just Know It' (Decca F11598)

1963   'I'm A Hog For You'/'Monster In Black Tights' (Decca F11747)

1964   'She's Fallen In Love With A Monster Man'/'Bye Bye Baby' (Oriole CB1944)

1964   'Dracula's Daughter'/'Come Back Baby' (Oriole CB 1962)

1965   'The Train Kept A Rollin''/'Honey Hush' (CBS 201767)

1966   'The Cheat'/'All Black And Hairy' (CBS 202080)

1966   *'Purple People Eater'/'You Don't Care' (Hep House HS04)

1970   'Cause I Love You'/'Thumping Beat' (Atlantic584321).

1970   'Election Fever'/'Rock The Election' (Atlantic 2091017

1972   'Gotta Keep A Rockin''/'Flashing Lights' / 'Hands Of Jack The Ripper' (Atlantic K10221)

1976   'Monster Ball'/'Rang-Tang-A-Lang' (SRT SRTS 76361)

1976   'I Drink To Your Health Marie' (Pts 1 and 2) (SRT SRTS76375)

1976   'Jack The Ripper'/'Dance And Jive' (Charly CS 1016)

1977   'Jack The Ripper'/'I'm A Hog For You' (Decca F13697).

1983   'All Black And Hairy'/'Monster Rock' (Monster Records; Monster 1).

1989   'Creepy Christmas Party'/'Rap Up Christmas' (Invitation Records: Korner 001)

1990   'Creepy Christmas Dance Party'/'Creepy Christmas Dance Party' (Zombie Mix) (Spiral Cut Records KOR 001/7R)

1991   'Number 10 Or Bust'/'Loony Rock' / 'Till The Following Night' (EMI LC0542)

2000   'Midnight Man' (Raucous RAUCD 070). Three-track CD single, including 'Thumpin' Drum' and 'Scream And Run'

12″

E P s

A l b u m s

    *Not generally available in UK.

Electionography

1963 15 August STRATFORD-UPON-AVON Stood for the National Teenage Party. 209 votes

1966 30 May (General Election) HUYTON Stood for National Independent Teenage Party against Prime Minister Harold Wilson. 585 votes

1970 18 June (General Election) CITIES OF LONDON & WESTMINSTER Stood for the Young Ideas. 142 votes

1974 10 Oct (General Election) STAFFORD & STONE. Stood for the GB-'Go To Blazes'-Party. 351 votes

1979 3 May (General Election) No record of Sutch standing anywhere.

1983 24 Feb BERMONDSEY Stood for the first time (as D.E. Sutch) for the Monster Raving Loony Party. 97 votes

1983 24 March DARLINGTON MRLP. 374 votes

1983 9 June (General Election) FINCHLEY. Stood for MRLP against Prime Minister Margaret Thatcher. 235 votes

1983 28 July CUMBRIA,PENRITH & BORDER MRLP. 412 votes

1984 1 March CHESTERFIELD Stood for the Monster Raving Loony Last Stand Party. 178 votes

1985 4 July POWYS, BRECON & RADNOR MRLP. 202 votes

1986 10 April HAMMERSMITH & FULHAM MRLP. 134votes

1986 17 July NEWCASTLE-UNDER-LYME MRLP. 277 votes

1988 14 July KENSINGTON & CHELSEA MRLP. 61 votes

1988 10 Nov GLASGOW GOVAN Stood for the Monster Raving Raving Loony 'I Bet I Will Beat William Hill' Party. 174 votes

1988 15 Dec EPPING FOREST MRLP. 208 votes

1989 23 Feb RICHMOND, NORTH YORKSHIRE MRLP. 167 votes

1989 4 May VALE OF GLAMORGAN MRLP. 266 votes

1989 15 June VAUXHALL MRLP. 106 votes.

1989 (European Election) LONDON CENTRAL MRLP. 841 votes

1990 22 March MID-STAFFORDSHIRE MRLP. 336 votes

1990 24 May   BOOTLE MRLP. 418 votes.

1990 27 Sep   KNOWSLEY SOUTH MRLP. 197 votes.

1990 8 Nov   BRADFORD, NORTH MRLP. 310 votes

1991 7 March RIBBLE VALLEY MRLP .278 votes.

1991 4 April   NEATH MRLP. 263 votes.

1991 16 May   MONMOUTH Monster Raving Loony Runner Bean Party. 314 votes.

1991 4 July   WALTON, LIVERPOOL MRLP. 546 votes.

1992 9 April   (General Election) Sutch stood against the three major Party leaders – taking on John Major, Conservative in HUNTINGDON where he polled 728 votes; Neil Kinnock, Labour, in ISLWYN where he scored 547 votes, and against Paddy Ashdown, Liberal Democrats, in YEOVIL where he ended up with 338 votes.

1993 6 May   NEWBURY MRLP. 432 votes.

1993 29 July   CHRISTCHURCH, DORSET MRLP. 404 votes.

1994 5 May   ROTHERHAM MRLP. 1114 votes.

1994 9 June   EASTLEIGH MRLP. 783 votes.

1994 9 June   BRADFORD SOUTH MRLP. 727 votes.

1995 16 Feb   ISLWYN MRLP. 506 votes

1995 25 May   TAYSIDE, PERTH AND KINROSS MRLP. 586 votes

1995 27 July   LITTLEBOROUGH AND SADDLEWORTH, GREATER MANCHESTER MRLP. 782 votes

1996 1 Feb   HEMSWORTH, WEST YORKSHIRE MRLP 652 votes.

1996 11 April SOUTH-EAST STAFFORDSHIRE MRLP. 506 votes

1997 1 May   (General Election) Plans to stand for a second time against John Major in Huntingdon scrapped owing to the illness of his mother.

1997 31 July   UXBRIDGE MRLP 396 votes.

1997 20 Nov   WINCHESTER MRLP 316 votes.

Sutch contested 41 Parliamentary Elections, polling 15,657 votes along the way, and also had a crack at one European Election, with the odd local council campaign thrown in for luck.

Index

beats UKIP 183
conferences 118–19, 121, 167,
  185–6, 230
decline 130, 227–31
manifestos 116, 117, 121, 126,
  130, 149, 164, 166–7, 185,
  186, 197
rifts 124, 127–8, 130
and Sutch's funeral 15
and William Hill 10, 124
wins council seats 123, 137,
  201, 228–9
see also by-elections; elections,
  European; elections, general;
  elections, local; Hope, Alan
Offshore Echoes 64
OK! 102–3, 109, 112–13, 155,
  163, 195
Oldham, Andrew Loog 219
Oliver, Linda 14, 164
Ono, Yoko 77, 131
'Oo Poo Pa Do' 43
Orbach, Susie 176
O'Riordan, Maggie 196
Orwell, George 119
Osbourne, Ozzy 43, 218
Outlaws, The 37
Over Exposed (film) 165
Owen, David 129, 185
Oxford Town Hall 42

Page, Jimmy 15, 68, 79–80, 81–2
Painter, Dave 162
Palais de Danse, Aldershot 32
Park Royal Hotel 30
Parker, David 197
Parker (Colonel) Tom 77
Parkfield Road (Reading) house 6,
  13, 100, 101, 172, 178,
  180, 183, 186–7, 191–2,

193–4, 207, 217, 222, 235
Parks, Peter 253
Patch, Chris 137
Paul, Brian 65
Payne, Cynthia 23, 24, 124, 126,
  139–45, 153, 161–2, 209,
  215, 222, 235, 237
  Sutch lives with 112, 141–2,
    159, 174
  and Sutch's death 15, 17,
    18–19, 208
  on Sutch's mother 141–2, 174,
    179
  on Sutch's problems 12,
    141–2, 143, 144–5
Payne, Ken 36, 40, 253
Percy Road Boys School 24, 25
Perry, Stephen 233
pet passports 186
Petts Hill 94, 100
Phillips, Pete 51, 253
Phillips, Sid 89, 253
Pickett, Bobby 'Boris', and The
  Crypt Kickers 47
Pink Floyd 96, 132–3
Pinner New Cemetery 17, 234
pirate radio 64–6
Pirates, The 15, 67, 75
Playboys, The 32, 35
Pollytone 122
Poole, Mac 212–13, 253–4
Potter, Bob 32–3, 47
Powys, Brecon and Radnor by-
  election (1985) 121, 261
Poyzer, Darren 137, 202
Presley, Elvis 76–7, 113, 166,
  209, 220
Pretty Things, The 52, 59, 72
Prince of Wales, Hammersmith
  200